ADDITIONAL PRAISE FOR
LISTENING FROM THE HEART OF SILENCE

"What an immensely worthy sequel to the first volume in this series, *The Sacred Mirror!* Like its predecessor, *Listening from the Heart of Silence,* should be required study—not just reading—for anyone seriously interested in the integration of effective enlightenment spirituality and deep, truly healing psychotherapy. Every single essay is not just a gem but a mine of them."
—Saniel Bonder, founder of the Waking Down in Mutuality work, author, *Healing the Spirit/Matter Split, Waking Down: Beyond Hypermasculine Dharmas*

"The dialogue concerning the nondual approach to psychotherapy is greatly enriched by this admirable collection."
—Swami Abhayananda, author of *History of Mysticism, The Supreme Self, Mysticism And Science*

"This book demonstrates that the nondual psychotherapist is able to facilitate and guide the leap into formlessness, the uncovering of the deepest psychological contractions, and the recognition that the body, or form, is not separate from the formless. This ability or function of the nondual psychotherapist is the same as that of the enlightened guru. This book, along with The Sacred Mirror, is a major contributor to a revolution in psychotherapy."
—Jerry Katz, founder of Nonduality.com, Editor, *One: Essential Writings on Nonduality*

"This book is at the same time a delight and strong medicine: a multi-faceted exploration of the relative and the absolute in the context of the therapy room, in language that manages to clarify rather than obscure this most subtle of subjects."
—Roger Housden, author of the Ten Poems series; *Seven Sins for a Life Worth Living;* and editor of *Dancing with Joy: 99 poems*

"This clear, insightful and deep book will assist lovers of reality."
—Isaac Shapiro, teacher, author of *Outbreak of Peace* and *It Happens by Itself*

"Whether you are a psychotherapist, a spiritual teacher, a client, or a student, each of the essays in this wise and elegantly written book will inspire you not only to listen but to think and respond from the heart of silence. Read, learn from, and be challenged and inspired by this book."
—Amy Weintraub, MFA, ERYT 500, is the author of *Yoga for Depression* and the founder of the LifeForce Yoga Healing Institute

"Along with its predecessor, *The Sacred Mirror,* this book addresses many of the major questions concerning the healing power of genuine nondual realization in the therapeutic relationship. I am grateful to the editors for extracting the essence of this monumental teaching and applying it to everyday clinical practice. Their book will inspire an ever-increasing number of therapists who intuit that emotional problems naturally begin to resolve as we open ever more deeply to the One Self beyond all selves."

—Bryan Wittine, Ph.D., Jungian Analyst, C. G. Jung Institute of San Francisco

"This is a breakthrough book that goes beyond the nondual school and enters into dialogue with the mainstream schools of psychotherapy."

—Brant Cortright, Ph.D., Chair of the Integral Counseling Psychology department, California Institute of Integral Studies, author of *Integral Psychology: Yoga, Growth, and Opening the Heart and Psychotherapy* and *Spirit: Theory and Practice of Transpersonal Psychotherapy*

"This inspiring collection of essays weaves together various threads that comprise the tapestry of modern transpersonal psychology: non-duality, contemporary psychological theory, religious philosophy and clinical practice. Rather than relying on spiritual theories and secondary sources, the authors' personal experience with non-duality and clinical practice informs the ground out of which the essays spring, imbuing them with a feeling of creativity and authenticity. This book is an important contribution to the transpersonal psychology literature and should be required reading in any transpersonal psychology graduate school curriculum."

—Laurel Parnell, Ph.D., Clinical Psychologist, author of *A Therapist's Guide to EMDR; EMDR in the Treatment of Adults Abused as Children,* former faculty at John F. Kennedy University, Graduate School for the Study of Human Consciousness, and adjunct faculty at California Institute of Integral Studies

"The experience of non-dual wisdom is beginning to penetrate the therapeutic process, as therapists who have known deep spiritual awakenings seek to bring the presence and truth of being into their meetings with others. In this remarkable anthology eleven therapists share moments of encounter with clients that go beyond doing, and have the potential for spontaneous healing of the splits in the human psyche. To see there is no other, to meet in the silence of Oneness, to discover a place within that has no problem, and to allow "spacious intimacy" brings a powerful new dimension into human relationship with Self and others."

—Bonnie Greenwell, Ph.D., Transpersonal author, educator and psychotherapist

"The pieces in this collection are not only *about* non-dualism, rather, almost every page is saturated with the unmistakable feel, touch, taste, smell of the freedom of the non-dual view. I read it hungrily—by the time I finished the text, I felt as though I had been through a transformative non-dual therapy myself! I highly recommend it—and not only for psychotherapists, but for all who are interested in seeing clearly."

—Stephen Cope, Director, Kripalu Center for Extraordinary Living, and author, *The Wisdom of Yoga*

"I was pulled in from the very first page, with the artful writing and compelling insights into the eastern wisdom traditions of Yoga and Buddhism. I started to only read a few pages and ended up reading the whole chapter. Now, this stays by my bedside, to read and reflect upon, a sip or two at a time, although I admit, I took the whole first chapter in one deep drink. I just couldn't put down the glass."

—John Kepner, Executive Director, International Association of Yoga Therapists

"*Listening from the Heart of Silence* deepens and expands on the wisdom expressed in *The Sacred Mirror,* the first book in the series on nondual wisdom and psychotherapy. John Prendergast and Ken Bradford have created an anthology of gifted writers, therapists and teachers, who inspire and move us to an awakened understanding of listening from the heart of silence. This book is a valuable addition to the field of spirituality and psychotherapy, drawing on both traditional and modern perspectives. Readers, be they students, teachers or therapists, will be invited into a larger radiance of being, truly touching on the wisdom of the nondual perspective."

—Ray Greenleaf, M.A., MFT, Chair, Counseling Psychology School of Holistic Studies John F. Kennedy University

"Listening from the Heart of Silence is an invitation itself to deeper listening. It is at the same time intellectually stimulating, professionally instructive, and spiritually inspiring. The authors take great care to connect nondual wisdom to the work of psychotherapy in a way that can be transformative of both the client and the therapist."

—Paul J. Roy, Ph.D., Academic Vice President, Institute of Transpersonal Psychology

"These articles by clinicians and academics carve fresh understandings for people interested in non-dual vision, adding considerably to the understanding and appreciation of this subject and vision."

—Mordechai Mitnick, LCSW, Adjunct Professor at John F. Kennedy School of Holistic Studies, senior clinician in private practice

LISTENING FROM THE HEART OF SILENCE

LISTENING FROM THE HEART OF SILENCE

NONDUAL WISDOM & PSYCHOTHERAPY
VOLUME 2

Edited by

John J. Prendergast, Ph.D.
G. Kenneth Bradford, Ph.D.

PARAGON HOUSE
St. Paul, Minnesota

First Edition 2007

Published in the United States by
Paragon House
1925 Oakcrest Ave., Suite 7
St. Paul, MN 55113

Library of Congress Cataloging-in-Publication Data

Listening from the heart of silence : nondual wisdom & psychotherapy / edited by John J. Prendergast, G. Kenneth Bradford.
     p. cm.
  Summary: "This companion volume to The Sacred Mirror is an anthology of teachings on how nondual spiritual realization and psychology work in the specialized relationship between therapist and client and in ordinary personal relationships"--Provided by publisher.
  Includes bibliographical references and index.
  ISBN 978-1-55778-862-7 (pbk. : alk. paper) 1. Psychotherapy--Philosophy.
2. Psychotherapy--Religious aspects. 3. Advaita. I. Prendergast, John J.,
1950- II. Bradford, G. Kenneth.
  RC437.5.L57 2007
  616.89'14--dc22
                          2007003433

Manufactured in the United States of America
10 9 8 7 6 5 4 3 2 1

The paper used in this publication meets the minimum requirements of American National Standard for Information Sciences—Permanence of Paper for Printed Library Materials, ANSIZ39.48-1984.

For current information about all releases from Paragon House,
visit the website at: www.paragonhouse.com

From John:

To my beloved wife, Christiane,
whose presence is a song in my heart

From Ken:

To my precious son, Galen,
And all of us who dare to cleanse the doors of our perception,
That we might see things as they Truly are
And laugh or cry out loud at the wonder of it all…

CONTENTS

Acknowledgments ix

Toward an Embodied Nonduality: Introductory Remarks 1
John J. Prendergast and G. Kenneth Bradford

Spacious Intimacy: 35
Reflections on Essential Relationship, Empathic Resonance,
Projective Identification, and Witnessing
John J. Prendergast

From Neutrality to the Play of Unconditional Presence. 55
G. Kenneth Bradford

Intersubjectivity and Nonduality in the Psychotherapeutic
Relationship 77
Judith Blackstone

Mystery, Mind, and Meaning 99
Dorothy S. Hunt

Listening and Speaking from No-Mind. 121
Peter Fenner

Nonduality: 151
A Spontaneous Movement "To" and "Fro"
Kaisa Puhakka

Experiencing the Universe as Yourself: 171
The Nonduality of Self and Society
David Loy

Walking the Talk:. 181
The Principles and Practices of Embodied Spirituality
Mariana Caplan

Healing from the Heart:. 197
Embodying Nondual Wisdom
Penny Fenner

Nondual Wisdom and Body-Based Therapy 217
Sheila Krystal

Nondual Awakening:. 231
Its Source and Applications
Timothy Conway

Selected Bibliography 255

About The Contributors. 265

ACKNOWLEDGMENTS

We wish to thank Lela Landman for suggesting the title of this book, and to the *Journal of Transpersonal Psychology* for giving permission to reprint Judith Blackstone's article "Intersubjectivity and Nonduality in the Psychotherapeutic Relationship."

TOWARD AN EMBODIED NONDUALITY:
INTRODUCTORY REMARKS

John J. Prendergast and G. Kenneth Bradford

PROLOGUE

This book continues the dialogue begun in *The Sacred Mirror* (2003), which was enthusiastically received by a small but growing community of therapists and clients along with a sophisticated public that is exploring the field of nondual wisdom and psychotherapy. Upon reading the first volume, one scholar commented that the authors were "on the cutting edge of the cutting edge." While this may have been a polite way of saying we are on the fringe, it may also be true that we are breaking some new ground. This volume will further develop many of the central themes that were interwoven within the essays in *The Sacred Mirror:* open listening, essential emptiness, spiritual awakening, embodiment, and, of course, the impact of nondual wisdom upon psychotherapy. In the first section of this chapter we will accent the theme of embodied nonduality, and in the second section briefly summarize the different chapters.

The role of nondual wisdom in psychotherapy is a paradoxical subject to write about, since we are using words in order to point beyond them. We hope that this new volume will broaden and deepen this subtle conversation, even as we remember that what we are trying to describe can never be adequately expressed through concepts. Still, if readers are able at times to follow these pointers and sense the fragrance of Silence behind and within these words, we have done our job well.

> First there is a mountain,
> Then there is no mountain,
> Then there is.
>
> —*Ch'an master Ch'ing yuan Wei-hsin*

LISTENING

First There Is a Mountain

Whether we go into psychotherapy, follow a spiritual path, or do both, our prime motivation is to free ourselves from some kind of malaise or self-limitation. "First there is a mountain" means that things are just as they appear—solid, substantial, and, above all, separate. On a psychological level it means that our self/world view is also taken to be completely real. As a result, in our daily life we may desperately long for material objects, for relationships, for recognition, or for meaning in order to fill an inner void. We may also hate or fear other people, avoid challenging situations, or resist experiencing disturbing thoughts or feelings. Whether we are grasping at or pushing away our outer or inner life, we definitely feel that the world and others exist "out there" and that we exist "in here" as a separate self. This consensual, dualistic reality seems as obvious and self-evident as the Sierra Nevadas, Alps, or Himalayas. This is the everyday experience of dualistic vision—the apparent separation between self and Other, between the experiencer and what is experienced.

This compelling, dualistic orientation to life leaves us with an inner sense of separation and alienation. If we look for support, advice, or therapy from professional helpers who are also enmeshed in this dualistic (mis)understanding, unaware of the constructed nature of consensual reality, we will only confirm and concretize the apparent objectivity of "the problem" as well as the "problem holder"—the client or patient.

It is only when our attention turns inward that we discover how we cocreate our suffering. Rather than taking ourselves as a powerless/rageful victim or self-improvement project, we begin to collect ourselves, withdraw our projections onto the world, and accept our situation just as it is. Looking and listening within, we may come to see how our mountain of a problem does not exist independently from how we see and hold it. Our open listening begins to reveal that things are not as they first seem.

Depth psychotherapy is, above all, the art of listening. True therapeutic speech arises from a listening presence. In its most mature form, listening is not limited to the two physical ears, but comes from a "third ear" that hears far beyond the words that are spoken. Such listening comes from the whole body and from that which is both beyond and saturating the whole body—the heart of Silence. By heart we mean the center or essence. The Silence that we are speaking of exists prior to the polarities of an active or quiet mind. It is the source of attention itself, regardless of whether attention is "evenly suspended" like a hummingbird poised in flight or busily searching for the next honeysuckle blossom. Trained or untrained, the mind's nature is to wander, yet there is an open, lucid, spacious, and intimate awareness that lies at its source.

If we are psychotherapists, we are trained to listen without emotional prejudice or judgment to what we hear with a more or less "neutral" attitude. Still, we are prone to listen from the eyebrows up according to our conceptual models. We tend to listen from a well-educated and highly conditioned mind. The result is often something like near-deafness. Our mental filters are like thick acoustic baffling that prevent any clear sound from coming through. And baffled we become, as we are lost in our thinking and unable to hear beneath our preconceptions or those of the person to whom we are listening.

Listening from the heart of Silence draws upon a different source of intelligence, a heart wisdom (*prajna* in Sanskrit) that Jung called *"l'intelligence du coeur."* This heart wisdom is like a silent master who remains unrecognized within the busy household of conventional thinking and identification. This unassuming master quietly listens, watches, and feels without judgment or demand in the background of ordinary awareness. Though unrecognized, he or she is the natural authority—the true king or queen of the inner court.

In contrast, the conditioned mind is like the self-appointed steward of the throne of Gondor in Tolkien's *Lord of the Rings: Return of the King,* who, pretending to be in charge, fiercely clings to power and generally makes quite a mess of things before giving up. Though inflated with pride, he or she is shadowed by a profound sense of inner lack—a dark gap in the center of his or her being, an unknown emptiness, an Otherness that is starkly foreign to the constructed, inauthentic sense of self. To make room for the true king, it is necessary to face this lack and eventually relinquish the pretense that covers it.

One of the purposes of depth psychotherapy, as we understand it, is simply to respond to the immensity of the world—the ten thousand things—from an opened heart and mind. This openness is possible only when the illusion of separation is deeply penetrated and we discover what is most true within ourselves. In this sense, authenticity is not an attribute of a special sense of self, but a release from the sense of any separate selfhood into that Silence, or empty-openness, which alone allows for the display, and nondisplay, of any number of selves. This is the secret meaning of the "Return of the King," in the sense of the fundamental Dzogchen tantra, *Kunjed Gyalpo* (The "All-Creating King")[1]—an embodied return to uncontrived presence.

Knowing this requires a profound letting go. Are we willing to release our tether to the familiar mothership of the known and free fall and float within the dark heavens of the Unknown and discover ourselves as That? Once entered, who returns from a journey into this Silence?

EMPTINESS

Then There Is No Mountain

We fear this barely sensed emptiness more than physical death. On a psychological level this manifests as a chronic sense of lack, of not being enough.[2] The core of human suffering lies in the resistance to *what is*—especially to this apparent lack. To the ego, or self-image, surrendering and opening to this dark, or blindingly light, portal of emptiness looks like the path to self-annihilation. It is rigorously repressed, avoided, and misinterpreted, so much so that it is barely mentioned in most Western psychologies, including even the Existentialists who focus on the fear of physical death. While religions, East and West, are quick to overlay the archetypes of God, Buddha, Christ, or the Great Mother upon it, the sages see through these masks. For example, the fourteenth-century Christian mystic Meister Eckhart writes in his remarkable sermon on the true meaning of poverty:[3]

Thus we say that a man should be so poor that he is not and has not a place for God to act in. To reserve a place would be to maintain distinctions. *Therefore I pray that he may quit me of god,* for (his) unconditioned being is above god and all distinctions…. I shall rise above all creature kind, and I shall be neither god nor creature, but I shall be what I was once, now, and forevermore. I shall thus receive an impulse which shall raise me above the angels. With this impulse, I receive wealth so great that I could never again be satisfied with a god, or anything that is a god's, nor with any divine activities, for in bursting forth I discover that God and I are One. Now I am what I was and I neither add to nor subtract from anything, for I am the unmoved Mover, that moves all things.

According to Meister Eckhart, once we are completely emptied, an underlying fullness—"wealth so great"—bursts forth. A similar multivalent theme of emptiness/fullness is found in the Buddhist notion of *sunyata.*

Although commonly translated as "emptiness," the root of *sunyata, su,* refers to a swelling, a fullness, which is not well conveyed by the word empty. This is not a mistake in translation as much as it is an unrecognized emphasis. The teachings of *sunyata,* emptiness of phenomena, and its stablemate, *anatta,* emptiness of self, emphasize that the path to freedom goes by the way of dispossession (from emotional clinging), disidentification (with a self-image), and disentanglement (from conceptual fixations). This psychological sobriety initially emphasizes the emptiness of beings (which we take for Reality) over the fullness of Being (which is obscured by our self-construed reality). Seeing into the actual emptiness of self and other *(vipassana),* and the projections that emerge from dualistic vision, allows us to appreciate the fullness of the Being of beings. "Then there is no mountain" expresses the breakthrough wisdom that objects, including an independent self, are inherently empty of any separate, self-existing nature. Seeing the empty essence of self and others relaxes the tense urgency of self-liberation projects and reveals the nature of the Self to be inherently open and inseparable from others and Otherness.

Most of us decline life's frequently fierce invitation to let go of the illusion of control and to accept what is. Whether through our own conscious cooperation fueled by our love of the truth or through painful contact with the sword of loss and disillusionment that rips through the fabric of an orderly conventional life, we all will eventually find ourselves on our knees, humbled before the great Mystery of life and death. When we are ready to abandon hope (and hopelessness) and meaning (and meaninglessness), there is room for something else—the truth of our being—to move. We are then open to what is sometimes called an awakening.

AWAKENING

Awakening, of course, is a metaphor. It points to a radical shift in our identity that is like waking up from a dream. There is the realization that what we took to be real—our constructed self/world-image—isn't. With this opening, however, unlike the change of state from dreaming to waking where the dream dissolves, ordinary life continues. Therefore, a spiritual awakening is more like becoming lucid within a dream where we are aware that we are dreaming while we dream. The dream continues, yet we no longer feel trapped as a character within it. This brings a sense of unbounded freedom, innocent bemusement, and quiet joy. We discover that we are in the world but not of it, or as Walt Whitman describes in his epic *Song of Myself*:

> Apart from the pulling and hauling, stands what I am,
> Stands amused, complacent, compassionating, idle, unitary,
> Looks down, is erect, or bends an arm on an impalpable certain rest,
> Looking with side-curved head curious what will come next,
> Both in and out of the game and watching and wondering at it.

It is important to realize that it is not the dream character herself who awakens. *That* character continues as part of the dreamscape.

A thought construct—my belief about who I am—cannot wake up, however, it is possible to see a thought and its related feelings and sensations for what they are. Awareness awakens to itself and recognizes the "me" as a character in the dreamplay. The self-image is not annihilated but, rather, *seen through*. It continues but without a belief in its ultimate reality. In the first movement of lucid self-recognition, there is the realization that I am <u>not</u> this dream character. With the full fruition of awakening we realize that we are that which creates the dream and everything in the dream, including the dream character called "me." As one of the great wisdom sayings from the Hindu Upanishads proclaims, "That thou art" (*Tat Tvam Asi* in Sanskrit): We discover that we are nothing less than the totality or wholeness of life.

The experience of awakening is paradoxical to the mind because it is sensed both as a deeply intimate and personal revelation of essence and as an impersonal event. The core of the individual is discovered to be open, unbounded, and universal—common to everyone and everything as a shared Ground. Although awakening registers to some sense of self in an individual body-mind, it cannot honestly be claimed by the "me." To believe "I have awakened," as if it were a personal accomplishment or attainment, is a contradiction in terms. Statements like "no one wakes up" or "awareness wakes up to itself" are closer to the truth. If we insist on how awake we are, especially in contrast to the lesser "unawakened" others around us, we are still confused—lost in the realm of the conditioned mind that divides self from other. Our real nature cannot in fact be asserted or denied even as the mind tries its best to do so. Everyone is inherently awake, whether we or they recognize it or not.

Initial awakenings or glimpses of Reality (*kensho* in Zen) are often quickly obscured by latent conditioning. This can be very frustrating, puzzling, and depressing for the spiritual seeker who, after a few hours or days of lucidity, experiences the veil of identity being redrawn like a thick curtain across a sun-drenched window. It can be helpful to remember at such times that whatever comes and goes is not *it*, but rather a transient state. What is prior to the comings and goings is always available and as ordinary as the clear sky. The well-educated spiritual mind thinks that awakening is a state to be attained in time, usually via some spiritual practice, yet it is never what we think it is. The mind gradually relaxes as it learns that it is not in charge of awakening and realizes that lucid Self-recognition is not an object or state, however subtle, that can be attained.

While some wisdom traditions identify various preparatory stages, there do not appear to be any ironclad rules for having or sustaining this radical shift in identity. Glimpses come unexpectedly to many people who are not overtly spiritual. They can happen during intense transitions like giving birth or witnessing death, while making love, or during calm moments of being in nature or contemplating beauty. They can definitely be helped along by deeply questioning one's core beliefs, being innocently available during silent meditation, and listening to and spending time with an authentic teacher. The most important factor seems to be the intensity of the desire to know one's true nature.

Generally speaking, a certain degree of inner stability, resilience, self-love, and self-acceptance are helpful for sustaining an authentic awakening. This does not mean that one must "have an ego before losing it"—a confusing formulation from a few decades ago. The issue is much subtler than this. Rather than speaking in terms of gaining and losing an ego, it is more useful to think in terms of discerning, and if necessary, strengthening the capacities of inner settledness and resilience. If there is too much inner conflict within the psyche, attention will not be available to let go of its familiar moorings, at least not for long. A deep letting go into the Unknown can further destabilize a psyche that is not sufficiently resilient to tolerate ambiguities, uncertainties, and decentering that typically accompany an opening of body, heart, and mind. It is first necessary to have or develop what Keats referred to as *negative capability,* that is, "[the capability] of being in uncertainties, mysteries, doubts, without any irritable reaching after fact and reason."[4] Sometimes structure-building, a reconstructive movement, is required before there can be a sustained deconstruction.

For this reason, it is important that therapists who have a first-hand understanding of awakening not be attached to inducing this in their clients. Pushing those clients to open themselves who are not prepared to do so can have the counterproductive effect of both strengthening their defenses against Unknowing and feeding their shame for not being good or brave enough. Both ways reinforce self-fixation. Any pushing in this direction reflects a therapist's, perhaps momentary, lapse into dualistic thinking with an idea of what clients should and should not do. In this case the therapist has slipped from being in empty-openness where "there is no mountain" into a dualistic vision that believes the client has (or is) a mountainous problem from which he needs to be awakened.

If we are not pushing an agenda for change in any direction, a client's own system will reveal where attention is needed and the pace to proceed. For example, a terrified or self-loathing "inner child" may first need to be addressed before any greater flowering can happen. Learning to listen to the body (one's own and the client's) greatly assists this process, since the felt sense of the body—including the "energy body" within the intersubjective field—is the most trust-worthy key to discern such inner guidance.

Even as we acknowledge the value of a certain degree of inner coherence and stability to sustain awakening, we also recognize that self-cohesion and stability refer paradoxically to the ability to release self-cohesiveness and to become destabilized and decentered in one's thoughts, feelings, and sensations. A sufficiently strong sense of self has the confidence to encounter Otherness without the terror of either being engulfed or annihilated by it. The stronger our sense of self is, the less we need to cling to a point of view. An awakening, at least initially, involves a radical disidentification from what we have taken ourselves to be. *It is not that our thoughts or feelings have transformed so much as has our relationship to them.*

This insight leads to the interesting topic of "spiritual bypassing"[5]—the well-known and extremely common tendency of spiritual seekers to try to avoid difficult personal issues, such as experiencing emotional vulnerability, being in an intimate relationship, or holding down a job, by "transcending" them. Although worldly involvement, especially an intimate relationship, has a way of bringing us down to ground—hard and fast, we can still spend years and even decades trying to meditate our problems away. As Chogyam Trungpa noted long ago, it is all too common for many of us on a spiritual path to subvert the teachings to conform to our neuroses, to practice a kind of "spiritual materialism" in which we may vacation in a blissfully detached *samadhi*, happy while we are meditating, but without letting the power of our concentrated mind penetrate our conditioning.[6] The willingness to honestly and vulnerably face whatever we tend to avoid or hold on to is critically important.

On the other hand, believing that we need to be utterly free of neuroses before we can wake up becomes the recipe for an endless and tragic self-improvement project. The luminous Indian sage Ramana Maharshi taught that the greatest obstacle to awakening is our belief that it is not possible. We can easily fixate to either position: trying to avoid our vulnerabilities while on a spiritual quest or engaging in endless self-improvement with the long-term goal of some mentally idealized spiritual realization. Each is a dead end.

How then to proceed? Do we focus our attention on spiritual awakening or psychological transformation? The mind enjoys dilemmas of this sort, yet the answer has a way of working itself out in each individual depending on a number of factors that largely hinge on discovering what it is that we most want. If we and our clients are willing to be stripped bare in our quest for what is most deeply true within ourselves, then our hearts and minds will be drawn to the polestar of awakening. If we are interested in making our daily lives better integrated and adaptive, we will gravitate toward more conventional psychological work. Each approach has intrinsic value. Assisting people to be more in touch with their bodies and feelings and clearer in their thinking is noble work that greatly reduces suffering and radiates out benefits to society as a whole, a point that some spiritual teachers undervalue.

In actual sessions with clients, spiritual and psychological insights and shifts often bubble up together. For instance, when we are immersed in a psychotherapeutic process, opening to Unknowing and releasing an "immature" fixation of some kind, the difficult and humbling work of being-with whatever the fixation may be is flush with self-transcending courage, unconditional presence, and

liberating insight that often releases an exhilarating swell of awareness and compassion for self and other. In other words, pre-personal
"psychological work"—when it is working—may be thoroughly
*trans*personal in experience, and the authentic occasion of a matur-
ing spiritual emergence and integration. By the same token—as
every spiritual warrior knows—when we are doing spiritual work at
an intensive meditation retreat for instance, it can involve confront-
ing and releasing sticky, decidedly immature psychological fixations.
Spiritual work unleashes elements that are thoroughly psychological, just as psychological transformations prepare the ground for
spiritual awakenings.

We may become rightly suspicious, therefore, that we must choose
one path over another. Can we not both awaken *and* transform our
body-minds, relationships, and society so that they become more
transparent and creative expressions of Spirit? As we discover that
the forms of daily life and our psychological constructs are truly not
separate from our deepest nature as open, lucid emptiness, cannot
phenomenal life come into greater harmony as a conscious and loving expression of essence? How best do we approach this possibility
of individual and collective transformation? These questions lead us
to the complex and nuanced issue of nondual embodiment.

NONDUAL EMBODIMENT

Then There Is

When entranced in dualistic vision, we are distracted and preoccupied
with our own emotional projections and mental constructions, which
we mistake for Reality. Shakyamuni Buddha called this confused state
of mind *samsara*. But when we see into the empty essence of this
virtual reality show, we discover that neither things nor ourselves
have any kind of independent existence. With this insight, the source
of suffering, clinging to apparent reality (and thereby resisting
Reality), is cut, and the freedom of *nirvana* is tasted.

We may think this path is a one-way journey or crossing from
the near shore of samsara to the far shore of nirvana. But even a
deep experience of unconditioned presence, in which one dwells in

peaceful stillness, does not necessarily effect a full embodiment of freedom. Rather, presence must penetrate our daily lives and conditioned minds, including the subtle karmic traces *(vasanas)* to which we are predisposed. This requires a further step beyond dwelling in a pacified state alone to realize, as the Buddha declares in the Heart Sutra, "nirvana is not other than samsara, samsara is not other than nirvana." While some nondual spiritual traditions emphasize the realization of emptiness as the final goal, we believe that a mature nondual realization fully embraces the paradox of emptiness and fullness: There is no mountain yet there is. In this understanding, the world reappears as an expression or play of unconditioned awareness rather than as a separate object. Longchenpa, the great *dzogchen* master of the fourteenth-century, sings the essence of this paradox,

> Know the state of pure and total presence to be a vast expanse without center or border.
> It is everywhere the same, without acceptance or rejection.
> Blend the nature of mind and its habit patterns into nonduality.
> Because entities, whether subjectively conceived or directly experienced,
> Are present as ornaments of one's own state of being,
> Do not accept or reject them.
> Because they are not divided into self and other,
> The apparitional, spontaneously present objects are the play of pure [unconditioned] experience.[7]

Most major Eastern nondual spiritual traditions recognize that awakening is the beginning rather than the end of an open-ended process of spiritual transformation. This recognition is particularly strong in Dzogchen, Zen and Kashmiri Saivism, while less so in Advaita Vedanta, which tends to favor the transcendent over the immanent. It is one thing to thoroughly wake up to one's true nature as the formless ground of being or no-self; it is another to *actualize* or *embody* this awareness in one's daily life in the body and in relationship and to transpose these changes to collective, societal structures.

Each body-mind holds different degrees and kinds of conditioning, both individually and collectively, from sources as varied as one's multigenerational family of origin, genetics, socioeconomic class, collective racial, ethnic, and national histories, and even possible "past lives." In a curious, awe-inspiring, and humbling way, each of us carries the collective conditioning and heritage of human evolution within our multidimensional body-minds as a kind of hologram.

The deeper the awakening, however, the less we are identified with this conditioning. It may still arise, but just as we awaken from or within a bad dream, we are not bound by it. There is a natural ability to be spaciously intimate with our lived experience, however roughly or smoothly it arises. This effortless capacity to be both clear and compassionate with our own and others' conditioned experience provides an optimal environment to dissolve long-standing knots. Tendencies of the body-mind that are not in accord with our true nature tend to stand out more starkly even as they are unconditionally accepted. One does not need to go searching for these incongruencies, since they will naturally arise in a spontaneous flushing out or decompression process. According to Integral philosopher Ken Wilber:[8]

> As you rest in that uncontrived state of pure immediateness or pure freedom, then strange things start to happen. All of the subjective tendencies that you had previously *identified* with—all of those little selves and subjects that held open the gap between the seer and the seen—they all start burning in the freedom of nonduality. They all scream to the surface and die....

Adyashanti, a contemporary American spiritual teacher with a background in Zen, starkly describes this postawakening process of embodiment as often being "a bloody mess." He elaborates on this "spiritual alchemy":[9]

> Certainly, when we have had some deep realization of our true nature, we have an intuitive or innate sense of what's arising within us that's not in accord with that true nature and

is the product of some element of divided mind or divided emotional body. We have this sense of it because we had a direct awakening to that which is undivided. Our own divisions tend to stand out much more clearly and vividly than before. In some way they often hurt much more than they did before… because they have this backdrop of wholeness. A lot of embodiment is simply remaining completely real and completely honest to our own experience in a very deep and authentic way, without necessarily trying to change it. Our conditioned tendencies are allowed to unfold into the field of awareness. It's the spiritual alchemy that takes place almost by itself, if we can just get out of the way enough.

This is a very different process than the "integration" normally described in the psychospiritual literature that conceptualizes a discrete somebody who is trying to integrate spirit. In the case of postawakening nondual embodiment, it is more accurate to say that the conditioned body-mind surrenders to and gradually aligns itself with the deepest truth within us. While one part may integrate with another, parts cannot integrate the whole—it is the other way around. When we discover the implicit, nonseparate wholeness that we are, all of the parts begin to spontaneously realign or reorchestrate themselves with That so that our lives move more harmoniously in service to our deepest truth. Nondual embodiment is an ongoing, open-ended individual and collective process.

We normally think of truth dualistically as the content of a specific statement or as a polarity to what is false. But the kind of deep truth we are invoking here is not bound to this dichotomy. The existential philosopher, Martin Heidegger, spoke of the essence of truth in its originary sense as *aletheia*, which means unconcealment, or disclosure.[10] In this sense, essential truth is a moment of opening-up, of pure and simple revelation. It is less a judgment about *what* is revealed—as true or false—than a description of the *process* of opening-up and responding from a naked presence. If we are open and opening ourselves, in speech or in silence, that is a moment of Truth. Conversely, if we are preoccupied with our own thoughts and feelings, and thus self-enclosed and self-constructing our own reality, we are not being True in this essential sense, in the sense of an arrow that flies "true" through an open sky, free and unimpeded.

There are two main schools of thought about the process of spiritual awakening and embodiment: direct and progressive. In the direct approach, assuming that there is enough interest and systemic resiliency, the initial focus is on waking up out of form into one's true nondual nature. In a Zen-influenced approach, which, along with Advaita, is currently the most prominent traditional form of nondual practice being woven into Western psychological and psychotherapeutic practices, the emphasis is primarily deconstructive—rigorously questioning core beliefs about one's self and the world and relaxing into a background silent openness. Once a deep awakening has happened, it is followed by a phase of "waking down" into form where inner splits and dense conditioning are faced and worked through at an accelerated pace due to the lack of identification with them.

Tibetan Buddhist Mahamudra and Dzogchen are somewhat different from this, especially insofar as they do not emphasize the deconstructive methods favored by the Mahayana Madhyamika approach which so influences Zen. The Madhyamika-Zen approach works on the level of mental constructs, conceptual and imaginal, that are deconstructed to reveal their true, empty essence. However, both Mahamudra and Dzogchen emphasize the natural wakefulness of nondual presence (*vidya* in Sanskrit / *rig-pa* in Tibetan), which is based on recognition of the mind's inherent emptiness.[11] While this principle is the same for both, the paths of each differ.[12] Mahamudra is a tantric discipline that works principally on the level of energy as a gradual path of transformation, transforming impure, conditioned vision into pure, unconditioned vision. Through working with visualizations (*guruyoga*) and subtle energy (*prana, nadis, chakras*), practices of tantric yoga are gradually "developed" to the point of "completion" in the Mahamudra proper: the embodied recognition that conditioned experience is not other than unconditioned presence. In contrast, Dzogchen works primarily on the level of the essence, or nature, of mind rather than on either the conceptual level of deconstructing psychological fixations or on the energy level of transforming felt experience. A nongradual path, Dzogchen begins with the direct, mind-to-mind transmission, or communion, of nondual presence between teacher and student. While work on both the energy and psychological levels may be valid and important to undertake in this approach, these are understood to be secondary practices distinct from Dzogchen proper, which is the instantaneous embodiment of our true, nondual condition, already complete and perfect as it is.

A progressive approach emphasizes the importance of a careful, gradual purification and transformation of the body-mind as preparation for a distant awakening. There is the assumption of someone working on bettering themselves, gradually progressing from confusion and fixation to clarity and openness.

Both direct and progressive paths have potential pitfalls. With the direct approach, there is the danger of inflation and dissociation, where we can believe that we have awakened when it has yet to happen and feel superior to others. With the progressive approach, one may work on laying the groundwork for an awakening that will never occur because the underlying assumption of the "me" who is trying to get somewhere is never effectively questioned. Tragically, freedom is endlessly postponed in the name of self-purification and improvement.

The most critical issue in this discussion as it relates to the practice of psychotherapy revolves around the theme of acceptance. Both direct and gradual approaches emphasize the importance of accepting *what is*—thoughts, feelings, and sensations just as they are. Yet where does this acceptance, this welcoming, this embrace of experience no matter how dark, painful, and humiliating, come from? It is very doubtful that it is the conditioned mind. *While the mind can learn to accept to some degree, this learned acceptance always has a hidden agenda —the hope that what we accept will change. The only "thing" that is totally and unconditionally accepting is that which is Total and Unconditioned—our natural Being or no-self. Any lesser form of acceptance involves a bargained-for exchange.*

If this is true, then the critical task is not so much to "practice" accepting or "trying" to integrate Spirit into the body, which sounds a lot like trying to stuff the infinite into a small space, as it is to be extremely honest in facing our shortcomings and vulnerabilities, to inquire deeply into and see through all of our cherished beliefs, to feel our feelings, to sense our sensations, to relinquish the illusion of control, and to surrender to the Unknown. In other words, we submit to being utterly stripped. This puts us on the doorstep of awakening, open and available to Openness.

Awakening itself liberates unconditional acceptance, which then speeds transformation and an embodied nonduality. A preawakening transformational process has, of course, already been happening. If this has gone quite deeply, as is sometimes the case, the postawakening unfolding will happen that much more quickly and smoothly. In any case, transformation happens at an accelerated pace because of disidentification and nonattachment to the results. A therapist with a deep nondual understanding can help facilitate both pre- and postawakening sides of this sacred process, monitoring and guiding clients through possible pitfalls, and supporting them during this sometimes difficult and frightening unfolding. A caterpillar cannot foresee itself as a butterfly, even though to be one is inherent in its nature. The metamorphosis can be harrowing, and an experienced guide, whether therapist, teacher, or both, can be extremely helpful.

NONDUALITY REVISITED

It will be useful to briefly revisit our understanding of the term "nonduality" since there is often understandable confusion about its meaning. Yet, we must be clear at the outset that any definition of That which is inherently whole is bound to fail. So *by definition* a definition of nonduality will be inadequate. How can thought penetrate the mystery of its own source? If we are honest, we must acknowledge that the best we can do is to offer a negative definition, that is, a definition of what nonduality is not. But even this will not help us much since nonduality excludes nothing, even these pale attempts to say what it isn't. After all, the discerning mind and its thoughts are also an expression of our true nature.

If we can agree that nonduality refers to an inherent reality that is prior to a mind-created split between an observer/observed, subject/object, and self/other, we are on our way to at least some intellectual understanding. The crucial difference is whether this understanding is experiential or conceptual. If it makes sense only on the conceptual level, it will fail to penetrate the conditioned mind, remaining only as another spiritually seductive idea. But even if nonduality is tasted experientially, pitfalls abound. In particular, confusion may arise if we equate nonduality only with the formless ground of Being or no-self—that realm that is experientially absent of polarities. *If we take the formless ground as something distinct from the world of form, then it is not nondual—it is notdual, absent in itself of polarities, yet still subtly separate from form.* This corresponds to what Ken Wilber calls the causal state because it is the source or cause of all manifestation:[13]

> This… causal state… is often likened to the state of deep dreamless sleep, except that this state is not a mere blank but rather an utter fullness, and it is experienced as such—as infinitely drenched in the fullness of Being, so full that no manifestation can even begin to contain it. Because it can never be seen as an object, this pure Self is pure Emptiness.

Yet in the "causal state" there still remains a subtle yet distinct sense of a witness separate from what is witnessed and the world therefore appears to be something separate. This eventually gives way to complete nonduality:

> The sense of being a Witness "in here" completely vanishes itself, and the Witness turns out to be everything that is witnessed. The *causal* gives way to the *Nondual*, and formless mysticism gives way to nondual mysticism. "Form is emptiness and Emptiness is form."…You don't look at the sky, you are the sky…. (A)wareness is no longer split into a seeing subject in here and seen object out there. There is just pure seeing. Consciousness and its display are not-two….The pure *Emptiness* of the Witness turns out to be one with every *Form* that is witnessed, and that is one of the basic meanings of "nonduality."[14]

Nonduality then is that ground that is prior to and inclusive of all divisions of emptiness and form or the absolute and the relative. It is undivided and nonseparate, not-one and not-two. Trying to define it, the mind stands at the threshold of its own understanding and peers into a dark Mystery. Yet we are always none other than this, even as we may read and puzzle over these words. The reader is not other than what is being read.

THE AUTHORS AND CHAPTERS

As with *The Sacred Mirror*, almost all of these original essays have been expressly written for this volume. One (Judith Blackstone's) arrived synchronously from an unexpected direction *as if* it were written for this anthology. Life is indeed surprising! Many of the authors have presented at the Conference on Nondual Wisdom and Psychotherapy.[15]

The authors come from an increasingly difficult to distinguish blend of roles: therapist/academic teacher, therapist/spiritual teacher, academic/spiritual teacher, and so on. As there is a deepening into nondual wisdom, and as the ground of Being is more consciously recognized, role identities become increasingly fluid and are more lightly held. We are wearing more hats these days and removing them more quickly. Please take a look at the "About the Contributors" section at the back of the book for details.

In the mere four years since *The Sacred Mirror* appeared, the "field" of nondual approaches to and enrichments of psychotherapy has matured, inviting us to make finer distinctions within this notoriously difficult to define subject. Having gone much more indepth into the subjects of emptiness, awakening, and nondual embodiment in the preceding introductory section, we now plunge into the substance of the specific essays. Eleven diverse yet complementary chapters explore in their own unique ways the cataracts, chasms, peaks, and plains that appear and disappear in this territory that we are calling the heart of Silence.

✳

In "Spacious Intimacy: Reflections on Essential Relationship, Empathic Resonance, Projective Identification, and Witnessing," John Prendergast explores several central themes in psychotherapy from the perspective of two apparently polarized qualities—the sense of open, nonattached spaciousness and the sense of intimacy or closeness. He suggests that the ground of Being or no-self is the source of each of these essential qualities, and that conscious recognition of this ground allows for their effortless and spontaneous expression in therapy. When this occurs, the therapist and client meet *right here*, not distant, not merged, and not limited to dialoguing as a discrete self and other in some interpersonal in-between space. An essential meeting can happen only when we are at home in Being or no-self. It feels like a host warmly receiving a guest into his or her home, but with some important differences:

> We meet the other in the same shared homeground, yet this "place" cannot be localized. Both parties can recognize that we are *here together*, but neither can say where this is or to whom this meeting space belongs. Further, we cannot say who is the host and who is the guest!

A case vignette illustrates the phenomena of empathic resonance where the apparent self-other split dissolves and John shares in his client's subtle feeling and accompanying energetic contraction while retaining the sense of a vast, open space. He describes nondual dimensions of "deep empathy" that can be recognized via open-mindedness, body sensing, and careful discernment. He also touches on the psychoanalytic concepts of projective and introjective identification, introducing the concept of introjective disidentification as an expression of spacious intimacy and a necessary ingredient for the functioning of empathic resonance. He ends with a discussion of witnessing, cautioning against the tendency to identify as a separate, spacious but unfeeling witness, or, to become caught in a disconnected emptiness:

An *inclusive disidentification* acknowledges that "we are not *only* this." We are not only these thoughts, feelings, and sensations: We are more (if we acknowledge our ultimate fullness) and less (if we acknowledge our ultimate emptiness). We are both more and less than what we have taken ourselves to be. And we are also what we have taken ourselves to be. Nothing is excluded. We come full circle: We are nothing and we are everything—between the two our life flows as a celebration of spacious intimacy.

Two chapters are devoted to revisioning the therapeutic attitude according to principles of nondual wisdom intertwined with the psychoanalytic sensibilities of Intersubjectivity theory.

In "From Neutrality to the Play of Unconditional Presence," Ken Bradford teases apart the compelling contradiction within the unconventional attitude of therapeutic neutrality, which, despite a full fifty years of critique, refuses to die. On the one hand and at its evocative best, Ken suggests that the radical heart of neutrality challenges therapists to meet the other nakedly, in *unconditional presence.* On the other hand, neutrality functions as a defensive stance that works against itself, insulating therapists from a naked, evocative encounter, whether with an other person or with the Otherness inside oneself. After a careful discussion of this contradiction, he considers how an *intersubjective* attitude of empathy and introspection mitigates the defensive posture but does not dissolve it. He proceeds to explicate intersubjectivity from a nondual perspective by noting how it is the *inter-ness,* or *interbeing,* of interacting subjects, rather than the subjectivities themselves, that is most evocative of authenticity. Discussing authenticity as the play of unconditional presence, Ken considers how nondual copresence opens the way for liberating therapeutic exchanges as noted in a case example.

An *inter*-ness as *subjectivity* aerates the therapeutic atmosphere, lightening the habitual tendency to reify ourselves and others as separate *beings* disjunct from *Being.*

Finding himself within the unconditional gaze and presence of a therapist, a client may be influenced to shift from taking himself primarily as an enduring Self, a kind of property owner who *has* problems, to being someone who is more of an *unfolding, open-ended awareness* within a shared field of subjective experiencing, in which problems arise, persist, and pass away. Allowing for enhanced spaciousness around problems naturally bodes well for dealing with them more effectively, as well as for loosening the core fixation of separateness that inclines us to take on and personalize problems, thus losing touch with the responsive sanity we were born with.

Judith Blackstone discusses nondual consciousness as the essence and ground of personal subjective experience that is not other than impersonal, or "transubjective," experience, and discusses how opening to this dimension facilitates maturation in "Intersubjectivity and Nonduality in the Psychotherapeutic Relationship." Through a critical reading of Intersubjectivity theory interfacing with nondual wisdom of Buddhism and Advaita Vedanta, she examines,

> the shaping of experience by invariant organizing principles…, describes the relational field, particularly in the psychotherapeutic relationship, as both intersubjective and nondual, and argues that nondual properties of the intersubjective field are revealed as both the therapist and the client relinquish invariant organizations of experience.

Judith addresses some pitfalls of nondual teachings that can unwittingly enhance fragmentation and dissociation rather than promote wholeness, especially as they promote a focus on the content of experience rather than on the embodied subject. The danger here is, "Rather than experiencing the integration of subject and object, the subject is simply negated, and the practitioner becomes fixated on the object."

In contrast, she notes theoretically and in a clinical illustration the therapeutic value of nondual awareness to enhance therapeutic skillfulness, such as subtle perception and empathy, including sensitivity to the constrictions and flows of the subtle energy body (*chakras* and *prana*).

> In the subtle core of the body we become disentangled from the material body as nondual consciousness. This does not mean that we are separate from the material body. It means that, as nondual consciousness, we pervade the body (and all phenomena) without interruption. The subtle core of our being is thus our entranceway into the transcendent space of nondual consciousness. However, it is also, at the same time, the source of the qualitative, cohesive experience of our individual being. Thus, nondual realization is the basis not only of subject/object unity, but of mind/body unity and cognition/affect unity as well.

Dorothy Hunt describes nondual wisdom as "the spontaneous *movement* of life responding to itself or expressing itself from true seeing and true listening in the moment" in "Mystery, Mind, and Meaning." This undefinable Mystery moves as a "compassion that meets suffering with what actually has the capacity to transform it, and the wisdom that knows how." In her view, this Mystery has two faces, dark and bright:

> Sometimes the great Reality reveals itself absent of all qualities, an unfathomable darkness that can consume all universes in a single gulp. Sometimes it reveals itself as a clear, awake, and shining presence that illuminates the world, speaks truth without fear, or moves to meet suffering with a tender love.

She further distinguishes between a natural sense of being and a *conceptually* separate self or "I" where Consciousness identifies with the conditioned body/mind, imagining itself to be separate and creating "an energetic field of resistance to what *is*." This ego is:

> a movement to survive that the self-reflecting mind has made into a supposed noun, a "me" that we imagine is our organiz-

ing principle. That imagined "principle" has taken on as its all-consuming job one thing and one thing only: to survive.

Awakening frees the body/mind to live increasingly from the Mystery rather than from the compulsion to control in order to survive. In psychotherapy this Mystery moves more directly and freely when we are not attached to meaning, which is often a subtle attempt to control experience. Dorothy notes, "Although nothing has inherent meaning apart from its sheer existence as *what is,* the mind continually attributes meaning to things and then acts from its self-created images." She elaborates:

> What seems important is our willingness to find out what meaning we have made of experience and to be willing to question it from the perspective of the Truth within us. It is Truth that sees untruth. It is also the case that when we speak *from* Truth, we naturally speak *to* Truth in the apparent other, inviting that deeper knowing.

Once the mind has surrendered to its unknowable and mysterious source, a new dimension of exploration can unfold:

> We cannot pretend to be somewhere we are not. However, if we happen to be working from an awakened perspective, we may discover that, naturally and spontaneously, we will be inviting this different dimension of exploration into the room and into our practice. The shift happens not because we intend to do so, but because when the embodied Mystery begins to move from its own wisdom, compassion, and clarity, mind is surrendered to that movement.

In "Listening and Speaking from No-Mind," Peter Fenner further articulates his practice of "nondual therapy," which draws upon the art of conceptual deconstruction rooted in Mahayana Buddhism. Understanding "therapy" in its essential sense as the removal of obscurations to unconditioned presence, he allows that this therapy

might include, and indeed, might focus on the discovery of unconditioned mind through "contentless communication," which occurs
through listening and speaking from no-mind. As a spiritual teacher,
Peter practices primarily in the contexts of group settings, including
workshops and long-term training programs, and presents deconstructive dialogues drawn from these contexts.

The explicit aim of his nondual therapy is to recognize and rest
in unconditioned mind. With this focus, Peter challenges psychotherapists to stretch their scope of practice beyond the conventional
boundaries defining the field of psychology. Challenging conventional assumptions, including those governing Transpersonal forms
of psychology, which privilege the discovery and creation of meaning, Peter presents an approach aimed at releasing meaningful—or
meaningless—constructions altogether so to discover the basic
openness which is their actual, uncontrived nature. The aim of this
deconstructive approach is to arrive nowhere, being nobody. That
is, the practice of no mind is to discover that there is nowhere better one need go to improve one's life and there is no need to either
defend or promote a self that has no independent existence. Thus,
the tensions of struggle and striving dissolve into "healing bliss."

Peter describes unconditioned communication as paradoxical,
and discusses the sense of this, foreign as it is to ordinary logic and
linear thinking. Through the use of specific skillful means, such as
deconstructive conversation and natural koans, which he exempli-
fies through nondual dialogues, the therapeutic power of unconditioned presence is revealed as relational *entrainment*, which cleaves
below dualistic thought and constructions of meaning to an unconditioned meeting of minds.

> By sharing our experience of nondual awareness without
> words or effort, we invite the people with whom we're in rela-
> tionship to entrain or attune to this experience themselves.
> As we rest in a state that is free of all ambition, the energy of
> serenity naturally transfers from one person to another like
> two bells resonating together. In nondual therapy, much of the
> work occurs through this process of energetic entrainment.

Kaisa Puhakka, along with several other contributors, addresses the challenges and paradoxes of talking and thinking about nonduality in "Nonduality: A Spontaneous Movement 'To' and 'Fro.'" She suggests that a simple way of doing this is by attending to the subtle flow of the "appearing" or "disappearing" of the self, leading readers through a phenomenology of self-fixation. In the process, she deconstructs the self's apparent stability, revealing the inherent emptiness and instability of selfhood.

> A self that is not fixated naturally disappears and appears, or "goes into" and "comes from" states of nonduality.

In the context of spiritual practices that cultivate the experience of no-self, Kaisa observes the paradox that "any attempt to make itself disappear only affirms the self's existence." Conversely, she notes that self-fixation also resists being dissolved in practices that foster expansion of the ordinary self into a "Higher Self" or Brahman, which may just be a higher order self-fixation. In contrast to the fixating of selfhood, and in terms of psychotherapy, she notes,

> In the natural coming and going of the self the problem of the self is gone—not solved but simply gone. We can see that the self need not be banished or even improved in any way. When it comes to the self's own projects, fixing is the same as fixating. When this understanding reaches deep into our bones, it allows us, as psychotherapists, to manifest a space of acceptance for our clients that is not just a matter of approach or even attitude on our part but is ontological, reaching into the heart of being with a tremendous power to heal.

Kaisa presents clinical examples of nonfixating therapeutic exchanges that do not reify the client's story or the therapist's own position by taking them so seriously. She discusses "original speech" as a speaking from emptiness and shows how this is both inherently creative in a therapeutic sense as well as a challenge to the therapist to face her own fear of possible self-disintegration.

David Loy extends his groundbreaking interdisciplinary study of nonduality and the central problem of *lack* in a succinct chapter addressing the psychosocial dynamics of the causes of suffering entitled, "Experiencing the Universe as Yourself: The Nonduality of Self and Society." He unpacks the three kinds of suffering *(dukkha)* described by Shakyamuni Buddha: commonly recognized suffering, which comes when we receive that which we do not want, such as sickness, infidelity, and traffic tickets, or the suffering that comes when we do not get that which we long for, like wealth, fame, peace, and quiet; the suffering of impermanence: the awareness that we are sure to lose anything and everything, including our own life; and the most unsettling yet least recognized form of suffering: the nagging sense that we, ourselves, do not exist in the way we think we do—that is, ungroundedness itself.

> This ungroundedness is like a hole at the core of my being. It is usually experienced as a sense of lack that tends to be a source of continual frustration because it can never be filled up. No matter how hard I try, my sense-of-self never becomes a real self.

David explicates the suffering of this lack by describing how modern, materialistic society caters to and exacerbates it by promising to fill inner emptiness with material goods and services, political/social security, and other handy distractions from the reality of emptiness. He expands the usual discussion of the ego as a solitary problem by both observing how consensual reality contributes to the ego's evasion of its own lack in the form of a collective we-ego, or "wego." And, he reveals how these social structures in which we are enmeshed institutionalize and promote the three poisons of greed, ill-will, and delusion.

In "Walking the Talk: The Principles and Practices of Embodied Spirituality," Mariana Caplan explores the challenge of integrating nondual wisdom "into every microfiber of dualistic expression." It is one thing to have powerful and illuminating experiences of nondual wisdom, but a very different matter for this wisdom to be integrated in the everyday life of the body, feelings, and intimate relationships. Mariana invites us to have a passionate curiosity about our own blind spots, particularly as Westerners:

> The primary arenas in which most spiritual aspirants fall unconscious, regardless of their degree of insight, boil down to money, power, and sexuality, the realm in which the fruits of our spiritual integration are expressed… or not.

She cautions against neo-Advaitic paths of instant enlightenment and "fast-food" spiritual technologies that do not educate students about the need to attend to gritty psychological issues or to prepare the body and the mind for the "tremendous energetic 'voltage' that such (nondual) states bring with them." Moreover,

> When an individual experiences a nondual state, the illusory nature of psychological constructs and relative reality is temporarily apparent. However, because such states are highly transitory, what is often left of the experience is a memory of the realization.

The memory can be useful if it reminds us that most of our problems are a matter of misperception, or if we are inspired to open to a deeper reality. It can be a hindrance if it is used as a strategy to avoid or bypass the messy business of daily life. Given the current human capacity for collective self-destruction, we are called to come off of the transcendental mountaintop and "to penetrate and transmute the dualistic world of form and manifestation with the diamond perception of nonduality."

Mariana identifies a spectrum of approaches to accomplish this integration, ranging from those that are "top-down" (commonly found in *The Sacred Mirror* as well as this volume) to those of conventional psychotherapy that focus on unwinding problems one by one. She locates her own approach, which she calls *enlightened duality*, somewhere in between:

It does not directly evoke nondual experience through teaching or technique, but instead this awareness serves as a silent, prevalent context from which the ordinary stuff of life is considered. When enlightened duality is applied to therapy, the nondual perspective is transmitted to the client through the energy or awareness of the therapist such that spiritual insight arises naturally with the client's own awareness, even though spiritual theory and technique may never be mentioned.

Regardless of the approach, she suggests that a full nondual realization will result in embodiment where, "our bodies… become the transmuted expression of our own integrated consciousness."

Drawing upon Tibetan teachings in her chapter entitled "Healing from the Heart: Embodying Nondual Wisdom," Penny Fenner sounds a cautionary note identifying pitfalls of nondual practice in general and nondual forms of therapy in particular. She discusses the importance of integrating relative and absolute truth, and emphasizes the value of cultivating loving-kindness as a way to facilitate this embodiment of nondual realization, which functions as a natural protection against the self-deceptions that can undermine the authenticity of unconditioned presence.

If we become fixated in either the relative or the absolute we are still trapped in dualism where one viewpoint is rejected for the other.

Clear preference or overconceptualization of the absolute, coupled with a lack of bodily grounding, can show up as avoidance or disidentification with emotions. When excessive, this can stimulate varying degrees of disconnection or even disassociation.

Without loving-kindness we typically become defensive against [and so fixated on] the pain of relative reality, keeping us deluded and trapped. We can become so lost in the relative that our pain seems more than real, our patterns solid and permanent. Instead of experiencing ego death, we become ensconced in the relative intensity of our patterns, unable to see their ultimately illusory nature.

With loving-kindness we can be more available to each moment, however it arises. This affords a capacity to attend to painful, tight aspects that occlude our true nature from shining forth! By directing loving-kindness toward such feelings we develop inner robustness. Instead of trying to talk ourselves into or out of what we are feeling, we are open to the full play of human experience. Dualistic fixations melt away.

Penny presents two case studies of her psychotherapy work aimed at embodying nondual wisdom. As this occurs, she notes,

Within the natural freedom of being we are enveloped in ever deepening acceptance, humility, and love. Alongside humility comes tremendous relief in letting go of conditioned or newly acquired concepts and theories, preferences, hopes, and fears, such that we can peacefully abide in "not knowing," grateful for the presence of each moment to be just as it is.

Sheila Krystal writes about the role of nonverbal, somatic therapies in the process of healing and awakening in "Nondual Wisdom and Body-Based Therapy," and notes that,

Body-based therapy can help people to relax completely, surrender to the experience of the vastness, and receive it fully. When the body is deeply relaxed, attention can more easily move beyond the body. Ironically, the ultimate body-based therapy leads to the realization that "I am not only the body."

Yet bodywork does not by itself bring true freedom. Despite significant and beneficial energetic shifts and healings that may happen during a body-based approach, if both the therapist and client are identified with their roles, the socially induced trance of separateness will continue.

Sheila describes her own clinical practice of using deep yogic breathing (*pranayama* in Sanskrit) along with an intuitive laying on of hands that arise from the sense of a unified field of love and kindness that she shares with her clients:

> Body-based therapy from this perspective becomes a mostly nonverbal inquiry into the psychological and physical patterns of trauma and conditioning and the holding of that conditioning in the tissues of the body.

As in other forms of psychotherapy, "therapeutic resonance" helps guide both therapist and client to sense and breathe their way through deep energetic contractions and releases.

She presents a lengthy case history of working with a client who went through many periods of recovery from and relapse into heroin addiction prior to therapy. Sheila's guided breathwork and intuitive touch gradually allowed the client to release old tensions and traumas, find an inner calmness, increasingly disidentify from her thoughts and cravings, and to rest in a silent, background awareness.

She concludes:

> The essence of body-based therapy from a nondual perspective is attention, relaxation, and inquiry into memory and habits of mind, behavior, and body. As they breathe and their bodies relax deeply, clients begin to wonder how many times they can persist in thinking the same thought while still believing that it is significant. They question their relationship with thought and the emotions associated with it and begin to ask the deeper question of who is thinking and feeling. Their attachment to thoughts and beliefs can loosen as they directly experience a deeper essence that is beyond thought and emotion.

Timothy Conway introduces us to the Indian sources of nondual teachings in "Nondual Awakening: Its Source and Applications." The historical roots of nondual awareness first emerged in India over three thousand years ago. Timothy traces this rich oral and written tradition of transcendent and immanent divinity from the Hindu *Vedas* to the

Upanishads and offers some samples of their "riveting aphorisms":

> "It is the notion of 'otherness' that results in fear."
>
> "There is no other seer but He, no other hearer, perceiver, thinker but He."
>
> "No one can see Him with sight. By heart, insight, and intuition is He contemplated."

Nondual teachings continued to be refined and expressed through the Brahma Sutras and famous *Bhagavad Gita* that contains Krishna's instructions to his friend and disciple Arjuna. Gaudapada and Shankara's teachings gave rise to the enormously influential school of *Advaita Vedanta*. Kashmiri Saivism developed nondual teachings in a different direction, asserting that the universe arises as "the eternal dynamic love-play of Siva and Sakti." Modern sages such as Ramana Maharshi and Nisargadatta Maharaj are recent exemplars of the vital nondual wisdom tradition of Advaita.

Timothy explores how nondual wisdom could impact the therapeutic relationship:

> Divine Awareness in the form of the client "approaches" Awareness in the form of the therapist… saying, on the personality-level, "I have a problem."…*Awareness compassionately, empathetically shares this client's pain. The drama of the Divine playing the noble role of a struggling human being is so utterly full of dignity and pathos!...* From this context of true Identity and enlightened Freedom, any personal issues, now "de-problematized," can then be therapeutically explored, worked through (played through!), and to some extent healed or resolved.

He goes on to note, however, that the ultimate "solution to all problems is waking up from the assumption of false identity. Then one is *fully Divine*, consciously playing at being *fully human*."

Timothy identifies four modes of awakening that therapists can encourage: 1) stopping/dropping/letting go of the illusion of being a separate, personal self, 2) re-cognizing or knowing again one's real nature, 3) returning Home or coming back, usually through self-inquiry and, 4) penetrating or bursting through/beyond the dream of limited identity.

He ends the essay with a section of common questions (and incisive answers) about nondual awakening, including: how to find or perceive the Self, what basic attitude to maintain, the purpose of suffering, how to deal with the experience of a dead, disconnected sense of emptiness, spiritual energies and powers, and how to sustain an expanded sense of Awareness.

ENDNOTES

1. N. Norbu and A. Clement (1999). *The Supreme Source: The Kunjed Gyalpo.* Trans. A. Lukianowicz. Ithaca, NY: Snow Lion.

2. D. Loy (1996). *Lack and Transcendence.* NJ: Humanities Press.

3. R. Blakney (1941). *Meister Eckhart.* NY: Harper & Row, pp. 231–32.

4. Quoted in D. Beres (1980). "Certainty: A Failed Quest," in *Psychoanalytic Quarterly* 49: 1–26.

5. J. Welwood, (2000). *Toward a Psychology of Awakening.* Boston: Shambhala.

6. C. Trungpa (1973). *Cutting through Spiritual Materialism.* Ed. J. Baker & M. Casper. Boston: Shambhala.

7. Longchenpa (1987). *You Are the Eyes of the World.* Trans. K. Lipman & M. Peterson. Novato, CA: Lotsawa.

8. K. Wilber (1996). *A Brief History of Everything.* Boston: Shambhala, p. 235.

9. Adyashanti.(2003). "Love Returning for Itself," in *The Sacred Mirror: Nondual Wisdom and Psychotherapy.* Ed. J. Prendergast, P. Fenner, and S. Krystal. St. Paul: Paragon House, p. 61.

10. M. Heidegger (1977). "On the Essence of Truth," in *Basic Writings.* Ed. D. Krell. NY: Harper & Row.

11. N. Norbu (1984). *Dzog Chen and Zen.* Ed. K. Lipman. Grass Valley, CA: Blue Dolfin Press.

12. For greater detail distinguishing the Tantric path of transformation from the Dzogchen path of instantaneous self-liberation, see C. N. Norbu (1996). *Dzogchen: The Self-Perfected State.* Ithaca, NY: Snow Lion.

13. K. Wilber, *Brief History*, p. 220.

14. Ibid., pp. 226–28.

15. Please see www.wisdompsy.com for more information about this annual conference.

SPACIOUS INTIMACY

REFLECTIONS ON ESSENTIAL RELATIONSHIP, EMPATHIC RESONANCE, PROJECTIVE IDENTIFICATION, AND WITNESSING

Love says: "I am everything." Wisdom says: "I am nothing."
Between the two my life flows.[1]

—*Sri Nisargadatta Maharaj*

John J. Prendergast

INTRODUCTION

As we awaken into our true nature as nondual awareness—that which is always and already whole and inseparable from the totality of life—all of our relationships, personal and professional, change. For me, this awakening and change of relationship toward life has been an ongoing, subtle process that has happened over many years, much like a river that at times rushes quickly forward, at other times meanders in back pools, and every once in a while goes over a precipitous waterfall marking a radical shift in identity. This process of awakening is, paradoxically, both sudden and gradual, where one may suddenly feel oneself in unbounded freedom outside of time while simultaneously experiencing a transformation and evolution in time on the level of the body-mind: both be-ing and be-coming. Equally puzzling to the mind, awakening is both intimate and impersonal, touching that which is most real within each of us, yet referring to no one in particular. As Nisargadatta suggests in the above quote, we eventually discover that we are both nothing and everything. The mind can't grasp any of this, which actually is quite good news, allowing it to relax into its natural role of being a faithful servant, rather than a false master, of the truth. The mind learns to bow down to the heart of Silence, relinquishing the illusion of control.

This awakened relationship to life brings an emergent sense of *spacious intimacy*. As I sat with clients over the past quarter century, two seemingly paradoxical themes gradually emerged. First, I noticed that over time I felt an increasing *intimacy* or closeness with my clients and their experiences. Of course there were exceptions to this, when I would have difficulty really understanding where a client was, due to my own reactions or lack of experience, but generally speaking there has been a steadily growing sense of closeness with whatever gets expressed, no matter how dark or unfamiliar. Second, I noticed that I felt more of a sense of *space* or nonattachment so that I am touched but not lost in the experience, close to it but not contained by it. An intense bodily contraction or emotion can be acutely felt along with a sense of unbounded space. The combination of the two brings the sense of knowing someone from the inside and at the same time accepting them exactly as they are.

Since I have trained and supervised clinical interns for many years, I know that it is very easy to get stuck in one of two poles as we listen carefully to someone else. On one hand, we may be pulled into someone else's feelings or stories so that we lose perspective. This is particularly true if we are emotionally sensitive or conditioned to be a caretaker in order to survive. For example, we may feel overwhelmed by clients' depressions and bleak views of life and begin to feel as helpless and hopeless as they do. In this case, *intimacy without a sense of space leads to merging*. When this happens, we lose the sense of our own experience and are subsumed by the other's. On the other hand, if we are more identified with our mind, we may tend to inwardly sit back and analyze the other's experience without opening to the inner feeling of it. While there may be a sense of mental clarity and intellectual spaciousness, the result is a feeling of disconnection. In this case, *space without a sense of intimacy leads to disconnection*. We lose touch with the other. Given the danger of becoming stuck in either of these polarities, we might imagine that there is an ideal balance point where we can experience a blend of the two without leaning forward or backward in our listening.

Experiencing both warmth and objectivity, emotional connection along with a clear perspective, is a therapeutic ideal that training and experience can help foster—to some extent. However, if we wish to experience the essence of both intimacy and spaciousness, we must deepen into the source of each. Remarkably, this turns out to be the same source—open, lucid awareness—the nondual ground of Being, or no-self. The more that we realize that *this* is what we really are, the more intimate and spacious we feel in our relationship to our daily life and the people in it.

ESSENTIAL RELATIONSHIP: BEING AT HOME TO RECEIVE THE "GUEST"

As our awareness of this spacious intimacy grows, the way we relate to or meet others is transformed—we feel increasingly like we are welcoming guests into our home, although with some important differences. I sometimes tell my counseling students that "we must be at home to receive the guest." This Rumiesque aphorism points to the foundation of an essential relationship where instead of leaving our self to meet the other, we meet them right *here* in our self. It is always *here* where the essential meeting and connection occurs in the "I" that cannot be made into some thing. Other kinds of meeting— "over there" in the other (merged), "over here" superficially from a safe distance behind the wall of an inflated/deficient self-image, or "in between" dialoguing and interacting as a discrete self and other (intersubjectivity, as conventionally defined; see both Bradford, Blackstone in this volume)—also can occur. Yet an essential meeting can happen only when we are at home in Being or no-self. We meet the other in the same shared home ground, yet this "place" cannot be localized. Both parties can recognize that we are *here together*, but neither can say where this is or to whom this meeting space belongs. Further, we cannot say who is the host and who is the guest!

Of course we first must be at home in order to receive the guest of our disguised self. If we are away on other business trying to fix or change the person to whom we are listening for example, a fully conscious meeting is impossible. This usually happens in conventional psychotherapy or when we listen to a friend or family member who is in distress. There are many ways to leave home while listening and we are often unaware as it happens. *Trying* to help the other quickly takes us away from home as we collude with the other's self-abandonment as they try to fix or change themselves. When we are at home in our Being or no-self, listening from and as presence, a liberating space is available that fully receives experience, inside or outside, just as it is. This receptive meeting eventually frees whatever is met.

CLINICAL APPLICATIONS

Since it is important to see how these broad and intuitive principles work with flesh-and-blood clients who present ordinary issues during psychotherapy, I will share a case vignette from my work along with my view of its key transformative elements. Over the years as I have researched the literature that attempts to explain the rich and often mysterious interchange that happens between therapist and client, I have found that conventional models, while useful, are limited because of their dualistic views of the self.

I would like to examine two important concepts in particular, empathy and projective identification, and see how well they hold up as nondual dimensions of the therapeutic encounter unfold. To analogize from the physical sciences: The relationship between dual and nondual understanding of psychotherapy is like the relationship between Newtonian and quantum physics. Newton got it right for the domain of experience that he was measuring (large objects), yet there was an entirely different level of subatomic reality that his formulas could not accurately account for. So, too, when therapists and clients drop out of their ordinary identifications as a discrete self and other, a different realm of relationship opens where conventional psychological descriptions lose their explanatory and predictive power.

A Session with Claire

Claire, with whom I have met for several years, begins the session by reporting that she is avoiding something in herself but isn't sure what it might be. I suggest that we sit with her curiosity. We easily fall into silence, quietly gazing in a relaxed way. After a few minutes,

Claire suppresses an urge to laugh.

"I think I got frightened," she reports with a slightly embarrassed grin.

"Frightened of…?" I ask.

"I don't know. I don't know what I am feeling exactly or how to describe it."

"That's fine. You don't need to understand or describe what is happening. Just be with it," I suggest, sensing that she is a bit caught in her thinking.

As we continue to sit quietly, I am increasingly aware of a sensation deep in my heart center. It feels very tender, something I haven't sensed before while sitting with Claire. We have met on a regular basis for some time, and this feels new to me. I am unsure of its meaning, but it feels important and I describe my experience to her, touching my hand to my heart area. She confirms that she is sensing something similar in the same area.

"Is there a fear of not being loved?" I ask.

"No, I don't think so." She pauses and senses into her experience more carefully. "It feels more like a fear of not being understood."

Somehow this feels right to me. There is a familiar sense of the truth being told that resonates in my body in a distinctive way, almost like an inner bell harmoniously ringing along with a light expanding somewhere deep inside.

"Yes. That feels right to me. Is this a new feeling?" I ask.

"It *is* new. There is also a sense of vulnerability," she offers.

"Hmmm. Vulnerability. And also something … (I pause searching for the right word)… very innocent?" I ask.

"Yes," she replies.

"Kind of how you felt last weekend when you wanted to tell your friends about how your relationship with me has changed, and you were concerned that they would not understand?" I inquire.

"Exactly….It feels like I am trying to protect something. I wonder what it is?" she asks.

We continue to sit without speaking for a few more minutes, gazing in a relaxed way. I have the distinct sensation of her settling into herself, resting more deeply into her heart. There is something very direct and simple in the contact, an absence of self-consciousness. It is an open, peaceful, mysterious meeting.

"The fear has fallen away," she volunteers several minutes later. "It doesn't feel like there is anything to protect. It seems strange that I avoid this, since once I am here it feels so comfortable and real. From this place it seems irrelevant whether someone else understands or misunderstands me. It doesn't really matter," she muses.

"What the mind thinks this is and what it actually is, are quite different. We scare ourselves with the stories we tell about it," I add.

The session ends soon after this. It is the end of the day and after Claire leaves, I sit quietly in my office for a few minutes, letting in the beauty of the contact. The heart feels graced by the innocence and openness that has unfolded and been shared. I recall the words of one of my spiritual teachers, Jean Klein, who invited me during a private interview many years before "to abide in the Heart, not knowing." Somehow, without any specific intent, Claire and I had found our way there.

Comments about the Session

Several years of prior therapy had laid the foundation for this session. Claire had reported in the past month a subtle but dramatic shift in her relationship with me. After going through many layers of terror associated with a survival fear that was rooted in a chaotic childhood marked by a critical, emotionally absent mother and a verbally abusive father with poor boundaries, she no longer felt dependent upon me and experienced a sense of solid ground beneath her feet. Her fairly sudden sense of solidity was strangely disorienting at first, but she was beginning to trust and acclimate to it. Once this underlying need for safety was addressed, attention spontaneously shifted from survival issues to matters of the heart—her fear of being misunderstood, which also derived from her childhood experience of being repeatedly misperceived. In those early years something very innocent felt threatened and was covered over—a tender and direct way of knowing and feeling about life. Whereas her earlier safety issues had localized in her body at the base of the spine, the issue of fearing to be misunderstood was sensed by both of us to be deep inside the middle of her chest. Once the fear was uncovered, faced and shared, it dissolved, at least temporarily. She could see that she was operating under the influence of an old, previously unconscious, story.

There are several aspects of nondual awareness operating in this session. The first is that we both felt like we were meeting in and as an open mystery. Something intangible and unnamable was being shared. We were both sitting with a question and an experience, yet without an agenda to fix, change, or solve anything. There was a shared curiosity and willingness to be with what arose, trusting in whatever would unfold. As I sat with Claire, I could feel myself letting her in, receiving her as if she were entering into a vast space of awareness. It felt like silence was meeting itself in this very specific form. Claire was at once familiar and unknown to me. We shared a history and yet were new in the moment.

This spacious meeting was also very intimate. I did not feel like some kind of distant observer. Instead, through a familiar but mysterious process, I could sense that I was receiving something important about Claire's experience—a certain deep, tender feeling in the heart center. This was another nondual aspect of our meeting—the experiential barrier between a discrete self and other had dissolved. Somehow I was accurately sensing and feeling what Claire was experiencing, yet without getting lost in it and, in this case, without at first fully understanding what it meant to her. It felt like a subtler level of my body was *resonating* with her body. I knew from many experiences like this over the years that it was her experience that I was feeling. There was also a knowing on a deeper level that the experience ultimately did not belong to anyone; it was happening within a larger, impersonal space.

Two other aspects of the session are worth noting. One was how I felt when Claire was "on the mark" with her experience—the "it rings true" feeling that I experienced when she identified her feeling as a fear of not being understood. I may or may not disclose this sense during a session when it arises, yet it is a clear and distinctive knowing when something said is true on a deep level. Our bodies have a sense of the truth, regardless of what our minds may be thinking. It is an inner felt sense of congruence and connection.

It was also interesting how the issue resolved for Claire; it happened in silence without any analytic process or emotional catharsis. There was a focus of attention on a sensation of vulnerability and an open inquiry into the truth of the related belief that something needed to be protected. A contraction dissolved and resolved into a feeling of openness.

This sense of openness was implicit within the contraction rather than a by-product of its release. The tightest places within us still have space right in the center of them, like the physical space that exists within the nucleus of an atom or a clenched fist. This experience of finding a sense of space within a contraction points to the inherent emptiness of form—all form is essentially an expression of open, spacious emptiness. This important insight allows us to approach contractions differently. Rather than trying to change or get rid of them, it is really enough to feel into and see through them. When apparent problems become transparent, they lose their compelling power.

The session ended with a similar silent, open contact as when we began, yet with a subtle shift. Claire's unconscious fear of not being understood had dissolved for the moment, leaving her resting even more deeply in her self. How well do traditional descriptions of the therapeutic encounter capture the essence of what happened in this session?

EMPATHIC RESONANCE

Empathy, a recent addition to the English language derived from the Greek *empathiea* (meaning passion, the opposite of apathy), refers to the capacity to enter into and understand another's experience. Heinz Kohut, the founder of Self Psychology, defined it as "the capacity to think and feel oneself into the inner life of another person." [2] Carl Rogers, who emphasized the importance of empathy well before Kohut, originally defined it as the ability "to perceive the internal frame of reference of another with accuracy and with the emotional components and meanings which pertain thereto as if one were the person, but without ever losing the 'as if' condition. Thus, it means to sense the hurt or the pleasure of another as he senses it and to perceive the causes thereof as he perceives them, but without ever losing the recognition that it is as if I were hurt or pleased and so forth."[3] Tansey and Burke, students of Merton Gill, defined empathy as the successful outcome of processing two forms of introjective identification (concordant and complementary) that "leads to emotional knowledge of the patient's experience."[4] While helpful, each of these definitions is partial and dualistic; in each there is the assumption of a separate someone entering into the experience of an other.

Surveying the field of empathy with sensitivity and insight, Tobin Hart, a humanistic/transpersonal psychologist, formulated the concept of "deep empathy," which includes nonduality. For Hart, deep empathy crosses a line into a process of direct knowing that "moves toward subject-object transcendence or a loosening of self-other boundaries."[5] For example, Carl Rogers's understanding of empathy evolved over time, "from 'as if' (an imaginative indirect knowing, a logical extrapolation) to actually entering a client's world—an act of alignment."[6] This act of alignment can also be described as fusion or merging. Ken Wilber's distinction between pre-egoic and trans-egoic states of fusion is relevant here, since a pre-egoic fusion results in the therapist becoming lost in the client's experience. For the therapist there would be no sense of space within which the experience was happening.

Hart also describes a state of deep empathy mediated by "a refined sympathetic resonance" where, "unlike the transient fusion in the experience of alignment ... *attunement* describes the experience of two selves connecting at a particular 'frequency' of experience."[7] This description of empathic resonance or attunement fits well with my experience with Claire. There was a definite sense of attuning to and inwardly vibrating with a specific level of experience as I sat with her. This kind of resonance is most commonly experienced in terms of feeling the same feeling as another, but it also may include subtle somatic sensations as well as thoughts. It feels like an attunement to an energetic field that is shared by two or more individuals. This is a well-known phenomenon when meditating in a group or spending time with an authentic spiritual teacher.

Hart takes his discussion another step to include the larger field of awareness or witnessing:

Empathy, refined still further, involves neither objective observation, nor seeing the world through the client's eyes, nor reacting to, nor fusing with, nor attuning to; instead, the center of perception seems to occupy multiple perspectives simultaneously. One seems to become the field itself while maintaining awareness since one is less identified with the perspective from a single self or vantage point.... *Witnessing* is experienced with more emotional detachment, although it would be erroneous to confuse it with a distinct subject-object schism of more inferential or conventional empathy.[8]

This is a critical addition since it describes the sense of space or open awareness that includes but is not limited to multiple perspectives. The reference to greater emotional detachment is also important and bears directly on the theme of spacious intimacy.

Focusing on the theme of empathic resonance, I have found that it can be cultivated by

- Intellectually acknowledging that it does or at least could exist

- Being attentive to one's body while listening to another, and

- Verifying the accuracy of one's perceptions.

Beliefs filter our experience in powerful ways; we often perceive only what our cognitive maps tell us exist. Many of us have heard the story about the native islanders in the Caribbean Sea who could not see the ships that Columbus and his crew sailed in upon because they had no concept of a ship. Whether or not this was actually true, it illustrates the point—we let in information that fits with our worldview and reject that which does not. For example, if we do not believe that it is possible to empathically resonate with another, we will ignore resonance when it actually happens. It will pass beneath our radar like a flock of geese or a cruise missile. If we are, however, conscious of an experience of resonance, our assumptions will also color how we think about it. For example, if I am sitting with my clients or friends and I begin to feel sad or agitated despite their report of well-being, I will discount my feelings. I may automatically assume that my feelings have nothing to do with the other's experience. This, of course, may actually be the case, but we are exploring the possibility here that we may be interconnected with and attuned to one another in unexpected ways.

Our bodies offer a wealth of information and inner guidance that we often ignore. When we listen to another, our attention is usually absorbed in thoughts and confined to our heads. We are listening and ascribing meaning to the words that we hear and usually ignoring the inner sensing and feeling that is happening in the rest of our body. It is a very limited way to listen. Eckhart Tolle writes movingly about this phenomenon and invites a different kind of listening:

> When listening to another person, don't just listen with your mind, listen with your whole body. Feel the energy field of your inner body as you listen. That takes attention away from thinking and creates a still space that enables you to truly listen without the mind interfering. You are giving the other person space—space to be. It is the most precious gift you can give. Most people don't know how to listen because the major part of their attention is taken up by thinking. They pay more attention to that than to what the other person is saying, and none at all to what really matters: the Being of the other person underneath the words and the mind. Of course, you cannot feel someone else's Being except through your own. This is the beginning of the realization of oneness, which is love. At the deepest level of Being, you are one with all that is.[9]

Tolle is pointing to a native sensitivity of the body, an "energy field of your inner body" that, when attuned with, allows us to offer a spacious quality of listening to the other, one that opens to essential Being. While there are many methods such as yoga, meditation, and martial arts like aikido that help develop awareness of this inner energy body, and while there are many centers, levels, and currents that can be discovered that apply to specific psychospiritual issues,[10] the main point is that the inner body is remarkably receptive during the therapeutic encounter. We can easily sense our multidimensional connection to others through it. On this level, creating a boundary between self and other is like drawing a line in the water with our finger. The deeper we go into our experience, the fewer boundaries we find. This can be unnerving to the conditioned mind that takes itself to be a discrete entity.

As important as it is to relax into and attune with the sensitivity of our inner body, it is equally important to be discerning and to verify that what we are experiencing is related to another. Humility, caution, and honesty are necessary. It may be best to at first just note our inner impressions and keep them to our self when we are sitting with others. We may begin to notice correspondences between our subtle sensing and feeling and what others verbally report. This was the case for me when this sensitivity first began to unfold in 1981. It was several years before I disclosed anything to my clients. I did so tentatively at first, and with curiosity as to whether my experience had anything to do with theirs. I wanted to make sure that I wasn't projecting my own reactions onto them. We also may want to first practice sharing impressions with friends or partners to see if they have any accuracy. When I introduce exercises to my students to listen to one another and disclose their body sensations and feelings, many are completely surprised by how relevant and helpful it is to share what they sense. For some of them it is a kind of revelation.

Sometimes, of course, what we are experiencing is unrelated to a client's experience and arises solely out of our own conditioning. This is important to acknowledge when it happens. Learning to listen to the inner body is not about trying to develop omniscience or special powers—a decidedly narcissistic agenda. It is important to be aware of the ego's self-aggrandizing tendencies. The point of including the body in our listening is to connect to what is real, not to look good or be special.

Returning to my session with Claire, we can see that Hart's definition of "deep empathy" can account for the experience of empathic resonance, a mutual attunement to a shared field or energetic frequency, as well as for the sense of our having shared in a vast, nonlocalized space of witnessing. Conventional psychology, however, does not acknowledge these nondual processes and instead describes empathy as a state gained through a process of projective and introjective identification. It will be useful to briefly visit these important conventional descriptions.

PROJECTIVE AND INTROJECTIVE IDENTIFICATION

In their book *Understanding Countertransference*, Michael Tansey and Walter Burke survey the evolution of the complex concept of *projective identification* from Melanie Klein through Thomas Ogden, eventually defining it as:

> an interactional phenomenon in which the projector, by actual influence, unconsciously elicits thoughts, feelings and experiences within another individual which in some way resemble his own. [11]

They are referring to the phenomena of when clients induce therapists to experience their inner world. In the authors' view, all empathy is mediated by this process. The most interesting part of this definition are the words "unconsciously elicits," which manage to name the phenomena of subtle interpersonal influence without actually explaining how it works. The concept of empathic resonance offers at least a clue of how this mysterious process occurs. In Buddhist and Hindu traditions, this same process is known as "transmission," although it refers to spiritual insights and energies rather than unconscious psychological material. In both cases there is a transmitter (or projector) and a receiver. The reception of the projective identification by the therapist is called *introjective identification* in psychoanalytic language. If the experience of the sender and the receiver are temporarily similar and harmonious, sharing a sense of poignant loss for example, it is called *concordant*, and if the experiences are dissimilar and disharmonious, where a client is masking intense feelings of rage, terror, or shame for example, it is called *complementary*.

The following is an example of how this can work: A client tends to arrive late to sessions or to not come at all, canceling at the last possible minute in order avoid the cancellation fee. When he does come, he tends not to look at or listen to the therapist. The therapist, normally kind and nonjudgmental, begins to feel uncharacteristically resentful and devalued, perhaps with a hint of abandonment rage. If the therapist has enough patience, insight, and support, she may realize that she is actually being unconsciously induced to think and feel as her client does and realize that her client's behaviors are defensive patterns that mask an underlying fear of being abandoned. The client will abandon or interrupt contact with others in order to avoid the greater vulnerability of being left or cut off himself. Beneath the client's behavior, that would be conventionally judged and shamed as being rude or insulting, lies terror, rage, and self-hatred. When the therapist can open to these raw states of experience within herself without becoming lost in them, she has a tremendous window into the client's inner world. In other words, when there is a sense of spacious intimacy, there is empathy. This empathy can then be fashioned into a therapeutic response that supports and allows the client to explore his unconscious defenses and bring them into conscious awareness so that they no longer need to be acted out, alienating anyone who threatens to get too close.

From a nondual perspective we can see that all introjective identification is a form of conscious or unconscious empathic resonance. The critical factor in determining if the reception of a projective identification is being consciously processed by therapists is the degree of spacious intimacy they bring to the interaction. When there is a sense of inner space and close contact on the part of the therapist, so-called introjective identification actually is or becomes *introjective disidentification*. The therapist is no longer identified with the feeling or view, no matter how intense or negative it may be. As a result, the experience is fully and intimately received, allowing for a natural empathic understanding.

WITNESSING/EXPERIENCING AND INCLUSIVE DISIDENTIFICATION

This discussion of spacious intimacy would be incomplete without touching on the topics of witnessing and disidentification. Many contemplative teachers and traditions encourage a practice of just noticing that phenomena, particularly thoughts, come and go like clouds passing through the sky. This practice is sometimes called witnessing. It encourages a stepping back and turning attention away from the contents of awareness (thoughts, feelings, and sensations) toward awareness itself. Here is an example of an instruction from Eckhart Tolle in his enormously popular and influential *The Power of Now:*

> When you listen to that voice (which comments, speculates, judges, compares, complains, likes, dislikes, and so on), listen to it impartially. That is to say, do not judge. Do not judge or condemn what you hear, for doing so would mean that the same voice has come in again through the back door. You'll soon realize: *there* is the voice, and here *I am* listening to it, watching it. This *I am* realization, this sense of your own presence, is not a thought. It arises from beyond the mind.... So when you listen to a thought, you are aware not only of the thought but also of yourself as the witness of the thought. A new dimension of consciousness has come in. As you listen to the thought, you feel a conscious presence—your deeper self—behind or underneath the thought, as it were. The thought then loses its power over you and quickly subsides, because you are no longer energizing the mind through identification with it. [12]

Witnessing can be a powerfully liberating practice, particularly for those of us who identify with our thoughts. A vast, spacious presence can be evoked that loosens the knot of identification with our chronic self-limiting stories. I use a related instruction based on this principle as one step in a structured process of deconstructive inquiry into negative self-judgments that I have developed as a variation of "The Work" created by Byron Katie.[13] Taken by itself, however, this practice of being aware of one's self as "the witness of thought" can become a subtle trap.

I know this well, since I was ensnared in the position of being just such a subtle witness for well over two decades in my meditative practice. The problem was that I assumed a new identity as "the one who is watching," despite my teacher Jean Klein's very pointed and earthy warning to me early on in our relationship to "not fornicate with the witness!" He could easily see where I was caught long before it was evident to me. There is a special suffering that comes if we take our self as a discrete witness because we still feel separate from that which is being witnessed. Although the mind may be very quiet for long periods, we are still in duality, unknowingly caught in a position and not really free. As noted at the beginning of this chapter, there is space without intimacy, a sure recipe for subtle disconnection or dissociation.

This position of being a discrete witness brings a quality of distant witnessing, much like an outsider who looks in or down upon something. The transformational power of this position is limited. Certain fairly superficial habits of mind will fall away—the thought "loses its power over you and quickly subsides" as Tolle wrote—yet more deeply rooted and often dysfunctional mental and emotional patterns persist in the face of this kind of witnessing. Longtime meditators who have watched their familiar patterns of reactivity fail to budge over the years know what I am talking about.

For such patterns to be penetrated by awareness, a different kind of witnessing is required, a witnessing from the inside or a watching-experiencing that includes a dimension of intimate feeling. Adyashanti, a contemporary American teacher, explains:

> What it means to be fully awake is to be not only fully conscious but to be fully feeling, to be fully experiencing. …If we don't try to play the watcher in our mind, there's this very natural and effortless watching-experiencing. One doesn't even have to try to do it. On the level of experience, when we're watching, we now feel that we're watching from inside the experience, or in the midst of it. The paradox is that the watching, even though it's inside experience and all around experience, it is not caught by experience. It's not identified even though it's so mixed in there that you can't distinguish it. …It is a

spontaneous act of love when we're watching from the inside with a willingness to yield back into our own experience.[14]

It is important to note that Adyashanti is not suggesting a practice here. He is offering a description, instead of prescription, of how awareness functions when it is fully awake to itself, when it is simultaneously spacious and intimate: "This is very paradoxical to the mind. The more detached you become in this way, the more intimate you become with your experience."[15]

Distant witnessing can be one of the hazardous way stations along the path of *exclusive disidentification.* Advaita Vedanta, the tradition of Ramana Maharshi and Nisargadatta Maharaj, for example emphasizes a *via negativa* (neti-neti: I am not this) where we are encouraged through a process of keen self-inquiry to disidentify from the body-mind and to see that we are not our thoughts, feelings, or sensations. Who is left? What remains? No-thing, the formless absolute. Phenomenal reality—the body, the world—is then described (some would say dismissed) as *maya,* an illusion, the product of a magician's sleight-of-hand.

However, seeing that the world is a kind of dream spun from pure consciousness does not end the life of form—the play goes on, the body continues. How do we then live in and as these bodies when we know that we are not limited by them? We have a hint from America's great bard:

> I pass death with the dying and birth with the new-wash'd
>   babe, and am not contain'd between my hat and boots,
> And peruse manifold objects, no two alike and every one
>   good,
> The earth good and the stars good, and their adjuncts good.
>
> I am not an earth nor an adjunct of an earth, I am the mate
>   and companion of people, all just as immortal
>   and fathomless as myself,
> (They do not know how immortal, but I know.)
>   —*Walt Whitman* (Song of Myself)

The fruition of awakening comes with the realization that everything is an expression or extension of nothing. Duality—the world of form with all of its inherent polarities—is intuitively realized to be inseparable from nonduality.

Exclusive disidentification can trap us in the subtlest duality—that of believing and feeling that absolute reality is separate from relative reality. If we take ourselves as only the absolute, we are only halfway home. On the other hand, an *inclusive disidentification* acknowledges that "we are not *only* this." We are not only these thoughts, feelings, and sensations: We are more (if we acknowledge our ultimate fullness) and less (if we acknowledge our ultimate emptiness). We are both more and less than what we have taken ourselves to be. And we are also what we have taken ourselves to be. Nothing is excluded.

We come full circle: We are nothing and we are everything—between the two our life flows as a celebration of spacious intimacy.

ENDNOTES

1. Sri N. Maharaj (1982). *I Am That*. Durham, NC: Acorn Press, p. 269.

2. H. Kohut (1984). *How Does Analysis Cure?* Chicago: University of Chicago Press, p. 82.

3. C. Rogers (1959). "A theory of therapy, personality, and interpersonal relationships, as developed in the client-centered framework," in S. Koch, ed., *Psychology: A Study of Science*. New York: McGraw Hill. pp. 210–11.

4. M. Tansey, and W. Burke (1989). *Understanding Countertransference*. Hillsdale, NJ: Analytic Press, p. 58.

5. T. Hart (2000). "Deep Empathy," in *Transpersonal Knowing* (ed. T. Hart, P. Nelson, and K. Puhakka) Albany: SUNY Press, p. 256.

6. Ibid., p. 259.

7. Ibid., pp. 260–61.

8. Ibid., p. 261.

9. E. Tolle (1999). *The Power of Now*. Novato: CA: New World Library, p. 105.

10. J. Prendergast (2000). "The Chakras in Transpersonal Psychotherapy," in *International Journal of Yoga Therapy*.: n. 10.

11. M. Tansey, and W. Burke (1989). *Understanding Countertransference.* p. 45.

12. E. Tolle (1999). *The Power of Now.* Novato, CA: New World Library, pp. 15–16.

13. See S. Bodian (2003). "Deconstructing the Self," in *The Sacred Mirror*, ed. J. Prendergast, P. Fenner, and S. Krystal. St. Paul: Paragon House, p. 242 for a brief overview of Byron Katie's "The Work." The unpublished protocol that I have developed is designed to invite a deconstructive inquiry into negative self-judgments. Clients are invited to first formulate a disturbing belief as a short sentence, step back from it as if seeing it written on a piece of paper or projected onto a screen in front of them, and then turn their attention to awareness itself with the instruction, "Notice that something is aware of this thought. What is your sense of this awareness?" Once a larger sense of awareness is evoked, attention is directed back to the original thought, and the question "Is it true?" is innocently posed. There are other important steps, but this gives the reader a sense of the approach.

14. Adyashanti. "Love Returning for Itself," in *The Sacred Mirror*, p. 62.

15. Ibid., p. 63.

FROM NEUTRALITY TO THE PLAY OF
UNCONDITIONAL PRESENCE

G. Kenneth Bradford

As we are liberated from our own fear, our presence automatically liberates others.

—*Nelson Mandela*

Any genuine encounter with an Other shakes us to the core. If we are not shaken, rattled, rolled, awed, or somehow blessed or blushed by an encounter, then it is not *authentic* in the sense of being open to and opened by Otherness, awestruck by the immensity of *being*. But caught in self-centered, everyday distractions and preoccupations, in the place we would encounter an Other we find instead self-absorption. Rolling along in our own preoccupations, hopes, and fears, we are hardly able to encounter the Other qua Other. And without the ability to encounter and so discover that Other, any effort at being a therapeutic interlocutor for that person is bound to fall short. Of course, it may be that in encountering an other person we come to the exchange already emptied and open. In that case, the exchange may elicit no additional shock since we are already meeting the person undefended and nakedly present. But whether self-absorbed or to some degree selfless in any given therapeutic exchange, the necessity and challenge of truly opening to an other person and to the Otherness within oneself has been a hallmark of the practice of depth psychotherapy since its inception.

The analytic attitude of *neutrality* is the primary and enduring attempt to address the twofold challenge of opening-up to and being opened-up by an other person. Unfortunately, the way neutrality has been understood undermines both the principle and practice it was conceived to serve and guide. Working against itself, the attitude of neutrality functions both to facilitate an honest and liberating therapeutic conversation as well as functioning as a defense against an authentic encounter, distancing the therapist from the client and so diluting a potentially liberating exchange. It is therefore important to untangle the courageous from the defensive intentions implicit in the notion of neutrality. The first part of this chapter teases apart these opposing agendas. The middle section considers how moving to an *intersubjective* therapeutic stance of empathy and introspection mitigates the defensive posture of neutrality. While the final section takes this further by considering the nature of intersubjectivity as *unconditional presence*, and discusses how this is evocative of authenticity. So, the chapter will progress gradually from reviewing neutrality as a sharply dualistic construct, through its softening through an appreciation of intersubjectivity, to a consideration of nondual awareness as an optimal therapeutic non-attitude. But this progression is really a sleight of hand. When depth psychotherapy is practiced with an open presence, its play occurs in an immediate, nongradual way .

Right from the start, I wish to revision neutrality in terms of *unconditional presence: the capacity and courage to be both open and responsive to the Otherness of self and other*. Minimally, this challenges us to not avoid the fear, attraction, or confusion that arises in an intimate encounter, but to enter into an exchange "*being present with our experience as it is*" (Welwood, 2000, p. 141), embracing the inevitable decenterings of interpersonal experiencing. In daring to be emotionally, intellectually, and psychically *open* to the Other and Otherness, unconditional presence also challenges us to *respond from within opened-upness*. Such presence allows for noncalculating communication, a kind of communion that is able to elicit the naturally liberating, unmediated intelligence of human being that conveys itself, as we say, "heart to heart". Chogyam Trungpa (2005) has referred to such fundamental openness as our "basic sanity," which is otherwise discussed in Buddhist thought as emptiness, or openness *(sunyata)*, or as naked, unconditioned awareness *(rig-pa)*.

NEUTRALITY

Neutrality was conceived both to facilitate receptivity and reduce countertransference reactions on the part of the therapist. Freud recognized that adopting an attitude of neutrality allows a therapist to be less personally invested in the outcome of a therapeutic exchange and thus be more able to attune to the vicissitudes of a patient's emerging subjectivity, wherever it leads.

In his seminal "how to" essay of 1912, Freud describes the technique of psychoanalysis, identifying the attitude most essential for practicing what has ever since been known as depth psychology. He advised that the various technical rules of psychoanalysis could "be summed up in a single precept...They are all intended to create for the doctor a counterpart to the 'fundamental rule of psycho-analysis' which is laid down for the patient" (p. 111 & 115). Of course, the "fundamental rule" is the practice of free association: spontaneously revealing whatever comes to mind without judging, censoring, or otherwise reviewing it for social acceptability. The counterpart to this rule enjoins the therapist to likewise open himself and respond freely, albeit in a particular sense. The therapist "must turn his own unconscious like a receptive organ toward the transmitting unconscious of the patient. He must adjust himself to the patient as a telephone receiver is adjusted to the transmitting microphone" (p.115). Freud thought it essential for the therapist to attune to the patient in a manner that is nonconscious and nonconceptual. But since this attuning involves an effort of will (a "turning") exerted in a specific direction ("toward" an other), it is not yet an unconditional, purely choiceless awareness. Although Freud did not recognize this potentiality, we can see today—aided by the nondual wisdom of the East—that the attitude of evenly hovering attention is a precursor to unconditional awareness, or "revelatory openness" (Adams, 1995), a listening from the heart of Silence.

Given the impressive power of self-centered hopes and fears to hijack selfless awareness, it behooves us to take to heart Freud's key insight, even though it will prove to be but a step toward a more mature unconditional copresence. Freud (1912) observed,

> The technique [of psychoanalysis]...is a very simple one....
> It consists simply in not directing one's notice to anything in particular and in maintaining the same "evenly-suspended attention" in the face of all that one hears.

Freud then explains why this is so important.

> For as soon as anyone deliberately concentrates his attention
> to a certain degree, he begins to select from material before
> him; one point will be fixed in his mind with particular clear-
> ness and some other will be correspondingly disregarded, and
> in making this selection he will be following his expectations
> or inclinations. This, however, is precisely what must not be
> done. In making the selection, if he follows his expectations
> he is in danger of never finding anything but what he already
> knows; and if he follows his inclinations he will certainly fal-
> sify what he may perceive. (p. 111 & 112)

The therapist is advised to relax any conscious "expectations,"
including theoretical and therapeutic preconceptions as well as
any unconscious biases, or "inclinations," including personal opinions, attractions, aversions or indifferences he may hold, in favor of
an unintentional, choiceless awareness in which he opens himself
nakedly to the conversation at hand. In concert with this, the therapist also must "not tolerate any resistances in himself which hold
back from his consciousness what has been perceived by his unconscious" (Freud, 1912, p. 116). The therapist is thus challenged to be
psychologically open both to the other person and to the Otherness
(unconscious) within himself that is stirred up by the intersubjective
exchange. While such psychological intimacy is clearly the corner-
stone of psychotherapy and the capacity most critical for and evocative of the "depth" of the analytic exchange, it is also the thing that
has proven the most difficult to actually practice. The challenges and
benefits of shared psychological nakedness are still being discovered,
in large part because the practice itself has remained vague, being
more an inspired ideal than a specific training.

Freud expressly advises the therapist to not consciously interpret
what he hears or doesn't hear, but to allow the unconscious to do that
work. I consider this understanding to be among Freud's most lucid
insights and to reflect the radical heart of any depth psychotherapy.
In this advice, he encouraged therapists to "get out of the way" and

be neutral in the sense that a mirror is neutral and does not pick and choose what it will or will not reflect, but reflects whatever appears without mediation, *as it is.* He was certainly not encouraging analysts to let their repressed unconscious have free rein to misinterpret the patient. Rather, he seems to have used the word "unconscious" in this instance to refer to a cognizance unmediated by personal or professional predispositions, deferring to an intelligence that is more intuitive than conceptual, more unconditional than conditioned.

Among the most immediate and difficult challenges in following this advice to open to an other person, as well as to the Otherness within, is the psychological decentering this entails. In opening oneself, self-centeredness becomes permeable to Otherness in that "I" become both more receptive and less defended. That is, I become more receptive *because* I am less defended, since I am no longer resisting subtle perceptions that have remained dim, occluded by my own preoccupations, whether conscious or unconscious. While an opening-up awareness allows me to tune in and perceive things about you, it simultaneously reveals the permeability of my "me." Psychologically porous exchanges of self and Other tend to evoke my own Otherness and something is liable to "come up" that I hadn't counted on. And as we know, the Otherness of what comes up often has the power to rattle my selfness. So, a key challenge to every therapist since Freud has been: How to handle the inevitable threats to the security of the therapist's sense of self?

The response proffered by Freud, and a common human response in any case, is to adopt a self-defensive position, and in particular (as a "professional") a neutral stance of emotional aloofness. It is one of the enduring ironies of depth psychotherapy that the essential attitude that allows the therapist to empathically attune to a client is also called upon to defend the therapist against becoming empathically resonant with that client. Freud advises therapists "to model themselves during psycho-analytic treatment on the surgeon, who puts aside all his feelings, even his human sympathy, and concentrates his mental forces on the single aim of performing the operation as skilfully as possible" (p. 115). The function of neutrality as a fertile shared openness is thereby confounded as its evocative power is compromised to the point of being undermined. Neutrality is construed as a withdrawal in the face of the Other in order to spare the therapist the anguish, confusion, and vulnerability that tends to arise within genuine intimacy (unconscious contact). As the old master honestly put it, "The justification for requiring this emotional coldness in the analyst is that it creates the most advantageous conditions for both parties: for the doctor a desirable protection for his own emotional life and for the patient the largest amount of help that we can give him today" (p. 115).

Thus, one reason psychoanalysis is an "impossible profession" is that the analyst must not tolerate any inner resistances in being open to the other while simultaneously maintaining an emotional distance from that person! It is tempting to criticize old Freud for his duplicity, but if we are honest with ourselves, we will find this ambivalence—wanting to be open to the Other but also wanting to remain safe within ourselves—to be a dilemma more characteristic of the human condition than merely a Freudian conundrum. The analytic attitude of neutrality tends to reify this dilemma and cannot, unaided, resolve it. What is called for is an understanding of therapeutic attention that does not advocate withdrawal in the face of Otherness, but is able to relate with the anxieties that inevitably arise within an intimate encounter.

EMPATHIC-INTROSPECTIVE INQUIRY

Among the critiques of neutrality, Orange, Atwood & Stolorow (1997) criticize the defensive deployment of neutrality on both theoretical and therapeutic grounds, and suggest an alternative therapeutic stance based on the work of Kohut. Theoretically they observe, as have phenomenologists before them (for instance, Husserl, 1970; Merleau-Ponty, 1968/1964; Giorgi, 1970), that the notion of an objective, neutral observer disjunct from an observed subject is a fantasy, and in this sense fallacious. Human experience in general and therapeutic relationship in particular takes place wholly within dimensions of *subjectivity*. The very possibility of a subject/object split, with objectivity as a separate, privileged position, is an abstraction construed by a thinking subject. That we do not notice our participation in the construal of dualistic perceptions and concepts that give rise to apparent independently existing "objects," including the positing of an objective, neutral observer, only means that these mental construals take place outside of our awareness.

Instead of the sharp dualism that posits a detached neutrality for the therapist and a detached (and diagnosable) selfhood for the client, Stolorow et al. (1997; 1992; 1984) advocate a relational approach, which acknowledges that the therapist's subjectivity intertwines with that of the patient. The optimal therapeutic attitude is shifted from the defensive autocracy of objectivity to the more vulnerable position of interacting subjects. With this attitude adjustment, therapists are no longer authorized to escape the experiential impact of the actual human encounter but "must be prepared to bear the profound feelings of vulnerability and anxious uncertainty that are inevitable accompaniments of immersion in a deep analytic process" (Orange, Atwood & Stolorow, 1997, p. 42). Renouncing analytic distancing, how does a therapist "bear the profound feelings of vulnerability and anxious uncertainty" that are inherent to the depths of intersubjective experiencing?

Kohut (1984) suggested a practice combining "empathic attunement" to the client with "vicarious introspection" toward oneself as therapist. "Unlike the posture of neutrality, the stance of empathic-introspective inquiry does not seek to avert, minimize, or disavow the impact of the analyst's psychological organization on the patient's experience. Instead, it recognizes this impact as inherent to the profoundly intersubjective nature of an analytic dialogue and seeks consistently to *analyze* it" (Orange, Atwood & Stolorow, 1997, p. 44). The emphasis on empathy and self-reflection goes far in reorienting the therapist to subjectively felt actualities and challenges him to take into account the impact his own fixations have on the therapeutic exchange. This intersubjective stance diminishes the defensiveness of the therapist's position by prohibiting his flight into an objectifying neutrality. Still more, it enjoins the therapist to understand the influence, including unconscious reactivity, he might inadvertently be bringing to bear in the exchange. This is a vitally important step in deconstructing the defensiveness of neutrality in the direction of greater relational honesty and intersubjective presence. However, this intersubjective turn is rather less effective in addressing the nondefensive potentialities of neutrality, especially the challenge and implications of practicing choiceless awareness.

The evenly hovering practice of choiceless awareness is underemphasized in empathic-introspective inquiry in favor of *"analysis"* of structures of subjectivity. This therapy seeks above all to illuminate "unconscious organizing principles," which remains consistent with the psychoanalytic privileging of cognitive insight over felt experiencing.[1] Although theoretical and therapeutic foci are spoken of by Stolorow et al. in terms of *"intersubjectivity"*, what they are actually focusing on are dialectics of *bi-subjectivity*. Their view of intersubjectivity is construed as an interaction between two discreet subjects with their respective formative histories and independent psychological structures. The work of the therapist proceeds dialectically, shifting between empathy toward the patient and introspection toward oneself, including how one may be feeling evoked and/or reactive in the conversation. The locus of therapy is no longer imagined as taking place inside a client's internalized object (relations) world, but in the oscillation between the client's subjectivity and that of the therapist. Shifting back and forth between my feeling into you and my sensing into me, understanding arises concerning the fixations of each of our internalized structures of subjectivity as well as of how these separate structures affect each other.

But even in this overtly relational context, with its enhanced ability to take into consideration subtleties of mutual influence, the therapy will still be limited by the clarity of the therapist's awareness, especially her ability to sustain intimate attunement to self and Other. The therapist continues to be at risk of misconstruing her perceptions by seeing only what she expects to see or is inclined to see; only now she is at risk of misconstruing herself as well as the client. This problem is addressed by allowing for the "fallability" of the therapist (Orange) and then trusting in the client's feedback to correct a therapist's miss. This is comparable to trusting in the democratic process to uncover unwanted or difficult truths. While it is surely better than authoritarian neutrality, is it the best we can do? Taking a further step suggests that we move from emphasizing the separate *subjectivities* aspect of *intersubjectivity* to giving more emphasis to the *inter*-ness aspect, and in the process release the healing potential of neutrality as unconditional presence. This requires a relaxation of focus into an attention that is more evenly suspended, remaining as much on the intersubjective *field* as it is on the subjectivities anchoring the field.

INTER-BEING AND THE SANITY WE ARE BORN WITH

Awareness that relaxes its focus on separate *beings* allows for the coemergence of the *being* of *beings,* the field quality in being-with others and Otherness. Although notoriously difficult to describe, Heidegger (1962/1927) refers to the field of human experience as *dasein,* our innate *capacity* as a *being*—that is not self-enclosed, but *open-to* and *embedded-in* the world. This is remarkably similar to the Buddhist understanding of the self as "no-self" *(anatta),* a phenomenon of "inter-being" *(pratityasamupada),* as *Thich Nhat Hanh* translates it, whose nature is inherently spacious—like the sky—both beyond and fundamental to any kind of self-limitation. Recognizing this self-nature is, as the Buddha taught, the greatest medicine, since it cuts through the core illusion of a separate selfhood and so loosens any and all of the various problems that seem to accrue to, and codefine, one's self. As Trungpa (2005) put it, unconstructed presence is "the sanity we are born with," but with which we lose touch, becoming lost in our own mental-emotional fixations, or "self and world constructs" (Bugental, 1978), or in psychoanalytic terms, "unconscious organizing principles."

We do well to appreciate our lostness in self/world constructs, which involve repressive barriers of impressive subtlety, including the repression of our own participation in construing the illusion of a separate Selfhood as a brace against the apparent Otherness of the world. As Marvin Casper (1976) put it,

> According to Buddhist psychology, the basis of ego is the tendency to solidify energy into a barrier that separates space into two entities, I and Other, the space in here and the space

> out there. This process is technically termed dualistic fixation.
> First there is the initial creation of the barrier, which is the
> sensing of other, and then the inference of inner or I. This is
> the birth of ego....The irony of the barrier-creating process is
> that we lose track of the fact that we have created the barrier
> and instead act as if it was always there. (p. 65)

Not recognizing the constructed nature of personal reality, but taking dualistic vision as "given" and myself as a separate, self-contained
entity, all kinds of reactions arise in regard to others and the outer
world, such as attraction, aversion, fear, and hope, which congeal into
a fixed set of attitudes to which I habituate. While an understanding of
the constructed nature of social reality is being more deeply appreciated (Berger and Luckmann, 1966) in the human sciences, experiential understanding of the illusory nature of these constructs as well as
an appreciation for what has been lost in this process has remained
largely beyond the ken of Western psychologies.

That the empty-open nature of human being and the lucid
awareness it bears sounds strange to conventional ears and is relatively unknown or inconsistently practiced among even well-trained
psychotherapists only means we have neither understood the nature
of human being well enough nor yet become practiced at embodying the unconditioned presence that accords to this sanity.

UNCONDITIONAL PRESENCE AS SKILLFUL MEANS

The crucial turn in evoking a vital presence moves from *knowing
about* to *knowing with* an Other and Otherness. This marks the
transition from conceiving of the Other *objectively:* as a self-existing
entity independent of the conceptions of the conceiver, through an
understanding of the other constituted *bi-subjectively:* taking into
account the mutual influence between the two subjects in dialogue, to
a knowing of the other *intersubjectively:* recognizing that knowledge
of the Other arises between partners in an open field of possibility.

Not construing the client primarily as a Self formed and deformed
by experiences of the past, invites a shift in how a client construes and

"takes" herself. Allowing for as much *inter*-ness as *subjectivity* aerates the therapeutic atmosphere, lightening the habitual tendency to reify ourselves and others as separate *beings* disjunct from *being*. Finding himself within the unconditional gaze and presence of a therapist, a client may be influenced to shift from taking himself primarily as an enduring Self, a kind of property owner who *has* problems, to being someone who is more of an *unfolding, open-ended awareness* within a shared field of subjective experiencing, in which problems arise, persist, and pass away. Allowing for enhanced spaciousness around problems naturally bodes well for dealing with them more effectively as well as for loosening the core fixation of separateness that inclines us to take on and personalize problems, thus losing touch with the responsive sanity we were born with.

CASE EXAMPLE

An example of the impact a lightly conditioned presence can have on a therapeutic exchange was described by Brenda upon her returning to therapy after a three-year break. We had worked together previously in the context of marital therapy in which I briefly saw Brenda and her husband, Jim, in both individual and conjoint sessions, until Jim decided to stop. Upon returning to do individual work, Brenda recalled an exchange we'd had three years earlier which she felt was extremely important and the reason she wanted to return for further work with me. It occurred in our first individual session, and went as follows.

> (1999) Brenda: (with urgency) I think I was molested by my father. My last therapist thought so; is convinced.
>
> Ken: (Making gentle eye contact, a long silence stretches out between us....I do not know how to respond. I am tempted to ask her more about it, to elicit her memories. But I see the purpose of my doing this would be for us to make some determination of truth about her statement of incest. Yet, I feel no particular urgency to make this finding, and I'm not sure that is what is being asked of me just now in any case. I sense there is some other pressing concern that has not yet declared itself, but not

knowing what that is, and not knowing Brenda well enough yet to probe it, I relax further into our shared space, opening more to the charged field I find us sharing, her attention riveted on me as she sits nervously on the edge of her chair. Settling in to the edginess of the silence, I notice how she is well able, even overly-able, to hold my gaze and sustain a visceral shared presence. It then strikes me that she is in a state of acute readiness, like an animal scanning a prey or predator, waiting for a cue to fight or flee. She seems to me both eager to open herself and terrified of doing so. Sensing that considerable vulnerability, along with the meaning of the words she has just uttered, my heart opens and eyes moisten, and without intending to, I find myself speaking,) Well, we'll see.

Three years later, as she follows up on this brief exchange, which I also recall vividly, Brenda makes her observation of those silent moments.

(2003) Brenda: Do you remember the session we had when I talked about thinking I was molested?

Ken: Yes, I do.

Brenda: That's why I came back. That 20 or 30 seconds of silence was the most important thing. It was "the work" I needed, and still need. I knew I could trust you.

Ken: Ah. I wonder if you also found you could more deeply trust yourself with me?

Brenda: Yes; that's it too. (stops abruptly)

Ken: Something stopped you just now.

Brenda: Yes, (meeting and holding my gaze with intensity) this [candor] just terrifies me, but it's so what I want. I wasn't able to stay with it before, it was just too much. But I'm stronger now and feel I can handle it, and want to take another step.

Ken: OK. (brief pause) Where to?

Brenda: (a big laugh and smile break over her face) Oh, right here! I want to stay right here and not go anywhere getting carried away. It's so easy for me talk about Jim and what an ass he is. We've had so much therapy. You know. And a lot of it has been good. But it always seems to come down to, "Why don't I just get on with things, divorce Jim, cause he's never going to change." I know I can't change him. (brief pause) Or, "What's wrong with me that I can't move on?" But somehow that all misses it.

Ken: The focus goes to what you can or cannot do about it rather than how you are with it.

Brenda: Yes, yes. It's like a reflex. I leap into trying to manage and fix things, it just takes me over. (then, emphatically) Enough of that!

Ken: There it is just now: "enough of that!"

Brenda: (momentarily arrested) Aagh. (a pause as Brenda breaks eye contact. The field between us remains charged as she seems to be sensing into herself. But I find myself wondering if she is now doing her "work" or if I've been too abrupt and she's withdrawing. A familiar guilt arises in me, and as I feel this old weight and recognize it, I release on it and re-attune to Brenda. Her body is still, her breathing full. "Ah," I think, recognizing the signs of an embodied presence, I see she is not withdrawing. Then, looking up to me with moistening eyes and a more gentle voice,) I really want to be kinder, both to myself and Jim.

Ken: Notice how well you're doing that just now.

Brenda: (slowly, letting that sink in) Yeah.

In this exchange, Brenda shared her understanding, which had been incubating in the intervening three years, of what her psychological "work" entailed. She came to understand that this involves deeply listening to herself, which can be facilitated by being closely listened to. She uses the word "work" to describe this. But what she actually means is "nonwork," as in nondoing, just being with her experience as it is without trying to manage it or to finally figure herself out. This is not to say that Brenda is not making sense of herself and her life and coming to a better understanding of things, as she is surely doing this. But her insight is only a by-product of her increasing ability to relax her striving for understanding and the security she hopes it will bring. As she intellectually knows, and is gradually letting sink in, her work is to relax her efforts to secure herself, and to risk just being herself, vulnerable, resilient, and radiant as she is. In the spaciousness—psychological nakedness—that she and I often share, and which she increasingly finds when alone, Brenda is paradoxically "getting" that she can find something like "closure" to her unsettledness through "opening" to it. This is not the closure of resolution, in which things are sewed up tight, but the settledness that arises through strengthening the capacity to be unsettled by the "outrageous fortune" of life without taking it personally.

Understood as a skillful means, unconditional presence facilitates the emergence of meaningful insights, be they fleeting intuitive flashes or more developed conceptual understandings. But of still more value is the recognition that unconditional presence is the play of genuine sanity itself.

THE PLAY OF UNCONDITIONAL PRESENCE

> And the end of all our exploring will be to arrive where we started and to know the place for the first time.
>
> —*T. S. Eliot*

Although unconditioned presence may sound rarefied, an elevated state difficult to attain, this is only because we are habitually distracted, lost in preoccupations (worries, hopes, fears) that obscure the innate intelligence that makes distraction possible in the first place. But even rudimentary psychotherapy works, when it does work, because self-centered fixations are not fundamental to our self-nature. Fixations are practiced only because they can be. It is also possible not to fixate. We have the *capacity* for fixating or not. This inherent freedom of *being* is too often overlooked. Psychology is adept at focusing on deficits, problems, fixations: all sorts of psychological things. But in doing so, it loses sight of the no-thing which alone allows for the sure release of troubling things, and is for genuine depth psychology, the secret cup.

Even the smallest breakthrough is possible only because the spin of an internal dialogue is interrupted, perhaps only briefly, thus allowing a gap to open within which the intelligence of basic sanity may express itself in a lightening insight. (This point is further developed by Kaisa Puhakka in her chapter later in this book.)

For example, in a routine passage common to many therapies, Amy, an engaging thirty-something mom who works part-time as an accountant, came in suffering from a low-level, garden-variety depression not uncommon to many of us. Over a two-year course of therapy she came to face that she was participating in her despair by continuing to tell herself a story about herself that echoed a foul opinion her mother had of her: that she was an embarrassment as a daughter, somehow fundamentally flawed and inadequate in any number of ways. As she became aware of her participation in these stories, she was able to examine the truth of them and the possibility then arose for her to release them. Not only did Amy recognize that she took herself to be the woeful person her mother nominated her to be, but that she maintained that "self" by reinforcing it. As she relaxed the severity of the self-criticism, her depression lightened, and with delight she discovered she felt more like herself.

Yet herein lies the paradox of selfhood. Even this modest therapeutic release was possible only because Amy's "self" was not herself (as a self-existing entity); rather, "she" was revealed to be a mental-emotional construction maintained through the subconscious conversation she kept having with herself. By facing who, and how, she was construing herself, Amy was able to open herself to who and how she was not who she was taking herself to be. In relaxing her self-stories, she was liberated from the self-limitations of those story lines; it was through not being—in the sense of *not construing*—herself that she found herself to be more authentically who she was. *Amy felt more like herself as she felt less like herself!*

While it might be fair to speak of selflessness, even a fleeting experience of selflessness such as Amy had in her release of negative self-statements, as a therapeutic attainment, who is it that could claim to attain such selflessness? Understanding that there is no Self that attains self-liberation, it becomes again evident that it is as important to be as oriented to inter-being as it is to a particular being. With this reorientation, a therapist is less liable to get caught up in and so reify the stories according to which a client is constructing his or her self-limitations.

Even though Freud recognized the optimal attitude and skillful means of practicing depth psychotherapy, he did not recognize that unconditioned awareness was no mere technique, but the nature of sanity itself: the nature of the undeluded mind.

The specific revelations that emerge through seeing things as they are have been seized upon by depth psychologists, displaying as they do psychological truths coemergent with emotional release. Although it has been well acknowledged that if an insight does not choke us up, make as laugh or cry or shiver, then it is an insight that is probably not very deeply felt, and so not likely to make much of a therapeutic difference, psychology has tended to privilege the cognitive, conscious side of knowing over the felt sensing. Insights are conceptually elaborated in order to bind the still shaky, new self-knowledge to consciousness. We know this is sometimes necessary, because a single glimpse of self-awareness is rarely strong enough to dissolve a fixation. Rather, it proves useful to "work through" *the way in which* one is fixated, which directs our attention to the way one tends to continue to practice a fixation in spite of intellectually knowing better. Through repeatedly observing oneself when getting caught, or when about to get caught, in an old fixation, one practices dehabituating to that old habit. In conventional psychotherapy this is accomplished by thinking about the fixation and its role in conditioning a person's sense of self and relationship to the world, rather than placing the emphasis on letting the experience of being non-fixated "sink in." This marks a critical difference between dualistic and nondual approaches, respectively.

What conventional psychotherapy has not recognized is that the glimpses releasing liberating self-understandings are glimpses only. Once this is experientially understood, it becomes possible to attend to openness itself as well as to that which emerges through it. This marks the "ontological difference" between what has been taken as the field proper to psychology to date: attending to confusion and its clarification through self-knowledge, and the potentially broader field for the practice of psychology in the future: attending to the sanity of unconditional wakefulness *(buddhi)* itself.

RELATIVE AND ABSOLUTE TRUTH

One way of understanding the "ontological difference" between beings and *being,* or dualistic and nondualistic knowing, is according to the Mahayana discussion of the *two truths*. This discussion appreciates that existence can make sense from two points of view, either in the ordinary, relative sense of discursive, dualistic thinking or from the unmediated, absolute perspective of nondual presence. This discussion is itself an artifact of dualistic thought, but is composed, as is this entire book, in the service of using concepts to go beyond concepts.

Far and away, most spiritual teachings, including moral proscriptions and meditative practices, operate within the relative perspective, as does virtually all of psychology. This makes sense since we ordinarily experience ourselves and each other on the relative level as separate beings caught up in our personal and shared (see David Loy's chapter on "wego") confusions, desires, and frustrations. Within this mind-set, non-dual awareness is known only as a memory or a concept, perhaps according to a theological, philosophical, or mystical reference system. Within the relative perspective, we are bidden to be psychologically honest with ourselves and recognize our various fixations and the suffering they cause both ourselves and others. It then makes very good sense to try to do something about this "full catastrophe" by pursuing a path of self-liberation that aims to reduce or eliminate confusion and suffering. As the Buddha said most succinctly, we follow a *path* from samsara toward the *goal* of nirvana, from dualistic fixation to nondual freedom. There is work to be done and somewhere better to get to. The Buddha even said that the dharma belongs not to the intellectually gifted or to those especially pious, but to those who "persevere" with their practice, who exert consistent effort to free themselves. Likewise, Jim Bugental has been a champion for many of us in encouraging and exhorting the psychotherapy client who would be crushed under the weight of self-defeat or self-deprecation, to "fight for your life!"

However, when we find ourselves on the "absolute level," it becomes clear that the effort to get somewhere other than where we are is both redundant and impossible. In a moment of unconditional presence, we know in a way that is beyond words and concepts that there is no essential difference between dual and nondual, samsara and nirvana, or relative and absolute truth. Within the space of such openness, or open suchness, there is neither here nor there, no inside or outside, no self or other, yet the spaciousness is saturated with awareness vividly awake to all manner of apparent differences. Lacking nothing, complete in itself, the natural capacity of the mind is not (yet) split into self and other, neither confused nor flustered in its basic sanity.

As any Buddha discovers, the psychological difference between the two truths is simply that of either clinging or not clinging to experience. Basic sanity entails the freedom to either take on perceptions and thoughts as "mine," getting caught up and lost in them, or to not grasp onto experiences, allowing them to arise and pass away as they do, without identifying with, rejecting, or ignoring them.

Within this nondual understanding, the reach and range of psychotherapy is expanded in two general ways. Since even a modestly liberating self-reflection requires at least a moment of relaxing habitual clinging to some position, so to glimpse and release what has remained unconscious, the ability of a therapist to allow and elicit unconditional presence will be facilitative for any depth-oriented therapy. But it is also possible to practice within unconditional presence in a more sustained way and more explicitly with those clients who are prepared and interested in doing so. With those who want to embody their openness more fully, therapeutic exchanges can serve as practice fields for the exercise, or play, of unconditional presence.

For instance, during unconditional exchanges, impulses to be distracted from what is happening *now* so to "get somewhere" other than *here*, presumably somewhere better, more clear or more peaceful perhaps, are recognized for what they are and may be released in conversations that turn in and return to the sanity we were born with. Just as a well-oiled hinge has "play," unintentional therapeutic conversations explicitly invite us to exercise a hinge that has become sticky, not in order to open and pass through a particular door, but in order to strengthen our ability—or suppleness—to open any door, and remain open and responsive in the face of whatever lies behind it.

So, in considering the reach and range appropriate for depth psychology, how deep should unconditional presencing go? Conventional wisdom, as an expression of dualistic thinking, observes that it is possible to go *too deep* with someone who does not have the requisite "ego strength." What this means is that "depth" work is understood to be the practice of "uncovering" unconscious fixations belonging to a client's "self." The uncovering is conducted in the service of searching for insights and conceptually understanding more about one's self. Within this approach, some kinds of self-knowledge are decidedly difficult to bear, either because they are narcissistically wounding or because they threaten a belief about existence that one holds tightly. Thus the conscientious therapist may back off from pressing a particularly upsetting therapeutic agenda.

But practicing with an unintentional attitude, with choiceless awareness, one is at less risk of going "too deep" with a fragile client. This is because there is nowhere the therapist intends to go. There is no assumption that a client's therapy should go anywhere other than where the person is in the moment. No therapeutic ambition is deployed by the therapist to get the client to go deeper, be more mature or more integrated than he is, or less repressed, less reactive, or less passive aggressive than she is. In short, practicing with unconᴏnal presence, there is little or no collusion in the co-construction of the client's self, which could otherwise be conceived as needing to be deepened or otherwise improved upon. At the same time, there is no ignoring of how a client may be invested in a particular self and world construct, and of the consequences she may be suffering due to this self-limitation.

THE THING IS THIS

Even though we are endowed with the capacity of natural resilience, free to either cling or not cling to experience, we find it difficult not to cling and to sustain unconditional openness. For most of us, our karmic propensities (unconscious fixations) have a deeply rooted momentum that is compelling, and releasing these knots may benefit both from work on the relative level and play on the absolute "level."

The rule is this: When emptied and open to self and other, in a moment of unconditional presence, there is nothing more to do. The challenge thus is that of doing nothing, of not filling in the openness with yet another self-improvement or self-liberation agenda. Instead, the "work" is to bear the shared openness and its inherent playfulness, getting more used to being emptied and opened, strengthening one's capacity for sustaining unconditional presence and so becoming more able to release its inherent qualities of compassion, appreciation, devotion, discernment, equanimity, and delight. On the other hand, when one is in the throes of an emotional reaction or caught up in a dense fixation, confused and miserable because of that, we can work as usual on the relative level. Within this approach, the therapist who experientially knows the difference and nondifference between the two truths may work on *both* relative and absolute levels, *if* he or she is so capable.

ENDNOTES

1. Although psychoanalysis understands its practice to involve *both* felt inquiry and the conceptual understanding arriving from it (as Ricoeur discussed at some length in *Freud and Philosophy*), still, the premium is placed on insight.

Freud, for example, understood the overriding aim of analysis to be that of "making the unconscious conscious," while Kohut noted that empathic "understanding" was conducted in the service of conceptual "explanation."

INTERSUBJECTIVITY AND NONDUALITY IN THE PSYCHOTHERAPEUTIC RELATIONSHIP

Judith Blackstone

INTRODUCTION

This essay discusses the potential for experiencing a nondual realm of consciousness, and the relevance of this experience for the psychotherapeutic process. One of the pivotal issues of this discussion is the relationship between the personal, subjective dimension of experience that is the arena of both individual differences and human suffering, and the transcendent dimension of nondual consciousness. If nondual consciousness is impersonal, as it is sometimes described, then it has little direct relevance to the psychotherapeutic project of personal development and emotional well-being. But if, as I propose, nondual consciousness is the essence and ground of personal subjective experience, then opening to this dimension can be understood as the direction of human maturity.

INTERSUBJECTIVITY THEORY

As my representative of the psychotherapeutic process in this discussion, I have chosen Intersubjectivity Theory a relational model of psychoanalysis developed by Robert Stolorow and his collaborators. My main concern in this essay is not to compare nonduality and Intersubjectivity Theory, per se. I am using this particular therapeutic model because its clear articulation of the mutuality of the therapeutic relationship and the cocreation of subjective experience provides an effective basis of comparison with the nondual experience of self/other oneness described in mystical traditions. Many contemporary forms of psychotherapy, such as Object-Relations, Gestalt, and Self Psychology, to name just a few, could be described as intersubjective. Like Intersubjectivity

Theory, they recognize that human development is both nurtured and thwarted within social contexts and that the therapist/client relationship has a significant influence on the therapeutic process. Intersubjectivity Theory offers a more radical assertion of intersubjectivity than most other therapeutic forms, in its placement of the therapeutic relationship at the very center of the therapeutic process and in its view of psychological healing as specifically the achievement of new ways of relating with other people. Stolorow and Atwood write, "More generally, it is the formation of new organizing principles within an intersubjective system that constitutes the essence of developmental change throughout the life cycle" (Stolorow & Atwood, 1992, p. 25).

Intersubjectivity Theory sees human identity as an emergent property of the relational field itself. It is a systems theory "in which experiential worlds and intersubjective fields are seen as equiprimordial, mutually constituting one another in circular fashion" (Stolorow, Atwood & Orange, 2002, pp. 95–96). Although not explicitly stated in the Intersubjectivity Theory literature, this suggests, or at least draws near to the idea of an underlying unity, a single system or field, which gives rise to human experience and behavior. It begins to explore the hard question of the relationship between individual perspective and fundamental unity.

As a systems theory, Intersubjectivity Theory resembles most nondual philosophies in its denial of the existence of the individual self as an "existentially independent entity" (Stolorow & Atwood, 1992). Arguing against an intrinsically separate mind-body entity, Stolorow and Atwood write, "This we contrast with the *experience* of psychological distinctness, a structuralization of self-awareness that is wholly embedded in formative and sustaining intersubjective contexts" (p. 10). Asian nondual philosophies view the goal of nondual spiritual practices to be the realization—that is, the *experience*—of the unity of self and other, or subject and object.

I also chose to focus on Intersubjectivity Theory because it speaks clearly for a prevailing contemporary philosophical perspective in the West: social constructivism. Although Intersubjectivity Theory espouses a hermeneutic "perspectival realism" (Orange, 1995), its view that "the principle components of subjectivity...are the organizing principles, whether automatic and rigid, or reflective and flexible" (Orange, Atwood & Stolorow, 1997, p. 7) aligns it with the postmodern constructivist viewpoint. It thus evokes a clearly drawn argument between the constructivist understanding that all experience is interpreted or "organized" and the claim of an unconstructed, essential dimension of experience, which is one of the defining aspects of nondual consciousness. It is this conflict that we must try to reconcile in order to understand the relevance of nondual realization for personal healing and development. I will attempt to show that the intersubjective, cocreated relational field and the nondual relational field are two views of the same relational field. Nondual realization is a subtler attunement and greater openness to the intersubjective relational field. As I will explain, nondual realization does not eradicate intersubjectivity; rather it encompasses and illuminates it.

DEFINING NONDUALITY

The experience of oneness—that the essence of one's individual being is the same as, or unified with, or dissolved in the essence of the cosmos—has been described throughout the world's spiritual literature, including the Jewish teachings of Kabala, Islamic Sufism, and the writing of Christian mystics such as Meister Eckhart. Many of the Asian spiritual teachings focus specifically on this experience, usually referring to it as *nonduality* (Sanskrit: *advaita*).

Perhaps because it has been a major focus of spiritual aspiration in the East, several different perspectives on nondual realization have developed there. They vary from the view, found in Advaita Vedanta, that only consciousness is real and phenomena are illusory, to the view, found in Madhyamika Buddhism, Taoism, and some schools of Zen Buddhism, that only the constantly changing flux of phenomena are real and there is no such "thing" as unified consciousness. David Loy (1998) makes the point that the various Asian nondual teachings are mainly differences in the philosophical interpretation of nonduality or in the methodological approach to nondual realization; the descriptions of the experience itself are markedly similar across different traditions.

Loy divides nondual experience into nondual perception, non-dual thinking, and nondual action. Nondual teachings that empha-size nondual perception describe a shift from dualistic subject/object perception to direct or "bare" perception, in which the perceptible world becomes vivid and immediate, unmediated by conceptual elaboration. Since there is no conceptual lag in one's perception, there is no discernible distinction between the subject and object of perception.

The same dropping away of conceptual veils enables nondual thinking, the spontaneous flow of thoughts associated with creativ-ity and intuition. Nondual action is spontaneous, un-self-conscious responsiveness to life. It is the ability to play, to interact with one's environment freely, without hesitation. Stephen Batchelor (2000) writes, "The awakened mind of a Buddha is nothing other than the pristine awareness animating one's ordinary mind at every moment" (p. 41). And, "By systematically stripping away any behavior that inhibits the spontaneous play of pristine awareness, one uncovers a freedom that is a dynamic response to each and every circumstance of life" (p. 43).

Indian Vedantic teachings also describe nondual experience as the dissolution of conceptual veils. Here is a description from Berthold Thompson (2002) of his experience with the Indian teacher Poonja: "Papaji's words were heard but there was no one left to whom he could address them. The speaking and the hearing were occurring as one single, impersonal event" (p. 29). Notice how the dropping away of conceptual elaboration is described here as "impersonal." We will return to this important issue shortly.

The description of nondual experience that I am concerned with in this essay includes the immediacy of nonconceptual perception, thought, and action, but adds another dimension. This is the experi-ence of a subtle, all-pervasive expanse of consciousness pervading one's internal and external experience as a unified whole. The Asian teachings that describe this type of nondual experience consider this subtle consciousness to be the essence of being. Tibetan Buddhist philosopher Longchen Rabjam (2001a) writes, "Within the essence of being…lies the spacious expanse of the ground of being" (p. 145). Vedantic scholar Eliot Deutsch (1969), referring to nondual consciousness as Brahman, writes, "Everything has its being in Spirit: everything, in its true being, is Brahman" (p. 110). And, "In the immediate, intuitive experience of non-duality, Brahman presents itself as the fullness of being, as self-luminous consciousness, and as infinite bliss *(saccidananda)*" (p. 28).

According to the Indian teachings, this subtle consciousness can be experienced without sensory objects, in deep meditative states (Forman, 1998). However, it can also be experienced along with the appearance of phenomena. The simultaneous experience of nondual consciousness and phenomena is most commonly described in the Mahamudra and Dzogchen schools of Tibetan Buddhism, but is also found in some schools of Zen Buddhism and in Indian Advaita Vedanta and Kashmiri Shaivism. In this experience, phenomena appear to be transparent or permeable, as if made of consciousness. Even one's own body is experienced as completely permeable (or open), all the way through, and made of consciousness.

This all-pervasive, nondual consciousness is described as "self-knowing" because it experiences itself. The Zen philosopher Hisamatsu writes, "The nature of Awareness beyond differentiation is that it directly knows Itself, in and through Itself" (cited in Stambaugh, 1999, p. 74). Longchen Rabjam writes, "The instant the bond between body and mind is loosened, self-knowing awareness—*dharmakaya* as original purity—merges with and becomes indistinguishable from supreme space—dharmakaya as the ground of being" (2001a, p. 186).

This is not just an experience of immediate sensory phenomena, and not just a shift in one's thinking or behavior. It is a clear-through openness and refinement of one's entire being. Not only one's mental awareness, but rather one's whole being is experienced as an expanse of subtle consciousness, pervading everywhere. Since this consciousness pervades one's internal and external experience as a unified whole, it transcends the boundary of the individual self. *However, since this consciousness pervades the internal space of one's own body, it is experienced as deep inward contact with oneself, at the same time as it is experienced as transcending oneself.*

Rabjam refers, in the citation above, to the "instant" the bond between body and mind is loosened. Although, theoretically, it is simply our beliefs that keep the body and mind entangled, in practice, that entanglement is usually so secure and complex that for most human beings, no single cognitive shift will undo it completely. One's first entryway into the nondual dimension may be experienced as a sudden, dramatic change from one's usual dualistically fragmented state, but this is only the beginning of a gradual process of uncovering or opening to the nondual ground of being.

In Buddhism, the subtle essence of being is also referred to as Buddha nature. Tibetan teacher Tsultrim Gyamtso Rinpoche (Gyamtso, 2001) writes, "Beings go through a process of purification from which the purified Buddha nature emerges" (p. 69). This understanding of nondual realization as a process does not mean that nondual consciousness is something that we create or develop. It arises spontaneously and effortlessly, once we have reached a degree of openness, and continues to become a more full, complete realization as we become increasingly open and refined. Gyamtso writes, "If the true nature of beings were not the *tathagatagarbha* (purified Buddha nature), they could never become Buddhas in the same way that a rock that did not contain gold could never yield gold however much it were to be refined" (p. 69).

THE INTEGRATION OF SUBJECT AND OBJECT

I have chosen to focus on this type of nondual experience for several reasons. I am interested in how psychotherapy can contribute to the type of transformation required for it, and also how this transformation is related to psychological health and maturity. I am also interested in how the experience of all-pervasive consciousness can enhance therapeutic skills, such as subtle perception and empathy.

I have observed that nondual teachings emphasizing only perceptual, cognitive, or behavioral shifts may lead to a particular type of confusion that is detrimental to psychological health. The methodologies of these teachings often present nonduality as a state in which one attends without distraction to the present moment, or understands that one does not really exist as a subject (as in the phrase "thoughts without a thinker"). Although I do not doubt that these approaches have brought some measure of relaxation and clarity to many people, they may also exacerbate one's fragmentation between subject and object (e.g., thinker and thoughts) rather than producing the wholeness that the term nonduality implies.

Sometimes it is taught that we cannot know that we are enlightened because there is "no one there" to know. This can be effective as a pedagogical strategy to help the novice practitioner (momentarily) shift from a dualistic self/object state to the openness of nonduality, but it can also be misleading, for students who will try to dissociate from themselves as the knowing subject.

If we actually could not know that we were enlightened, we would not have the many descriptions of it available in the world's spiritual literature. For example, Longchen Rabjam clearly and gleefully describes his experience of nondual realization as "Within the spacious expanse, the spacious expanse, the spacious vast expanse, I, Longchen Rabjam, for whom the lucid expanse of being is infinite, experience everything as embraced within a blissful expanse, a single nondual expanse" (2001b, p. 79).

In the type of nondual experience in which one realizes one's own nature as all-pervasive space, the subject (as nondual consciousness) does not vanish. It becomes one with the object of experience. In this type of realization, we can have any kind of experience without disturbing our realization of the stillness and pervasiveness of nondual consciousness. Nondual realization does not eradicate our "lesser" mental functions, such as the ability to reflect on, learn from, or enjoy our experience, to have preferences, or to remember past events.

Spiritual teachings that train one's focus on the content of experience, especially on the sensory world outside of one's body, or that claim that nondual consciousness has nothing to do with personal experience (e.g., that is "impersonal") may contribute to the common psychological problem of dissociation. Rather than experiencing the integration of subject and object, the subject is simply negated, and the practitioner becomes fixated on the object. This is a manipulation of experience that obstructs both the wholeness and the fluidity of nonduality. It censors our participation in life, placing us in the mode of observer rather than experiencer.

I have found that many spiritual practitioners attune to awareness outside of their bodies rather than experience consciousness pervading their body and environment at the same time. In my observation, when nondual consciousness pervades the whole body, even the quality of the pervasive space changes. Instead of simply being empty, it has an intrinsic radiance as well as a quality that might be described as the quality of "being." Hisamatsu writes, "For the nothingness of Zen is not lifeless like emptiness, but, on the contrary, is something quite lively *(lebendig)*. It is not only lively, but also has heart and moreover, is aware of itself" (cited in Stambaugh, 1999, p. 79).

Some degree of dissociation is, in my view, typical of the human condition. Defensive patterns, developed in childhood to protect against ordinary occurrences of emotional or sensory abrasion, produce a degree of numbness and fragmentation even in highly functioning adults. This manifests as a general diminishment or lack of development in one's capacities for contact with oneself and others, including one's capacity for understanding, emotional responsiveness, physical sensation, and sensory perception.

As we will see, the type of nondual experience that reveals nondual consciousness as the essence of one's being actually heals dissociation. Nondual consciousness is experienced as the basis of contact, the most intimate contact one can have, with oneself and others.

INTERSUBJECTIVITY AND NONDUALITY

Intersubjectivity Theory, as I have said, specifically rejects any claim of a realm of experience that is beyond the subjective organizations of experience, and the shifting contexts of intersubjective dialogue. In this outlook, as in the prevailing Western constructivist viewpoint, all experience is subjectively created. In sharp contrast, nondual consciousness is considered, in the above-mentioned Asian philosophies, to be uncreated, arising spontaneously as mental elaborations and body-mind entanglements are relinquished. Moreover, a defining characteristic of nondual experience is that our perceptions, thoughts, and actions appear to function spontaneously, without conceptual mediation.

These two perspectives seem completely opposed. Yet if we explore them more closely, we see that both Intersubjectivity Theory and nondual spiritual practices are aimed at the same goal: healing the fragmented, constricted relational field. As a therapy, Intersubjectivity Theory focuses on the "structural invariants of the patient's psychological organization" (Stolorow, Atwood & Brandchaft, 1987, p. 13) and "limiting world horizons…which reflect patterns or organizing activity formed and maintained within living, intersubjective systems" (Stolorow, Atwood & Orange, 2002, pp. 49–50). Nondual practices seek to dissolve the rigid, habitual patterns of experience that obscure nondual consciousness. I suggest that these two disciplines both facilitate the same process of human development, toward inward contact with oneself and openness to one's environment.

In order to understand this, we need to look at how nondual consciousness is related to one's personal subjectivity. Nondual consciousness is often called "impersonal," as we saw in Thompson's description above, but to what exactly does this word "impersonal" refer? Thompson had the feeling that there "was nobody there," that the words of his teacher were simply occurring without anyone being there to hear them. However, he obviously did hear them, and was able to reflect on the experience afterward. So, although he felt that he was not there, he actually was. He experienced a radical shift in how he was there, in that he had no reflexive awareness of himself as being there, but he was still there.

For me, this is one of the great mysteries of nondual experience, which is often hidden behind the term "impersonal." We can feel that we are as much the tree or the lamp or the person facing us as we are our own self, but at the same time, we are always our own self, our own personal subjectivity. For example, we cannot perceive the room from the perspective of the other person, or get up and leave the room as that other person. As nondual consciousness, we do not sense ourselves as being separate from our experience, we are suffused in the stimuli of the present moment, and yet we are still experiencing and knowing. We experience ourselves as transparent, dissolved in empty space, and yet it is our own subjectivity that experiences this.

Zen philosopher Nishitani (1982) writes, "The existence of things is seen to be at one with the existence of the subject itself by the subject that has become its original subjectivity" (pp. 109–110). Explaining the Vedantic teacher Ramana Maharshi's teaching, Godman (1992) writes, "You must distinguish between the 'I,' pure in itself, and the 'I'-thought. The latter, being merely a thought, sees subject and object…But the pure 'I' is the pure being, eternal existence, free from ignorance and thought-illusion" (p. 49). As our habitual, created representations of ourselves and our environment dissolve, we discover our original, uncreated dimension of subjectivity. In this view, subjectivity is inextricably personal (the core of one's own being), and at the same time it is the essential nature of the self/other field.

Interestingly, nondual realization does not eliminate the shifting contexts that characterize human discourse. Just as the laying bare of nondual consciousness does not eliminate the movement of one's emotions, thoughts, sensations, and perceptions, but rather frees and illuminates that movement, it does not eliminate the dynamic exchange and reciprocal influence of culturally and psychologically shaped responses within a relational dyad. The richness of human dialogue, which depends upon differing contexts of personal memories, education, culture, gender, and so forth, is not eliminated, but revealed more clearly in the openness and spaciousness of nondual consciousness.

The only types of context that are considered problematic in the Asian nondual teachings are those habitual or invariant modes of subjective organization that defensively bifurcate subject and object, or that reify, through mental elaboration, either subject or object. In other words, those organizations of experience that limit one's experience of the present moment. I am not speaking here just of perceptual limitations, but also of limitations in our capacity for thought, emotion, and physical sensation. These rigid or repetitive patterns of experience that obscure nonduality are the same subjective organizations that are considered problematic in most forms of psychotherapy, including Intersubjectivity Theory, where they are called "transference" phenomena.

Stolorow, Atwood and Brandchaft (1987) define transference as invariant or repetitive organizations of subjective experience based on "archaically rooted configurations of self and object" (p. 36), and as the "assimilation of the analytic relationship into the thematic structures of the patient's personal subjective world" (p. 45). In other words, certain types of subjective organization can cause us to experience our idea of the present moment, based on our memories and interpretations of past events, rather than the moment itself. The more we assimilate others into our own thematic structures, the more isolated we are in our own hermetically constructed world, and the less we can participate in the mutuality of the relational field that concerns both Intersubjectivity Theory and nondual teachings.

The view held by Intersubjectivity Theory, that all experience is subjectively organized, means that it does not consider the psychotherapeutic process as moving toward the dissolution of organizations. Stolorow and Atwood (1992) write, "Successful psychoanalytic treatment, in our view, does not produce therapeutic change by altering or eliminating the patient's invariant organizing principles. Rather…it facilitates the establishment and consolidation of alternative principles and thereby enlarges the patient's experiential repertoire" (p. 25). However, the authors of Intersubjectivity Theory also write, "The rigidity that we associate with various kinds of psychopathology can be grasped as a kind of freezing of one's experiential horizons so that other perspectives remain unavailable" (Orange, 2000, p. 489).

As rigid organizations of experience are recognized in the psychotherapeutic process, an openness or availability to experience emerges. Nondual realization, as we have seen in Batchelor's description quoted above, signifies a high degree of flexibility and spontaneity of responsiveness. I believe this flexibility is experientially (if not philosophically) similar to the unfreezing of experiential horizons and expansion of experiential possibilities described in Intersubjectivity Theory.

Nondual realization, as I have said, is a gradual process. Although we may enter into it abruptly, we can then spend the rest of our lives continuing to open to the pervasive space of nondual consciousness. Thus, the claim, by Intersubjectivity Theory, that experience is always to some extent organized, is for practical purposes, true. However, nondual consciousness emerges as "limiting world horizons" and "structural invariants" of psychological organization are relinquished. In this sense, the major difference between the perspectives of Intersubjectivity Theory and Asian nondual philosophies is in the greater reach of the latter's vision into the more advanced phases of human development.

The spaciousness of nondual consciousness is experienced as vast stillness, within which all of the movements of life—our perceptions, thoughts, emotions, physical sensations, and actions—occur. As our realization of nonduality progresses, all of these dynamic aspects of our experience gain their optimal fluidity and freedom. In other words, we are able to allow experiences, such as emotion, thoughts, or perceptions, to occur, or to flow, without impeding them. Examples of this unimpeded experience are an increased subtlety and vividness of perception, a greater depth of emotional responsiveness, as well as greater emotional resiliency and a more spontaneous flow of creativity. For this reason, nondual realization is often referred to as freedom. It is freedom from our own constraints upon ourselves, from our rigid organizations of experience.

NONDUALITY AND INDIVIDUALITY

The founders of Intersubjectivity Theory present their systems perspective as an antidote to Cartesian fragmentation. They write, "Descartes's philosophy not only segregated inner from outer and subject from object; it also severed mind from body and cognition (reason) from affect" (Stolorow, Atwood & Orange, 2002, p. 10). In my view, this anti-Cartesian project of Intersubjectivity Theory is in complete accord with and can be facilitated by nondual realization.

When we realize nondual consciousness, we experience that it pervades the whole internal space of our body at once. This is not body-sensing in the ordinary sense; it is not simply an internal sensation. Rather, it is an experience of internal transparency, as if one were made of space. This experience requires no volitional action, as does body-sensing. It appears spontaneously as part of the sponta-neous arising of nondual consciousness, when we reach a degree of openness or sensitivity. This internal space is completely empty, and at the same time, it is suffused with a very subtle quality of being. We feel as if we have no boundary between ourselves and our envi-ronment, because we are made of the same space that pervades the environment as well.

In order to experience this subtle clear-through space, we need to inhabit our body all the way through to a subtle channel that runs through the vertical core of our being. This channel is called *sushumna* in Indian Yoga and the "central channel" in Buddhism. If we inhabit our body without reaching this core (if we inhabit only the surface of ourselves), we do not enter into the subtle, pervasive essence of our being. Above, I quoted Longchen Rabjam as saying that the bond between the body and mind is loosened in nondual realization. In the subtle core of the body we become disentangled from the material body as nondual consciousness. This does not mean that we are separate from the material body. It means that, as nondual consciousness, we pervade the body (and all phenomena) without interruption.

The subtle core of our being is thus our entranceway into the transcendent space of nondual consciousness. However, it is also, at the same time, the source of the qualitative, cohesive experience of our individual being. According to Asian spiritual teachings, the essential (uncreated) qualities of our being, such as awareness, love, power, and sexuality, and the subtle vibrations, or energies, associ-ated with each of them, emanate from points (called *chakras*) along the subtle core of the body.

In this subtle dimension of ourselves, the internal space of our body is directly correlated with our essential qualities and functions. If we inhabit our head as nondual consciousness, we experience the quality of mental clarity, and we can also think more clearly. If we inhabit our chest as nondual consciousness, we experience the quality of love, and we can feel all emotions more deeply. If we inhabit our pelvis as nondual consciousness, we experience the quality of physical sensation, and we can experience physical sensations more intensely.

As our realization of nondual consciousness gradually progresses, it pervades more of our body at once. This develops an internal
coherence. We can feel, think, and sense at the same time. We experience that we are coming alive within our own skin, not as an idea of
ourselves, but as a qualitative being. Thus, nondual realization is the
basis not only of subject/object unity, but of mind/body unity and
cognition/affect unity as well.

This quality-rich internal coherence provides a felt sense of one's
own existence. Especially for people who feel overwhelmed or dis-
placed by their environment, the experience of internal wholeness
provides the basis of genuine boundaries; that is, boundaries that
are not maintained by the defensive limitation of one's participation
in life.

NONDUALITY AND THE THERAPEUTIC
RELATIONSHIP

I will end this essay with a brief description of how nondual realization
can enhance therapeutic skills and the therapeutic relationship (for a
fuller account, see Blackstone, 2007, in press). One aspect of nondual
realization that has not been explored in the Asian literature is the
relational. Nondual realization changes the way we experience and
relate with other people and this affects the psychotherapeutic
relationship in several ways.

For example, nondual realization deepens our capacity for contact. We experience nondual consciousness pervading everything in
our environment, including other people. This means that we are
able to encounter people not just on their surfaces but also within the
internal depths of their being. This gives us a qualitative, felt sense of
the other person. In the therapeutic relationship, it can help clients
feel seen and met in a dimension of basic human kinship, beyond
the narrative aspect and shifting dynamics of the encounter.

One of the main tenets of Intersubjectivity Theory is the col-
laborative nature of psychotherapy. In keeping with postmodern
thought, Intersubjectivity Theory seeks to dismantle the prevailing power structure, particularly within classical psychoanalysis, in

which the analyst is considered to be an authority on the patient's psychological life. The authors of Intersubjectivity Theory reason that since there is no truly objective view of reality, and no position that can separate the observer from the observed, the interpretation of events or behaviors by the analyst cannot be assumed to be more valid than the patient's. They write, "The analyst's frame of reference must not be elevated to the status of objective fact" (Stolorow, Atwood & Brandchaft, 1987, p. 6). Nondual realization provides the therapist with a felt sense of equality with the client, because the defensive boundary between self and Other has been dissolved. Rigidly organized attitudes, including the attitude of authority, have been dismantled. The therapist who has realized nonduality experiences that the essence of his or her own being is unified or continuous with the essence of the client.

The realization of nondual consciousness refines the therapist's ability to experience and respond to the specificity of each moment, without manipulating or obscuring those moments with therapeutic strategies. A therapist who lives in the nondual dimension brings a receptive stillness and silence to the clinical setting, out of which "news from the self" (Bollas, 1987, p. 236) can emerge spontaneously for both the client and the therapist.

Although the therapist's responses are still informed by contexts of belief and knowledge based on education, experiences with other clients, memories of his or her own developmental process, and so on, these contexts become transparent. The therapist can see through them, to remain open to the stimuli arising in each moment of the therapeutic dialogue. In other words, he or she will not be bound in rigidly fixed patterns of understanding or response, or mistake his or her own historical influences for objective reality. The therapist's ability to be present and immersed in each moment, to be involved and affected by the therapeutic dialogue, means that the therapeutic process is cocreated, or even "trans" created. Healing emerges from the relational field, affecting both the client and the therapist.

Nondual realization also deepens the therapist's ability for empathy. Just as one's own body is experienced as transparent, permeable consciousness, the bodies of other people also appear as clear-through transparent forms. Within this transparency, the fluidity of a person's responses, and the qualities of their being, can be seen and felt. Instead of observing just the surface of the client's body, such as their facial expression and bodily posture, the therapist can, to some extent, see through to the movement of thoughts, feelings, and sensations that occurs within the client's body. This enhances the therapist's ability to know what it feels like to be the client, and how the events that the client is relating have affected them.

Since nondual realization is experienced pervading the therapist's and client's body equally, it allows the therapist to maintain inward contact with himself or herself at the same time as experiencing unity with the client. Since the therapist has not energetically left his or her own body and entered the body of the client, this is not experienced by either party as a merging, nor as an energetic invasion of one person into the other. The therapist can maintain clear boundaries at the same time as he or she refines attunement to the client.

THE TRANSUBJECTIVE FIELD

If both the therapist and the client know about the potential for nondual realization, the therapeutic process can be experienced as a progression toward uncovering the unfragmented, nondual relational field. When we realize nonduality, everything appears to be made of the same one consciousness. This is why some Asian philosophies have concluded that in fact everything actually is made of a single consciousness, a single Self that can be realized, or uncovered, in each individual being. At this point we have no way of knowing whether the experience of unity is an ontological or a phenomenological reality. However, when two people both experience nondual consciousness together, they have a vivid experience that the same one consciousness pervades them both. They experience that their consciousness is unified, or continuous, with each other's consciousness (Blackstone, 2002). We might call this mutual space of subject/subject unity a "transubjective field."

This does not mean that two people can think or feel as proxies for one another, or that they lose their individual agency in any way.

The nondual field of consciousness retains its paradoxical nature of being individual and transcendent at the same time. But they experience that they are both made of the same fundamental ground of being. Since they have both reached the subtle core of themselves, they experience deep inward contact with themselves and unity with each other, at the same time.

As nondual consciousness, two people can connect with each other from within the internal space of their separate bodies. This produces a vibrational resonance between their essential qualities. For example, the love that they experience within their own body resonates with the love in the other person's body. The mutual stimulation of this resonance is healing in itself. Wherever one person is more open in their own being than the other, it will help dissolve the rigid organizations of the other person. Thus the nondual encounter facilitates each person's realization of nondual consciousness. There is a discernible shift in the depth and quality of contact and in the spontaneity of dialogue, whenever the subjective organizations of either person give way to the mutuality of the nondual field.

CLINICAL ILLUSTRATION

Background

I have developed a method, called Realization Process, to help people experience nondual consciousness in the clinical setting. This is a series of exercises that attune directly to the pervasive expanse of nondual consciousness, and to the subtle core of the body as an entranceway into this dimension. Particular emphasis is placed on attuning to nondual consciousness in the whole body, and on experiencing nondual consciousness while in relation with other people.

These exercises are not nondual realization itself, which is an effortless, self-arising state. Rather, they can gradually help the client become open enough for nondual consciousness to appear. The exercises also serve as diagnostic tools for both the client and therapist to discern whatever holding patterns in the body are obstructing this openness.

The following clinical vignette describes a session with a woman named Terry, about four months into our work together. Terry had been a meditation practitioner for ten years. She came to work with me because she was experiencing anxiety and loneliness. She felt awkward in social situations and could not bring herself to pursue friendships. She was an extremely sensitive woman and described herself as feeling "rattled" after being with other people.

Terry described her father as emotionally remote, and her mother as often either depressed or frantic. She had spent much of her childhood trying to avoid her mother's emotional turmoil by spending long hours in her own room, reading and daydreaming.

In the first four months of our sessions, we had explored her childhood background and also practiced the beginning of the main Realization Process exercise, in which the client inhabits her body, first part by part, and then all at once, also attuning to the essential qualities of being within the body. I use the analogy that the body is the temple, and the person can be inside of the temple. This is practiced with the eyes closed, and then with the eyes open. It was most difficult for Terry to feel that she was still "inside her own temple" with her eyes open. She became energetically diffuse with her eyes open, as if she were being absorbed into the environment. Terry described this as being "pulled" out of herself. I suggested that she practice purposely leaving her body in this way, and this helped her recognize that it was something she did herself so that she would not feel overwhelmed by the environment.

It is important to note that nondual realization is not an energetic expansion, or an internal vacancy. As I have said, we need to inhabit the body through to the subtle core, in order to arrive at the pervasive stillness of nondual consciousness.

Gradually, this exercise helped Terry experience that she had internal depth. This shift is visible to a sensitive observer; it looks like a ripening inward, a deepening of a person's presence. She said that it was a relief to feel that she was not "right up against the world." As she had begun to feel more comfortable in her body, I suggested that we might go on to the next part of the exercise in which the client attunes to nondual space pervading her body and the environment equally.

Vignette

Terry seemed particularly anxious as the session began. Her eyes were unfocused and diffuse and I had the sense that she was floating up above herself.

> T—"I wanted to go on to the next part of the exercise today, but I feel very nervous about it."

As I nodded and waited for her to go on, I could feel her settle more deeply into her lower body. This calmed her a little, but she seemed to be very reluctant to tell me what was upsetting her. Finally, she spoke.

> T—"I'm afraid about what I might see if the space pervades us both."
>
> J—"What might you see?"
>
> T—"Your pain."
>
> J—"What would it mean if you see my pain?"
>
> T—"I don't know."

Terry agreed to try the exercise. After she inhabited her whole body at once, I asked her to find the space outside of her body, and then to experience that the space inside and outside of her body was the same, continuous space. Then, she practiced this same process with the eyes open. I then asked her to experience that the space that pervaded her also pervaded me. At first she energetically came toward me in order to pervade my body. I said, "Try to stay in your own body as you experience the space pervading us both. You do not have to move at all from your own body; it is as if you are attuning to the space that is already present, pervading us both."

> T—"I don't think I can do that. I don't know what you mean."

> J—"Okay, then just feel again (as in the first part of the exercise) that you are inhabiting the internal space of your chest."

She did this easily.

> J—"Now find the space inside your own chest and inside my chest at the same time."

Terry did that for an instant, and then felt fear.

> J—"Are you afraid to do this?"

> T—"Yes. I'm afraid that I'm going to feel your pain."

> J—"What might happen if you feel my pain?"

Terry sat with this question for a moment.

> T—"I will have to fix it. I will be responsible for fixing it."

She sat a while longer, attuning to the space inside her own chest, and then inside both of our chests. Suddenly I could feel intense grief inside Terry's chest.

> J—"She was very sad."

In general, I do not think it is helpful to tell a client what I see regarding her own feelings, let alone her mother's feelings, unless it is in the form of a question. But this response welled up in me as part of the spontaneous flow of our exchange. Terry began to cry very deeply.

> T—"She was so sad. And there was nothing I could do. I was just a child. I could never fix it." Then she paused, and looked at me with surprise. She said, "I've never felt compassion for her before. I only wanted to get away from her."

After this release, Terry was easily able to find the space inside her chest and my chest at the same time. When she did this, love flowed between us spontaneously. At first she seemed embarrassed by this, but then she said, "Oh, I see, I'm in my own body, so it's okay. It feels safe." Her eyes focused and for the first time in our relationship, she made eye contact with me.

She then practiced experiencing the space pervading her whole body and my whole body at the same time. As she did this, the internal space of her body seemed to become more subtle and "clear-through."

Comments

This vignette illustrates how attunement to nondual consciousness can help us open to other people, and also recognize the psychological patterns that obstruct that openness. It requires some sensitivity to be able to experience the subtle expanse of nondual consciousness. However, this attunement is particularly helpful for sensitive people who have difficulty tolerating the emotional and perceptual stimuli in the environment. They find that, even though they have become even more sensitive, they no longer feel overwhelmed by stimuli because they have made deep contact with the essence of their being. With practice, one no longer has to "attune" to nondual consciousness, but simply finds that the luminous transparency of this subtle dimension is everywhere.

---

*This chapter first appeared as an article in the *Journal of Transpersonal Psychology* as:

Blackstone, J. (2006). "Intersubjectivity and Nonduality in the Psychotherapeutic Relationship. " *Journal of Transpersonal Psychology,* 38(1), 25-40.

MYSTERY, MIND, AND MEANING

Dorothy S. Hunt

Absent of qualities, yet intimate with a blade of grass,
this Mystery swallows opposites in a single gulp.
Thoughts are useless here.

Tears were streaming down the face of my client as she described her pain and disillusionment with life. At one point in her litany of reasons for self-hatred, she sobbed, "Sometimes I want to kill myself." At that moment, deeply present to her without any thought of what should happen next, I called her by name and unexpectedly said, "I have a very important question to ask you. It is a serious question and an important one." Her tears stopped, and she was suddenly present. I continued, "The question is: Who is the 'I,' and who is the 'myself'?" Immediately she seemed to be operating from a completely different dimension of her being, and without thinking, she responded, "The 'I' is the perpetrator, and the 'myself' is the victim; and neither one of those is who I really am!"

Something released her from her trance of self-judgment, and she sat deeply and profoundly experiencing the mystery of herself beyond opposites. From that vantage point, she could not relate in words who or what she was, but both of us were aware of the shift. Truth had revealed itself spontaneously, illuminating the roles the "I" and the "myself" were playing in that moment. The Mystery that was aware, clearly seeing that "neither of those is who I really am," was beyond both.

WISDOM MOVES SPONTANEOUSLY FROM MYSTERY, NOT CONCEPTS

To call this mysterious movement either dual or nondual is to try to define it conceptually in time, but neither the Mystery nor its

99

movements are concepts. Something moved spontaneously in that moment during the functioning called psychotherapy. It moved as compassion that meets suffering with what actually has the capacity to transform it, and the wisdom that knows how. Both my invitation and my client's immediate clarity arose from beyond our thinking minds.

In speaking about nondual wisdom in a book such as this, I would caution the reader not to imagine that it is something that can be learned the way one may have learned about diagnoses or treatment options in the practice of psychotherapy. Neither is it expounding teachings from spiritual traditions or philosophies that claim to teach nonduality. Nor is it labeling states of mind by thoughts of mind and imagining we "understand" the Mystery that is "not one, not two." Nondual wisdom, if it can be said to be anything at all as it pertains to psychotherapy, is the spontaneous *movement* of life responding to itself or expressing itself from true seeing and true listening in the moment. It is fresh, new, and "on the mark." It moves from Totality and not from conditioned thought.

In referring to this mysterious movement operating (or not) in psychotherapy, I have no knowledge or clinical skills to impart to your *mind*. Neither have I a desire to add to the mind's collection of information. The rational mind, in its pursuit of knowledge, has no choice but to compile, interpret, weigh, criticize, compare, judge, and fix conclusions. That is what minds do, which is perfectly fine, but as long as that is the primary way we take in the world, we do not see and we do not listen from our wholeness.

True seeing requires emptiness; true listening can happen only in silence; and a true response is applicable only in the moment in which it arises. As an example, some time later, I found myself in a group in which someone seemed equally en-"tranced" by self-judgment, self-hatred, and a desire to harm herself. I was neither facilitating nor functioning in any official capacity as therapist or teacher in that group, but at one point I began to share elements of the above "I"-and-"myself" story. I had hardly spoken a sentence when this person became furious with me for not meeting her where *she* was—in the vulnerability of admitting the truth of her deep pain in the group. My mind had done what minds do—remembered the results of a similar situation and attempted to use the remembered experience. Making no judgment that the moment should have been different, the Truth within recognized this moment as an example of mind trying to find a place to hold on to, wanting to effect a result—actually attempting to control experience rather than seeing it clearly and responding directly.

Having an agenda (to be helpful) and wanting to effect results seems to be what most psychotherapy is all about. But when we are moving directly from our true nature, and not conditioned thought, there is no agenda, no future, and no result to achieve. There is simply life moving spontaneously, now, from the Mystery that is awake. This does not mean that we are not helpful or that no transformation occurs. But we are working from the Mystery of our own *being*, rather than preconceived notions. What is wiser than thought "knows" even when our minds do not, and moves in its own wholeness with clarity and compassion. When we are deeply listening from the heart of Silence, each moment is new. The Mystery may use our experience or training in its functioning, but it does so in a fresh and living way. Transformation happens simply by seeing clearly from the Truth of our being rather than by the mind's attempts to manipulate its experience.

Of course, even when we are moving from our own deep truth, we will not necessarily be understood or appreciated for doing so. Truth does not require approval to move as it does. Even a relevant question will simply not be heard if it is not the right moment. Yet seeds are planted before they begin to take root. The deepest compassion may or may not move to offer solace and comfort to a suffering ego, but may invite a deeper seeing from beyond ego, beyond the mind of conditioned thought.

It is our unborn nature, naturally open, awake, and present, that can meet life with love, compassion, and wisdom. It is unconditioned Truth, and not concepts, that liberates untruth. Whatever has been unseen, unmet, unloved arises in order to be seen, met, loved, and liberated within ourselves and within life. When the whole of life is seen with the single eye of Truth, every experience is a doorway to the vast Mystery of what we are. Are we willing to walk through?

BEYOND DUALITY OR NONDUALITY

What I am calling the Mystery cannot actually be defined, although words may be used to point toward it. To call it something or nothing, nondual or dual, can so easily become a play of words and not an invitation to the Truth beyond words. Minds may read "about" the Mystery, as though it were an object to be found, but Truth reveals that we *are* this vast Unknown, and always have been. It is only the Mystery that knows Itself. Such knowledge has nothing to do with what we *think* about it.

Sometimes the great Reality reveals itself absent of all qualities, an unfathomable darkness that can consume all universes in a single gulp. Sometimes it reveals itself as a clear, awake, and shining presence that illuminates the world, speaks truth without fear, or moves to meet suffering with a tender love. Sometimes it shows up as a cloud, a kiss, a moment of grief. As a coin is whole and not just "heads" or "tails," so the Mystery has its absolute and relative expressions, neither being more or less the whole. But what is awake to both aspects? What is the essence of your *being*? Can you say? Do you know? In looking for its Source, the inward-seeking mind can reach a place where it is stopped completely and consumed, where no words of description are possible. I call it the dark face of the Mystery.

MYSTERY: THE DARK FACE

By "dark" I do not mean something sinister or shadowy; I simply mean unknown and unknowable to the thinking mind. Within each of us, there is a serene, unfathomable Darkness that swallows up all ideas and images and leaves nothing outside of itself, at the same time allowing nothing and no one to enter. It is impossible to describe this imageless space, this profound Abyss that empties everything into a poverty like none other. This poverty speaks no words, has no thoughts, needs no understanding, has no will, and assumes no form. Everything you ever imagined about God, Self, enlightenment, or ignorance ends. In fact, "you" end. We cannot really call this mystery Awareness, Consciousness, Emptiness, or God (although we try), or even Void. Our minds make meaning of these words, and this is beyond all mind-made meaning. In this dark Unknown, there is no seeking, no perfecting, no deepening. Experiences of peace, bliss, freedom, presence, insight, and understanding are rendered irrelevant. Here is where, in the words of the great Christian mystic, Meister Eckhart, "distinction never gazed."[1] Here, in the words of a Buddhist sutra, lies "the depth of unthinkability."[2] Here, "not even a thousand sages are aware."[3] In the face of such Mystery, Silence consumes all.

If it seems that you have never encountered such Silence, let me remind you that each of us is consumed by this Mystery on a regular basis. Each night, in dreamless sleep, there is (experientially) no self, no other, no world, no time, no space, and nothing known to our mind. Our existence is unknown to us, and yet we awaken without imagining we have died. We are actually nourished in this Unknown. When mind is consumed by this dark Mystery in the *waking* state, likewise there is experientially no self, no world, no other, no time, no space, nothing known. Even though our mind cannot survive as separate in this unknowable Silence, when mind emerges again, it has no sense of death. In fact, there is a sense of the truest, deepest Mystery of what we are having revealed itself as formless, deathless, timeless, and utterly unfathomable. When there is no longer anyone aware of silence, there is Silence. Here, in the words of the Indian sage, Ramana Maharshi:

> There is neither creation nor destruction,
> Neither destiny nor free-will;
> Neither path nor achievement;
> This is the final truth. [4]

MYSTERY: THE BRIGHT FACE

While the dark face of the Mystery cannot be defined in substance, its bright face appears to function as *Being* itself and, simultaneously, what is *conscious* of being. What seems to arise most directly and spontaneously from this dark Mystery is a clear, vast, transparent Awakeness that both illumines and continually moves the whole of life. Indeed, the Mystery appears to create out of itself everything that is, including the constructs of time and space necessary for the appearance of life in form. It appears to do this in a manner similar to our nighttime dreams—creating out of its own consciousness universes and forms that can move, feel, be born, and die. When the Mystery moves to wake itself up out of identification with its dream of "me," there is no "one" who awakens. Although the dream itself continues, the Mystery has awakened to itself.

Love emanates from the Mystery, a love of life in its totality. This love includes what we once took to be a separate "me," as well as the ones we imagined were "not-me." It encompasses not only what we judged as "worthy," but all we judged to be "unworthy." Life is experienced as a single whole, moving from a love and wisdom that the mind cannot fathom, yet with an intimacy that is deeply felt. In awakening to this reality, we see that each moment is a manifestation of the same Mystery, that we are life's expressions rather than its victims, that our thoughts, feelings, actions, doubts, confusions, and insights are ALL the movements of the Mystery that is "not one, not two." We realize that despite what our minds once imagined, there is *only This!* Rather than imagining we are human beings looking for the Infinite, we discover our Infinite Being here, having human experience.

Peace, love, presence, clarity, wisdom, compassion, beauty, bliss, understanding, self-reflection, creativity emanate spontaneously from the Mystery awake to itself. These qualities cannot be said to *be* the Mystery, yet neither are they separate from it. Most minds—which savor and protect the thought of their separate identity—are longing for these divine qualities and not the Mystery itself. Even those spiritual personalities searching for God, enlightenment, or Truth continually turn to the known in the face of the Unknown in order to maintain the illusion of separation. To discover oneself as the infinite awake Mystery, however, and to live consciously as That, means our mind is surrendered to the Unknown continually and unreservedly. The mind then returns to its natural functioning. It operates from the Whole in the service of the Whole, rather than operating out of fear solely for its own survival, or out of a will to control the experiences and pleasures of a "me."

MIND: A SELF-REFLECTING QUALITY OF THE MYSTERY

When I speak here of "mind," I am referring primarily to that aspect of human consciousness that manifests as thought, and includes memory, feeling, will, imagination, and reflection. It is what most of us think of when we use the term "mind," although mind itself is much broader than this definition. This particular movement of the Mystery reflects on the perception of the five senses (which are essentially thoughtless and timeless) and ascribes meaning and time to them. It remembers and can also contemplate its own thought-creations. It is, essentially, a movement of thought reflecting upon a collection of information, including information about the physical body, the environment, and the behavior of other forms. However, most human beings take this movement of thought to be an identity, a self-organizing principle called "me" around which all other movements revolve.

At its inception, the development of a sense of "self" in distinction to "other" is quite innocent. After all, a rudimentary sense of self allows sentient beings to know which stomach is hungry and which mother is "mine," among other attributes necessary for physical survival. Over a child's early years, the movement of a body with flailing arms and legs, and a stomach that periodically becomes empty and wants to be fed, is gradually coupled with the ability to remember and reflect on these things and many more. The child is taught by everyone around her that these activities of Consciousness mean she is a "self." Gradually, the innocent and functionally necessary "sense" of oneself evolves into a vast array of concepts that are taken to be a defined and separate "self," separate from *being*, separate from world, separate from other forms, even separate from itself (as when a thought called "I" reflects on another thought called "myself").

The alive, aware, sense of *being*, which we all share as our common reference "I," turns into a *concept* of "I." What began as a "sense" of self (*Being's* unique form as this body-mind) now becomes a conceptually separate self—a good self, bad self, lovable self, unlovable self, smart self, shy self, willful self, aging self, etc. It is the overlay of the conceptual thought of "I" and not the underlying experience of

"I" that is called "ego." Here, I am not using "ego" in distinction to Freud's id or super-ego, but rather as Consciousness identified with the thought of separation. The Mystery moves as thought, memory, and reflection, but in identifying with these movements, creates an illusory intermediary between Consciousness and the body that actually has no independent existence but "thinks" it does.

Let me be clear: To perceive or sense a unique body-mind to which a name is attached is not a problem. Even the most "enlightened" being imaginable turns when his or her name is called, and realizes which mouth to feed! A *sense* of self is an operational necessity as long as there is existence in form, and is neither an enemy to defeat nor an obstacle to liberation. In fact, our felt-sense of *being* can lead us beyond our self-limiting concepts when we are deeply interested in the question, "Who/what am I?"

EXPERIENCE OF "EGO"

What seems to be the *experience* of the so-called "ego," however, is Consciousness fused, or identified, with a conditioned body-mind, imagining itself separate. This goes far beyond a "sense" of self needed for the Mystery's functioning as form. This separation from our wholeness is experienced as an energetic field of resistance to what *is*. It manifests as effort, tension, thought, contraction, and a will to control, that motivates our waking lives and carries an enormous emotional attachment. An ever-chatting inner commentator holds itself separate from Life and continually believes that things should be other than they are. The result is often a perpetual sense of wrongness, and a perceived need for an unending project of improvement of self, other, and world. Concomitantly, a sense of lack is unavoidably present when we imagine we are a limited and conditioned "self-image" rather than the Self (or no-self), which lacks nothing. Somewhere there is a nagging feeling that who we are is never enough (See Loy, this volume). And indeed, the phantom ego will never *be* enough, no matter how much it tries to polish its persona.

Arising from this "nagging feeling," egos experience a continual desire to 1) not feel this lack; and 2) fill the perceived void. We attempt to manage these feelings by our addictions—primarily our addiction to thought. Thought continually separates a "me" from the experience of the moment and perceives a future in which the "me" will have more of the desired experiences or will rid itself of the undesired ones. Other well-known addictions to acquiring "more" of anything in order to feel full (fulfilled) include those to approval, power, food, alcohol, drugs, sex, relationships, money, shopping, and spiritual experiences, to name just a few. This last addiction is one of the most seductive because spiritual egos believe their experiences are leading them to some end-state of God, Truth, or Consciousness *that is not already here now.* Thus, we are never looking here for truth, but continually project it to some future.

This panoply of egoic need, lack, projection, desire, and fear is based on a whole collection of concepts that go far beyond a sense of self or a particular personality. Indeed, what is usually experienced as "ego" is based on one thought (the thought called "me") seriously believing that all the other thoughts it has about itself are true! These other thoughts are often experienced as labeling, judging, interpreting, defending, projecting, protecting points of view, deciding what should or should not be present in experience, and operating with the illusion (whether deemed to be successful or unsuccessful) of being in control of its destiny.

But what has come to be known as "ego" is not really a thing. It is a movement to survive that the self-reflecting mind has made into a supposed noun, a "me" that we imagine is our organizing principle. That imagined "principle" has taken on as its all-consuming job one thing and one thing only: to survive. For as long as it does, it holds on to a self-identity that is centered on the thoughts called "I," "me," "myself," and "mine," and lives in fear of not existing as such. (This movement to survive as a psychological entity is distinguished from the biological instinct for physical survival that appears naturally in all species, including human beings, in the face of actual danger.)

In between the innocent birth of a "sense" of self necessary for form to function, and the awakening out of *identification* with a particular body-mind, we have the life that most of us know, love, or hate—the world of ego run amok. This is the world we read about in our newspapers, encounter in our psychotherapy offices, and imagine we are actually living from. Here is mind—whether consciously or unconsciously—operating out of conditioned concepts, out of fear, out of a desire to maintain, protect, change, or improve an *image* of self rather than operating from Truth.

WHO/WHAT AM I?

But when you do not go to a thought, what is the actual *experience* of being, of existing? Who or what is reading these words? What is noticing your reactions to them? Your mind may answer, "I am." Who is this "I"? What is your *experience* in *this* moment? What is your experience of "I" without the mind's judgments, memories, or comments about it? What is aware of *that* experience? Do you at any point come up with "I don't know?" What is here experientially when you allow yourself *not* to "know"? Do you actually find an "ego" when you go to look for it?

Reading about nondual wisdom or an identity beyond ego makes no difference whatsoever to our lives if we do not know for ourselves what is true. We are not what we think we are, and what we are cannot be thought. Herein lies a conundrum for the mind. All of us have a sense of some kind of continuous consciousness from day to day, year to year. The sense of "I" seems to be that continuity. But our bodies and our collection of thoughts, memories and feelings keep changing. None of those things remains the same throughout all of our states of being—waking, dream, and dreamless sleep, nor through all moments, from prior to our birth to the present moment. What is here continuously that does not depend on any particular state or memory of states? What is noticing your thoughts moving right now? Find out for yourself, if you are interested!

FROM EGO TO MYSTERY

The body-mind in which awakening has occurred is increasingly freed to live from the Mystery rather than being consumed by ego's nearly single-minded attempt to control and to survive. Mind is emptied of its *belief* in its conditioned thoughts and begins to embody What has been realized. Conditioning may or may not disappear, but one is no longer identified with it. Actions, thoughts, responses seem to arise from a deeper, truer place and move spontaneously, no longer attached to the question of "what will it do or not do for ME?" The experience seems to be one of Life or Truth moving spontaneously without fixation, and without emotional attachment to a "me." In this there is a sense of freedom, but it is not a personal freedom. In other words, the Mystery, as it lives awake in us, is no longer concerned with maintaining any state that the mind once imagined defined a "self." All states come and go, except for the nonstate that is natural and unchanging, even as It is aware of all that changes. From this perspective, there is no attempt to refuse the experience of the moment, whatever it may be, or to live from a point of view that imagines life is all about a "me." Life is moving as what is. We are then devoted to Truth and trust its movements.

When I speak here of Truth, I do not mean a "true" concept. *No concept is truth*, even the ones I use to attempt to distinguish between them! The true "I," or Self beyond ego, knows itself and all of life as its own movement, but this is not a knowing with the intellect. Rather, it can be experienced only by consciously *being* the Mystery, *being* the totality of What we are, without conceptualizing about what that is. None of these words are IT. Truth remains when thought disappears.

Living from Truth is not based on the mind's figuring anything out, or maintaining an image, spiritual or otherwise. The Mystery simply moves as it does directly—more directly and clearly the emptier we are, less directly and more veiled the more beliefs we imagine are true. When we are empty, we are still, silent, and unknowing inside as in deep sleep, yet simultaneously awake, present, aware as in our waking state. Life simply happens. Ego has been surrendered to its Source, which means we have discovered that the so-called ego, identified as "separate," never actually existed! Mind gives up its arguments with what is and starts following the movement of Truth rather than attempting to manipulate it.

Although personality continues to flavor our expressions of the Mystery, we are no longer identified with form, flavor, or masks. The deep emotional attachment to a "self" disappears, and with it, the suffering that was created by this attachment. Fear of the loss of survival, or fear of nonbeing, is no longer our central energetic moving force. We finally see that everything we wanted or hoped to attain, even *spiritually*, was an attempt to protect the ego from its fear of nonexistence.

For example, the spiritual ego that is addicted to spiritual experiences—beautiful as such experiences may be—has no idea that it fears encountering what is *prior* to experience of any kind. It could be said that our spiritual ideas and ideals about what should and should not be thought, felt, or experienced are attempts to defend against the dark silent Mystery we cannot know, manipulate, or control—in other words, against Nothing (No-thing definable). Once when I was offering a group instruction for meditation, inviting minds to "resist nothing," a man commented that that was his problem. He humorously, yet honestly, admitted he had spent a lifetime "resisting Nothing." How true! The mind of resistance is very fearful of this mysterious No-thing. Yet how full it turns out to be! The Emptiness is the infinite potential constantly expressing itself, flowering as everything that is, including the functioning we might call psychotherapy.

PSYCHOTHERAPY WITHOUT DIVISION?

What has any of this to do with psychotherapy? Psychotherapists have the distinct privilege of meeting many beings in deeply intimate ways. But where do we meet ourselves or one another in this work? When our clients express their emotions, thoughts, stories, and fears, do we meet these with or without judgment? With or without identification? With or without fear? Do we imagine our clients are separate from this Mystery of Being, or do we see that they, as we, are expressions of a Truth beyond division? Are we operating in a way that heals divisions or rather increases them?

If we take conditioning to be an identity, we will try very hard to rid ourselves or our clients of unwanted conditioning. But how much simpler it is to see conditioning for what it truly is. While conditioning may be present, it does not define us unless we *believe* the thoughts that tell us that it is who we are. Can we actually experience that thoughts (wisps of nothing we can really define) are simply thoughts and not reality? Can we notice that thoughts create and sustain most emotions? Can we invite nonseparation from emotions by inviting awareness *inside* the experience instead of operating from outside experience, trying to get rid of experience?[5]

A client asked if we could explore the fear she was feeling. I asked her where the sensation she was calling fear was located. She put her hand to the center of her chest. I invited her to allow her awareness to go into that area without any attempt to change the experience, just to touch intimately the sensation with her own awareness. She initially softened but then reported that she was having a terrifying image. She saw herself as very small, walking alone in a vast desert. I invited her to "Let yourself be the desert." Immediately she relaxed completely and said she felt a safety and spaciousness untouched by anything. Her fear seemed immediately transformed. "How did you know to invite that?" she asked; "That is exactly what I needed." During the remainder of this hour, and in sessions that followed, this experience stayed with her.

There was no agenda to "move" the client away from fear. The spontaneous movement in the moment was simply to invite nonseparation from the desert image. Whenever we are not separated from our vast Totality, we will see an instantaneous reduction or disappearance of fear. When we see the Vastness from the perspective of being small, we may feel overwhelmed; when we see the small from the perspective of being the Vastness, the experience changes everything.

Often in our attempts to connect with others (or in our attempts to remain separate), we do not listen deeply or precisely before imagining we know what someone's experience is or what they need. But do we? How many times have we shared something with someone and been met with judgment rather than curiosity, advice rather than presence, interpretations rather than exploration? Isn't this what minds do? How often do you or others respond internally or verbally with "I know exactly what you mean; let me tell you about *my* experience!"?

In contrast, to listen deeply is to follow experience with our whole being. Words, meanings, feelings, energies, body sensations, nonverbal language are all taken in and perceived with the intimate Seeing that is not separate from the moment. True Seeing is independent of thinking; it contains no judgment whatsoever although it is capable of precise discernment and wise action. Much of what the mind imagines is discernment is simply mental commentary. True discernment sees from the perspective of Truth, which is not in time.

MEANING

Although nothing has inherent meaning apart from its sheer existence as *what is*, the mind continually attributes meaning to things and then acts from its self-created images. Until we see from beyond our thoughts, we will continue to believe that thoughts are reality, that our interpretations are accurate, and that the meanings that mind attributes to things—from the "right" way to wash dishes to the "right" beliefs to have about the mystery called Life—are actually true.

However, to discover there is no meaning apart from a moment's intrinsic *being* is not to render life meaning*less*. Seeing the emptiness or illusory nature of life does not demean or devalue life in any way. In seeing all moments and all forms as the manifestation of the Mystery, we are freed to experience the moment fully, richly, intimately, completely, without judging it. We discover experience is simply an expression of Totality itself, and not a statement about a "me." Thinking is having thoughts, sadness simply being sad. Life, including the life we once imagined belonged to a "me," is the manifestation of a divine Mystery, unborn yet continually birthing, infinite and impermanent simultaneously. Such an experiential realization can only leave one in deep gratitude, speechless, humbled, and in awe. Meanings can be questioned freely; they no longer are lived as an identity.

My mother died when I was a child. While her death had a profound effect on my experience of life at the time, my imagining she "left" because I was not "enough" was an addition of meaning that simply did not exist in her death. It was an addition of thought in the ego's attempt to find meaning and to defend against the experience of helplessness. Mind could create a story of tragedy: A young mother had a heart attack that was misdiagnosed and resulted in her untimely death, leaving a widower and two motherless children victims of a cruel fate. (In this story, "victim" could become an identity.) Or mind could create a story of heroism: A young mother dies out of such love for her children that they have to find a deeper meaning, strength, and love in life in order to survive, eventually provoking them to discover what lies beyond death. (Spiritual seeker could become an identity.) Or mind could create a story of karma or chaos, a God's will or a doctor's mistake, or a thousand other possibilities. On the relative plane, any story or attributed meaning may have its time, place, or purpose. But from the place of the clearest Seeing, the Seeing that comes from the Mystery, my mother's death was none of these. It was not even about a "me" or a "mother," or "death," because from the deepest Seeing, none of these things exist independent of the movement of mind. Yet mind experienced all of those things in this dream of life and death.

PSYCHOTHERAPEUTIC MEANING

The question that seems most relevant in psychotherapy is not what meaning we "should" make of experience, not what meaning is the "true" one, but what meaning we *do* actually make. And can we *know* that that meaning is true? What if we imagined for even a moment that perhaps we don't really know? What if we do not really know *why* life moves as it does, but only *that* it does? What if the causes and conditions of this moment are so vast and interwoven with all moments as to be incomprehensible to the mind? What if the meaning that we attribute to life, whether positive or negative, is seen to be added? Would your world collapse or would you be relieved of an enormous burden? Who would you be if you ceased to *believe* your beliefs, theories, or stories even if they arose? If you are a psychotherapist, how would your practice of psychotherapy change?

Psychotherapy continually adds meaning where none exists, and subtracts meaning where none exists, both of which can be beneficial (or not), depending on the skill and motivation of the people involved. From the perspective of evolution, attaching significance to things that threaten life is useful. But from the standpoint of human psyches, if we look deeply, we will find that we often create "meaning" (commentary of mind) to avoid experiencing fully what is here now, whether that is pain, sadness, anger, joy, or blissful cosmic oneness. Meaning requires mind. "This experience means I'm getting 'closer' to some desired outcome"; or "this one means I'm moving farther away." Yet, all the while, experience is just experience—simply what it is, with or without stories about it.

One of my clients had recently experienced the death of a very dear and close friend. She was somewhat surprised that during the previous week she had been functioning fairly well, had not been overcome with sadness, yet when she came into my office, she immediately began to weep in grief. Immediately she made an interpretation, "I guess I must have been repressing this all week."

Now many psychotherapists (which she herself happened to be) might agree with such an assessment, at least on some level. However, I saw, because I knew her mind of "shoulds," a judgment that if she had been "doing it right," she would not have been functioning well all week and now crying in my office. She would somehow have been "doing grief" better, "working through" it in a particular way, being more "conscious."

I asked her if it could just be the case that she had functioned well all week and was now feeling grief in this moment. She cried even harder. Eventually we spoke about how much more authentic it feels to meet what is here rather than to judge it.

Thoughts, analysis, judgments, and interpretations are often ways mind attempts to control experience by separating from it. To the mind, this seems like a very good idea at times of intense or unpleasant emotion. However, if we experience what is here in the moment from the Awareness that does not divide itself from experience, we continually see what the moment is made of. When we intimately meet experience from the perspective of the awake Mystery and not the "me," we discover that there is no moment and no experience that is not a doorway to our true nature.

In discovering this Reality within each moment of experience, we are freed from the necessity of trying to control life in order not to feel what we do not want to feel. The enormous energy spent in trying to control thoughts, feelings, ourselves, others, or life is freed up for other things. We discover the very awareness of the moment, which both transcends the moment and is deeply and intimately present to it, is always here. We just didn't notice because we were so busy trying to figure life out, or imagining we had to change ourselves or improve ourselves to be okay in our own limited and conditioned vision. In other words, we are so used to viewing everything through the thought of separation, through conditioned mind, that we fail to notice the intimate, unconditioned presence and the deep Intelligence that is always right here when we are open to the Unknown.

A client was contemplating suicide from a very detached place of "emptiness" and said to me, quite assuredly, that from "emptiness" it would not matter whether she lived or died. I sensed both fear and detachment present in this very likable woman who had a history of self-destructive behaviors as well as a lot of "awakeness" operating within her. Although my thoughts wanted to shuffle through the mindfiles of "what to do when . . . ," I found myself totally and utterly unable to do so. The mind seemed dark. And so I sat, both listening and truly not knowing in my mind how to proceed. However, another level of intelligence was operating at a level deeper than the mind of thought, deeper than my training, or anything "known." From here, the moment moved. I agreed that from the perspective of Emptiness it would not matter whether she lived or died, but that embodied truth was actually intimate with experience and not detached from it. So I invited her to become more intimate with her feelings, to bring them down from the detached sense of emptiness and into her heart. As soon as she did this, she began to relax and was no longer gripped by fear. I said to her at that point that it certainly appeared that something wanted to die, but did she really think it was her body that wanted to die? She responded, "No, what wants to die is my living from untruth." We then had a rich discussion about what this meant to her. In my willingness not to "know," and in both the invitation to be intimate with experience and her willingness to do so, something totally unexpected opened up.

In a different moment or with a different person, the movement might look quite different. The point here is not what to do or not do, but to ask whether the mind is willing to *not know* when it doesn't. It is actually in *unknowing* that we are open to and guided by the deeper levels of Consciousness in any given moment.

This vignette also speaks to the functional side of meaning-making. What wanted to die was "living from untruth." There was deep meaning for her in this recognition. Meaning helps us to make sense of our experience and sort it out so that it falls into place in a way that resonates with a deeper knowing. What seems important is our willingness to find out what meaning we have made of experience and to be willing to question it from the perspective of the Truth within us. It is Truth that sees untruth. It is also the case that when we speak *from* Truth, we naturally speak *to* Truth in the apparent other, inviting that deeper knowing.

"COCREATION" OF REALITY

Each moment creates reality; reality creates each moment. When we are sitting with someone, together we are giving "reality" to some things and not to others depending on where awareness and words are moving in the moment. Clients of Jungian therapists, for example, do not necessarily have *more* dreams than anyone else, but since much of Jungian analysis focuses on the significance and meaning of dreams, these clients often increase their remembering and reporting of dreams. We do not need to judge this cocreated reality as being good or bad, but to see it for what it is. Similarly, if each time that a client mentions "sex," or "mother," or "anger," the therapist seems more or less interested or engaged, this will alter what gets mentioned, and in what ways.

Even in our own experience of daily life, we see that giving attention to some things and not to others creates a certain reality. When we have a headache and yet are attending to an interesting and creative project, we may not notice the headache. In those moments, it is gone because it is unperceived. Likewise, when we are "thinking about" our conditioning, we are creating it. In fact, we are creating duality. A judging "me" is separating from the actual experience of the moment, projecting a different future free of some conditioned response. What are the implications for psychotherapy of actually seeing this?

All psychotherapists who identify with their "role," even those practicing with some degree of awareness of the Mystery of their own being, operate from their conditioning. This set of ideas, or theories, is based on life experience, education, professional training, emotional, intellectual, or spiritual insights, mind or body consciousness, or other additions that are unique to them. Clients arrive with their own unique experiences and perspectives. When psychotherapist meets client, two sets of individual conditioning meet in the mix, as well as the collective conditioning of culture, ethnicity, socioeconomic class, gender, age, etc., and the even deeper conditioning that resides in the collective of human beings as a species.

What is created then when each of us is identified with this whole host of conditions? Do we imagine we have "answers" and our clients don't? Or that one of us is "savior" and the other needs "saving"? Or do we see from the eye of Truth that here, sitting before us, is an expression of the same whole and divine Reality that we are? Do we see our client from a divided mind or from our undivided *Being?* It makes an enormous difference to the experience we both will have. Where do our words and actions come from? Do we imagine we are seeing pathology that needs fixing or life moving to meet itself in the places that are not yet awakened and liberated? Either mode of interpretation could be said to be an added "meaning"; either one could become a "position" that could render us less open to the truth of the moment. Yet what is most deeply true for you? What is most deeply true for the person in your office?

One client was rather exasperated by the judgments encountered in her education to become a psychotherapist, judgments that continually referred to dissociative states as pathological. "Don't they know that dissociation is the only way some of us could survive trauma?" We spoke together about the total innocence of all so-called pathological states at their inception and what it might feel like to honor the coping that had taken place in her very challenging circumstances. She deeply under-

stood that the circumstances that triggered dissociation were no longer externally present, and she was courageously facing the experiences still held in mental, emotional, and bodily memory that had been unmet years ago.

How different it feels to see and embrace one's innocence rather than something termed "pathology"; to view "symptoms" as Life's way of pointing to what has yet to be met, loved, and liberated rather than as evidence of our "lack."

Traditional psychotherapy gives "problems" great reality. An enormous amount of time and energy is frequently expended trying to get rid of emotions that would simply pass through, like changing weather, if we weren't judging them to be a problem to be solved, or a statement about a "me" rather than about a moment. Years can be spent trying to change a negative self-image into a positive one without ever questioning whether an image is really who we are. Clients want to feel better, and they come to a therapist in order to effect that change. That is fine. But while a positive self-image may feel better, it is just as limiting, untrue, and temporary as any other image. What is here *beneath* the image? "What is actually true?" becomes a much more interesting question than "How can I manipulate life, 'me,' 'you,' or 'them' to feel/be a certain way?"

Often, in psychotherapy as well as in life, "self-images" are busy meeting other "self-images." But what kind of meeting is this? How authentic does it feel? How can a "mask" perpetuate truth? Yet Awakeness encountering *itself* invites entrainment. (See Peter Fenner, this volume.) Clients often comment that they had problems before entering my office, but those problems seem to disappear when they are here. This is not because life has ceased being life; it is because unconditioned Awareness is so much stronger than thought that it attunes to itself. Where opposites can meet without struggle, in awareness resisting nothing, the perception of "problems" disappears.

In each moment, truth transmits what is actually present—judgments, fear, and division, or stillness, love, and whole being. We cannot pretend to be somewhere we are not. However, if we happen to be working from an awakened perspective, we may discover that, naturally and spontaneously, we will be inviting this different dimension of exploration into the room and into our practice. The shift happens not because we intend to do so, but because when the embodied Mystery begins to move from its own wisdom, compassion, and clarity, mind is surrendered to that movement.

Many imagine that we can "awaken" and still maintain a sense of a separate "controller." However, we are either *being* What we are, or we are attempting to *control*.[6] To supposedly "know" we are the undivided Mystery and still imagine our ideas are the only "right" ones is no knowing at all. Does unconditioned Openness have a point of view? Is it Buddhist or Christian, Republican or Democrat? Does it call itself anything? Does it try to convince anyone of anything? Does it have an agenda? No. And yet, the Mystery is not passive; it is continually creating. It can move decisively and precisely when that movement is needed, tenderly and intimately when that is needed, or it can remain unmoving. Do we actually imagine mind can wrap itself around the infinite and figure it all out? Or are we able to see the limitation of mind from the Mystery beyond it? If so, are we willing to live that realization, wherever we happen to find ourselves—in or out of the psychotherapy office?

ENDNOTES

1. *Meister Eckhart: The Essential Sermons, Commentaries, Treatises, and Defense,* trans. Edmund Colledge, O.S.A., and Bernard McGinn. New York: Classics of Western Spirituality, Paulist Press, London, SPCK, 1981, Sermon 48.

2. Lex Hixon, *Mother of the Buddhas: Meditation on the Prajnaparamita Sutra.* Wheaton, IL.: Quest Books, 1993, p. 12.

3. Yamada Mumon, lectures on *The Ten Oxherding Pictures,* given to the monks of the monastery of Shōfuku-ji in Kobe, Japan, translated by Victor Sogen Hori, distributed by University of Hawai'i Press, Honolulu, Hawaii, 2004, p. 95 (Picture Ten).

4. Ramana Maharshi, *Essential Teachings of Ramana Maharshi,* ed. Matthew Greenblatt, Inner Directions, 2001, © by Sri Ramanasramam, p. 120.

5. For a more detailed description of this type of invitation, see "Being Intimate with What Is: Healing the Pain of Separation," by Dorothy Hunt, *The Sacred Mirror: Nondual Wisdom and Psychotherapy,* ed. John J. Prendergast, Peter Fenner, and Sheila Krystal. St. Paul: Paragon House, 2003, chapter 7, pp. 164–84.

6.   For a particularly clear and direct exploration of the phenomenon of control, see Adyashanti, *Emptiness Dancing,* chapter 15, "Control," Los Gatos, CA: Open Gate Publishing, pp. 149–61.

LISTENING AND SPEAKING FROM NO-MIND

Peter Fenner

The final aim of all nondual approaches to therapy and healing is to introduce people to a way of being that exists beyond pain and ordinary pleasure and helps them become more and more familiar with this mode of being. A critical skill that's needed in order to open up an experience of unconditioned mind with clients, friends, colleagues, or in a group setting is a capacity to listen and speak from no-mind.[1] When I say no-mind *(mushin)*, I could also use the terms buddhamind, openness *(shunyata)*, unconditioned mind *(asamskrta-citta)*, pure awareness *(vidya)*, witness consciousness *(sakshin)*, suchness *(tathata)*, contentlessness *(nihsvabhavata)*, and so on.

In this chapter I want to explore "listening and speaking from no-mind" as a vital dimension of nondual approaches to psychotherapy. Listening and speaking from no-mind represents a specialized form of relationship in which it's possible to effect a transmission of contentlessness. The chapter describes the structure of contentless communication and identifies some of the sensitivities that nondual therapists need in order to be able to listen and talk in ways that directly reveal and transmit the experience of no-mind or pure, unconditioned presence.[2]

Most of my own teaching and transmission of contentlessness occurs in a group setting in workshops, retreats, and long-term trainings. Within these settings I offer individual sessions. I also work with individual clients from around the world, mainly by telephone. The teacher-student, counselor-client relationship I will describe here, particularly in terms of listening and speaking from no-mind, represent the nondual heart of my work.[3]

When they first hear about what I have to say about "pure listening and speaking," some therapists can make an erroneous generalization that pure listening and speaking represents a very clinical, neutral, and even detached way of relating to others. They may think that the human dimension of relationship could be lost if a therapist was to function exclusively from this place.

My experience is quite the converse. The pure listening and speaking that I will describe shortly has a multitude of expressions. It's at once precise and open, sensitive and tender yet rigorous and exact, intimate yet detached, smooth and totally still yet full of potency and capable of erupting in any moment into joyous laughter and communion. I should also add that the pure listening and speaking that I describe occurs within a container of warm affection. I have the fortune of not being a "therapist." When I'm not "teaching," I have the freedom to share and join in the lives of my students in a very demonstrative and uninhibited way.

PURE LISTENING: LISTENING FROM NOTHING

We can distinguish three different ways in which we can receive what people are communicating to us. We can listen to people through a positive filter (positive listening), a negative filter (negative listening), or with no filter (pure listening). Negative listening occurs when we listen through a filter of boredom, disinterest, invalidation, annoyance, arrogance, anger, frustration, and so on. Positive listening is marked by moods of interest, enthusiasm, excitement, approval, and validation.[4]

Pure listening is a quality of being that we can bring to all our relationships. Pure listening is also a central skill that therapists with an affinity for nonduality naturally bring to their clinical relationships. When our listening is pure we listen without being diverted by, or identified with, the filter of our own interpretations. We receive our client without static or interference. We neither add to nor take away from what is being communicated. When we listen from nothing we're like a clear mirror, receiving exactly what's communicated.

Pure listening neither encourages nor subverts another person's communication. We don't need the conversation to continue or stop; we don't need to "understand" it conceptually. We listen without projecting or interpreting, without anticipating what someone is going to say next or attempting to reconstruct or interpret their experience for them. From our point of view, it makes no difference whether a client, friend, or partner is talking or not talking. If they stop in the middle of a sentence, we're complete. We don't need them to complete what they're saying. We're completely satisfied with the communication exactly as it is. Such listening arises naturally out of unconditioned mind.

We're not being attentive in an expectant and encouraging way that invites the person with whom we're communicating to continue. Nor do we discourage communication by being inattentive or distracted. We're neither engrossed in our own thoughts nor immersed in the story that we're hearing. We're just listening, being purely present to what's here. John Prendergast (this volume) describes this as the experience of "spacious intimacy."

In contrast to pure listening, positive and negative listening distort the nature of a relationship in which we are fully and totally open to others. Positive and negative listening respectively disconnects us from ourselves and the people with whom we're in communication. Our attention becomes biased, privileging either our own experience or the experience of "the other."

I define positive listening as a form of listening in which we become wrapped up in other people's experiences and seduced by their stories. When this happens we lose connection with our own thoughts, feelings, and values. Positive listening can be identified by thoughts in our own mindstream such as, "This is fascinating. I can really relate to what they're saying. This makes total sense. I can really see how I can help this person."

When we listen negatively, we become preoccupied with our own thoughts and feelings and trivialize the significance of what we're listening to. "How can I wrap this up? I wish I could change the subject. I've got more important things to do than listen to this." In negative listening there is an attentive bias toward our own experience. In contrast, in pure listening our field of awareness embraces everything equally. We rest within a field of awareness in which the difference between self and other cannot be found (see Loy, this volume).

When people first begin to explore pure listening, they may confuse pure listening with a feeling of disinterest. If the therapist is familiar with Eastern teaching on the illusory nature of reality (*maya*), he may even superimpose a judgment that a client's experience is unreal. But pure listening is definitely not disinterested. When we're disinterested, we switch off; we're not fully present to the person in front of us. Usually we're involved in our own thoughts, and we may be lightly judging the person who's communicating with us. By contrast, when we listen from the unconditioned mind, we're neither attentive nor inattentive. We are neither focused nor distracted.

We hear and understand everything that's communicated. It is a state of pure receptivity in which we are effortlessly present to everything that arises. If our client is talking, we could repeat everything that she has said, word-for-word. We're aware of the content, structure, nuances, and tonality of what is being communicated. As Ken Bradford explains in his contribution to this volume, nondual approaches to psychotherapy are based on a state of unconditional presence that is open and intimate, and to this extent quite unlike the "neutral stance" of classical psychoanalysis, which can be accompanied by a sense of psychic withdrawal and distance.

The difference between positive and pure listening is that in pure listening we aren't "looking" for anything, and we don't do anything with what's being heard. As a result, the person with whom we're communicating may find that they no longer need to communicate something that previously seemed important. In the face of this pure listening, there may simply be nothing to say.

Because we listen without projecting or interpreting, we don't anticipate what the speaker is going to say next, nor do we consciously search for a common reference point by attempting to relate their experience to our own. We don't feel uncomfortable if they say nothing or don't complete what they're saying; it doesn't matter whether they're talking or not talking. We have no needs either way.

Often we tend to think it's important to hear what we're about to hear, and we listen as though it's going to make a significant difference. If our listening is interrupted, we may feel frustrated, which shows that our listening is anything but pure. Even though pure listening is receptive and responsive, it isn't the same as what is often called empathetic listening. The difference is that when we listen *with* empathy, there is often an identification with a client's story that isn't counterbalanced by the wisdom *(prajna)* that sees through the narrational fabric of all constructed experience. Empathy is often accompanied by expressions of active interest, focused attention, conscious availability, and even an active contribution of our own personal experience. When we're active and attentive in this way (even nonverbally), we're consciously or inadvertently encouraging the person with whom we are communicating to continue her or his constructions.

In pure listening we neither encourage nor discourage the process of interpretation and meaning-making: We're fully present, without distraction, intention, or effort. When a therapist is in this state of effortless, evenly distributed awareness, people who aren't familiar with the experience can see the therapist as being focused, penetrating, and intense, when actually the converse is the case.

Pure listening changes the structure of what the other person is saying because they're talking into an awareness that isn't conditioned, and they aren't receiving a conditioned response. In fact, they're talking into nothing. When constructions are neither encouraged nor discouraged, they tend to dissolve by themselves.

ENTRAINMENT

By sharing our experience of nondual awareness without words or effort, we invite the people with whom we're in relationship to entrain or attune to this experience themselves. As we rest in a state that is free of all ambition, the energy of serenity naturally transfers from one person to another like two bells resonating together. In nondual therapy, much of the work occurs through this process of energetic entrainment.

In fact, one of the greatest contributions we can make in nondual therapy is to offer others the experience of our own serenity, especially when people are agitated or distressed. By remaining in equanimity, unperturbed, we share with others the possibility that there's nothing wrong with what's happening. We model the possibility that there's actually no problem, not because we're creating or inventing that position as a particular therapeutic role or professional identity, but because it's true for us. We share this possibility by staying intimately connected with whomever we're in relationship, yet at the same time the experience of unconditioned mind is uncompromised.

By doing so, we may occasion a creative dissonance between ourselves and those with whom we're in communication. Rather than "coming down" to meet the other on their own terms, we're inviting people to "step up" to meet us in the space of unconditioned mind, where there are no problems. Like the pacing and leading of Ericksonian hypnosis, the entrainment generally occurs in incremental steps.

To this end I have a sense of the "gradient" at which I am introducing people to nondual awareness. If I move too fast or too steeply, I will disconnect from a client and lose the opportunity for contentless sharing. If I move too slowly, I waste a unique and precious opportunity that happens every time we meet someone within the framework of engaging in result-oriented psychospiritual work.

When people share their problems into the nondual space of pure listening, their experience becomes *our* experience; there's no separation. We experience other people's immediate reality—their thoughts and feelings—as though they were our own. We feel totally open and profoundly connected with whatever anyone is experiencing. We have no resistance at all to their confusion, anxiety, fear, anger, or torment. We don't wish that they weren't suffering. We *know* that they're suffering but, at the same time, we *know* that there's no suffering. This is love without pity or sympathy. Pity and sympathy take people's suffering to be real, and they thereby compound people's problems and pain.

You could say that our pure listening creates a clearing for the liberation of other people's suffering. From this pure listening we can authentically question the structure, the texture, and the nature of other people's suffering in a way that begins to dissolve contracted experiences of the present moment. We identify with our clients' suffering and let this dissolve into our own experience of identitylessness. If our experience of the unconditioned mind is firm and deep, and people stay connected with us, they have no choice but to experience the evaporation of their problems.

We don't push for change. Through the energy of love we're drawn into the structure and full intensity of other people's pain and suffering. And with wisdom we know that this pain is unreal—it isn't what it seems to be. In reality it doesn't exist anywhere. We know that despite our conditioning, even the most intense pain can't be sustained in the presence of the unconditioned mind.

PURE SPEAKING: SPEAKING FROM "NO-MIND"

While the act of listening from unconditioned mind is powerful in its own right, the process of introducing people to the experience of unconditioned mind can be greatly accelerated if we are also able to verbally communicate from non-mind. By using words we're able to capture someone's thought-stream, lead it in the direction of having nothing to think about, and thereby help someone rest in a state of nonthinking. When I say nonthinking, I'm referring to a state in which we aren't using our thoughts to get someone, to arrive at a conclusion or experience. Nonthinking includes thinking and not thinking.[5] Certainly it isn't necessary to stop thinking in order to experience unconditioned mind. If this were the case, unconditioned mind would be a conditioned experience.

Pure speaking arises spontaneously from no-mind. In ordinary communication we tend to formulate our ideas as we listen, and our goal is to deliver these ideas through our speech. But in pure speaking we don't try to convince anyone of anything. Instead, we focus on responding to what's happening in the here and now. We speak without forethought or strategy, without knowing how (or even whether) we'll finish and without anticipating the future consequences of what we're saying. In pure speaking we don't try to convince anyone of anything.

Ultimately, the point of such communication is to reveal no-mind. Since we're speaking from nothing, the subject matter of our communication is also "nothing."

When we speak from no-mind, our speaking is continuously accommodated and adjusted to the listening of the other person.

As we attune to their body language, their verbal responses, and other signs of their receptivity or confusion, we calibrate our speech accordingly, not as a strategy but as a natural response in the ongoing dance of communication. For example, we may sense that the other person has "gotten" what we've said and we don't need to continue. By acknowledging their receptivity, we may deepen the connection between us. Or we may begin to communicate something and realize, by the quality of the atmosphere surrounding the communication, that it isn't necessary or won't be received. By acknowledging this apparent lack of receptivity within ourselves, we may create a bridge to the other person that invites more intimacy and reception.

DECONSTRUCTIVE CONVERSATIONS

Speaking from no-mind produces different kinds of conversations, all of which move in the direction of dissolving or deconstructing different types of fixations or rigid ideas about ourselves and the world. I call these "deconstructive conversations."[6]

These conversations dismantle the structures of our conditioning and introduce us to the experience of contentless awareness. They are the lifeblood of nondual traditions of spirituality and therapy. They penetrate the seeming reality of our reactive feelings and emotions in a way that dissolves their existence. They are rarely encountered in daily discourse. Most of the conversations we engage in are constructive. They unfold as a commentary on our experience. We interpret what's happening in the moment. We produce histories to explain what has happened, and project into the future, anticipating what will happen. One thought follows the next as we elaborate, modify, develop, rework, add detail, change direction, validate, invalidate, approve, disapprove, and so on.

Deconstructive conversations move in the opposite direction to most of our conversations. They reverse the process of elaboration and complexification. They locate the "core distinctions" upon which a conversation rests. They then show that the core distinctions don't refer to anything. The conversations may have an air of casualness about them, but they're also highly precise. They can unfold gently or as a dynamic and fast-paced exchange of questions and responses that deconstruct a nest of ever more subtle assumptions and fixations.

TYPES OF DECONSTRUCTIVE CONVERSATIONS

In order to communicate the distinctive structure of nondual communication, I've identified a number of different conversations that naturally arise when a therapist or facilitator is resting in no-mind. Here I will describe some of the conversations I use in my work with groups and individuals. The conversations aren't original. The same, or similar, ones are used by other teachers and practitioners. They can also be found in the spiritual texts of Buddhism and Hinduism.

The fact that I'm distinguishing "different conversations" might give the impression that nondual therapy can be broken into discrete elements. To some extent it can—at least for training purposes; though in practice this work is organic, spontaneous, and highly interactive.[7]

The primary role of the therapist or facilitator is to be aware of the opportunity to drop into this space of effortless being, in which there is nothing more to do; in which we come home to that state of complete fulfillment—the space of nondual awareness.

When I'm working with people, I don't predict what will happen next. I don't know in advance how a session will unfold. I don't know if it will be punctuated by periods of deep, meditative silence, or whether it will consist of a dynamic exchange of questions and answers. In any particular session, a number of the conversations I will describe might come into play, with each one blending fluidly in with others. In order to facilitate nondual work, we need to have some fluency in these conversations.

INQUIRING INTO THE UNREALITY OF AN INTERPRETATION: UNFINDABILITY CONVERSATIONS

Normally when we listen to people talking, we assume that there's some truth or reality to what they're saying. Or at least that what they're saying could be true or false. In ordinary conversation, there's a strong consensual pressure to listen in this way. When we don't understand what people are saying, we still assume it's meaningful, and we typically try to work out what they mean by inviting them to say more.

When we listen to a "story" from the unconditioned mind, we don't take what's being described as true. What seems to be happening may *not* be happening. For example, we no longer assume that people's problems and difficulties are real or fictitious. This innocence and freshness opens up the possibility of engaging with people's constructions from the viewpoint of "beginner's mind."

From the viewpoint of nondual wisdom, there is no intrinsic meaning. Meaning is a human construction. We may join people in their constructions, agreeing or disagreeing, but we're not compelled to do so. There is another listening in which we may understand that what they're saying is meaningful to them, but we actually don't find any meaning there. This is pure listening, which has been described previously. Out of this pure listening, or listening from no reference point, comes pure speaking.

So how does the experience of unconditioned mind guide the deconstruction of our constructions. Let's look at a claim that someone could easily make when in therapy.

"I think I'll be happy when I find someone who loves me."

Usually when someone says something like this, we assume that this is meaningful, even if we disagree with it. We know what thinking is, we know what it is to be happy, and we think we know what love is. However, when we listen to this statement from unconditioned mind, we find that we don't take things for granted in the way we usually do. At one level we can identify the person's longing and aspiration by presencing our own histories and memories. But at the same time, we can't find any reference to the terms they're using; they have no intrinsic meaning for us.

The way to inquire into the reality of an emotional construct is by first identifying the foundational concepts upon which it is built. Having identified any core concept we can inquire into the existence of the reality behind the concept, and dissolve the painful feelings associated with fixed ways of thinking. We find that suffering dissolves when it's examined by the mind that rests in unconditionality. In fact, we discover the truth of the *Heart Sutra:* that there is no suffering, never has been, and never will be.

If someone says, "I think I'll be happy when I find someone who loves me," this statement replays like an echo in our mind. We gently scan the statement for any intrinsic meaning we can unlock. We hear what has been said, but the statement deconstructs because we fail to find anything that our thoughts can lock into. The process works something like this:

Client says:	We think:
"I"	"You? Who are you? I don't know who *you* are. Who am I?"
"think"	"What is thinking?" "Where does that thinking happen?"
"happy"	"What does happiness mean?" "Where is that?"
"find"	"How do you find someone?" "I can't find someone by looking for them because this presupposes I haven't found them. For as long as I'm looking I haven't yet found them. So how can I find someone by looking? But how can I find them without looking? How *do* I find someone?"
"love"	"What is love?"

With this going on in our minds, we might say, "I hear what you're saying, 'that you'd be happy if someone loved you.' And I'm sure that the word 'love' has many associations for you, but what does that word refer to? What actually is love?" We say this in a way that invites them not to elaborate or come out with their story, but to join us in an inquiry into the possibility that we *don't know* what love is. Or we may simply say, "I do not know what you're talking about." We communicate this in a way that doesn't in any way imply any deficiency in the person with whom we're talking. We ask these questions because *we* don't understand what's being said. They may think that we should know. However, if their words are deconstructing in our mind, then we actually don't know what they're talking about. We don't know what we could be expected to know, and we admit this. In fact, our admission becomes a tool entering the unknown.

Even though we understand the language that's being used, when we listen to the above statement from the nondual experience, we can't find any reference to the key descriptors and concepts. Also, because we're not identified with our network of thoughts and associations, the pace of therapy slows down, resulting in the emergence of silence, serenity, and peace. We can't respond to the construction in any immediate way. This is what we've called listening and speaking from the unconditioned mind.

In a therapeutic or teaching relationship, the therapist or teacher usually has a combination of personal and professional authority, and this helps people stay connected despite our unexpected response. If we want to make sure that our response is accessible, we might say something like, "Love—I hear what you're saying, but I don't know what that is. I know that might sound strange, because I use the word myself. However, right now, I hear what you're saying, but I don't know what it means." The critical point is that they know we heard them, yet we don't get it. At this juncture the conversation moves to a different level and leads to the opportunity for the client to join us in an inquiry into her or his original construction: "I think I'll be happy when I find someone who loves me."

To respond with these queries in a scripted way won't produce the same results in the client. We're not just learning some technique, saying, "I don't know what you're talking about," while we're still inhabiting our own constructions. In such a case, we would just be comparing our own opinions with those of our client. Whereas, if it's an authentic experience, we can genuinely say, "I do not know what you're talking about."

Deconstructive inquiry should be used only when we sense that the timing is right. We're inviting people to join us in the space of wonderment and uncertainty; to experience what it feels like not to take things for granted. For this to occur, there must be a certain readiness and a level of trust in the relationship.

Any interpretation can be deconstructed in this way. The primary limitation is the extent to which we identify with the interpretation in question. Stories that may be deconstructed include:

- personal beliefs (for example, "I'm a serious person.")
- spiritual beliefs (for example, "By doing this practice, I'll gain this result.")
- constructions about suffering (for example, that it is bad, it shouldn't be happening, and that it is happening)
- constructions about fixations (for example, that we shouldn't have them, and that we're not enlightened until we remove them, that they exist or don't exist)
- stories about enlightenment
- stories about the deconstructive process itself.

Here's an example to give you the flavor of how our unfindability conversation[8] can unfold.

Joanna:	What's happening for me is that I'm breaking up with my partner, but I feel a lot of attachment. I'm thinking about him a lot of the day.
Peter:	Is the feeling of attachment (the feeling of being fixated) a sensation in your body or a thought?
Joanna:	It's in my body. It's a feeling of not wanting to be separated.
Peter:	That sounds like a thought, "Not wanting to be separated."
Joanna:	It's an uncomfortable feeling in my heart area. It's a feeling of longing.
Peter:	Where is it?
Joanna:	In my chest.
Peter:	Can you feel it now?
Joanna:	Yes.
Peter:	How big is the feeling?

Joanna: About the size of my hand.

Peter: Let's just stay with that a little while. Is it stable or is it changing?

Joanna: It's changing.

Peter: How?

Joanna: It's becoming more intense.

Peter: Okay… And now how is it?

Joanna: It's lessening.

Peter: What are you feeling?

Joanna: It's a sensation. I can't say what it is.

Peter: Is it still uncomfortable?

Joanna: I don't know. I don't think I like it.

Peter: What don't you like?

Joanna: The idea that I'll be living alone.

Peter: We can come back to what you are thinking, but let's stay with what you are feeling at the moment. How is the sensation in your heart area?

Joanna: It's gone, but I can't help thinking about my partner.

Peter: [Allows some silence.]

Peter: Are you still feeling attached?

Joanna: Yes, I can't get him out of my mind. Sometimes I forget about him for a few minutes, but then he comes back to my mind. I like to think about him only occasionally, not all the time.

Peter: Okay…can we look at that?

Joanna: Sure.

Peter: Let's be silent for a couple of minutes and see how much of your thinking is tied up in thoughts about your partner.
           [Silence]

Peter: How is it going?

Joanna: Well it's interesting because I only thought about him twice.

Peter: What do you mean?

Joanna: Most of the time I was thinking about other things—what we're doing, you, my work….

Peter:	In terms of time, how much time did you spend thinking about him?
Joanna:	Perhaps ten seconds… Can we do this again?
Peter:	Sure.
	[Silence]
Joanna:	It is really interesting. I barely thought about him.
Peter:	But there are still some thoughts about him.
Joanna:	Yes. The worst thought is that "It's going to be terrible without him."
Peter:	Can we look at that thought?
Joanna:	Of course. It's the word "terrible" that makes it bad.
Peter:	"Terrible … terrible …"
Joanna:	Yes, the thought "terrible."
Peter:	Can you think that thought a few times and tell me what happens?
Joanna:	[Silence, while thinking the thought "terrible".]
Peter:	What happened?
Joanna:	Nothing really. It's not the thought "terrible." It's the thought that links "me," "Michael [my partner]," and "terrible" together.
Peter:	You're saying that each one individually is okay, but when you think them together or in a stringed sequence, then it makes you feel heavy in the heart.
Joanna:	Yes, it must be.
Peter:	Can we test this out?
Joanna:	Of course.
Peter:	So can you put together the set of thoughts that make you feel heavy and think them several times?
Joanna:	Okay.
	[Silence]
Peter:	So what happened?
Joanna:	Nothing. I thought, "It will be terrible without Michael" and I feel fine.
Peter:	Interesting. Just as an experiment, can you think of any way you could make yourself feel heavy hearted at the moment?

Joanna:	Right now, that's impossible [laughing]. This is ridiculous.
Peter:	Is that a problem?
Joanna:	Of course not. It's ridiculous in a completely liberating way. It's amazing what we do, isn't it?
Peter:	Yes.

If we're identified with our own history, it will be difficult to help clients see through the reality of their attachment or aversion. Our questions need to come from a place of innocence. We're like an empirical scientist who wants to "see" the fixation, or suffering. If we find ourselves agreeing with our clients, we've become caught in their construction. We're buying into their experience. And this can happen only as a consequence of moving out of "beginner's mind" (no-mind) and into our own emotional history.

NATURAL KOANS

In our journey from a structured (knowing) to an unstructured (not knowing) state of consciousness, the conceptual mind can naturally generate thought forms that are rightly called "natural koans."[9] Natural koans are questions that can't be solved with the analytical mind and whose resolution opens us up to the experience of nondual presence. In nondual forms of therapy, we provide a space for natural koans to arise.

They may be questions or declarations like:

- Why am I doing this?
- Is there any point in this?
- Who is doing this?
- This is a waste of time.
- I am bored.

A common feature in all of these questions is that they refer to "this"—the experience that's happening, or "I"—the person who is meditating. Often we don't go on to ask the next question—"What is this?" or "Who am I?" We assume that we know what we're thinking about in those first set of questions. These two questions—"What is this?" and "Who am I?"—are at the heart of many forms of deconstructive inquiry.

"WHO AM I?"

The classical Hindu form of nondual inquiry is called "self-inquiry" *(atma-vichara)*. It dates back to Shankara (seventh-century) and Gaudapada (sixth-century) before him. It was popularized last century by Ramana Maharshi. It is based on the question "Who am I?" and involves an inquiry into the subjective foundations of our experience. This form of inquiry invites us to discover the experienc*er* of whatever is being experienced. It's an unfindability inquiry that has the potential to connect people with "consciousness that witnesses all without there being a witnesser *(sakshin)*."

In a therapeutic setting, I find that it's best to introduce this type of inquiry by saying something like: "I hear what you say you're experiencing, but I'm wondering who it is that's actually experiencing that?" Sometimes we may have to add, "I know that might be a strange question, but I'm wondering who or what it is that's actually having those experiences." Once we've signaled that the conversation is moving in a different direction, we follow the inquiry by asking questions such as: "I hear what you're thinking, but I'm wondering *who* is thinking that? Who is actually thinking that thought?" If they answer, "I am," then we respond by saying, "Yes, but who thinks, 'I am.'" Ideally, this line of inquiry proceeds until the client arrives at an experience of "not knowing," of not being able to find himself.

"WHAT IS THIS?"

The question "What is this?" is a well-known koan in Zen Buddhism.[10] So, in nondual therapy, we ask ourselves this question in an authentic way. We don't know what "this" is and we are seeking to know what "it" is, whatever "it" is that we are seeking to know. At some point we see that "this" isn't anything. There is no it. It does not exist. What does not exist? The "this" that we are now experiencing—that we are always experiencing—in fact, does not exist. It is and it isn't. In fact, it is because it isn't.

I personally prefer the question "What is this?" over "Who am I?" The question "Who am I?" is more introspective. It tends to point us inward. Some people on the spiritual path can become confused by the question "Who am I?" It can disconnect them from their problems rather than deconstruct them. The question "What is this?" doesn't point us in any direction whatsoever, because "this" includes everything inside *and* outside of ourselves. We don't know where to look! And this is what the question is designed to do.[11]

WHEN AND HOW TO POSE THESE QUESTIONS

With skill, these questions can be consciously introduced into the practice of nondual therapy. However, the same questions that can be used to release us from our thinking can also embed us further in our thoughts. Generally, someone needs to be in a fairly refined, unstructured state of mind before we invite them to contemplate these koan-type questions. If they're introduced prematurely, the effect can be counterproductive. If we ask these questions too early, when people are in a thick interpretation, the questions will only invite elaboration. The questions will lock into people's belief systems and lead them to construct responses. They'll produce *more* thinking rather than a disidentification with thoughts. If the questions are well-timed they lead directly into an unmeditated experience of the present moment. The questions are asked without any suggestion that they should be thought about or contemplated. They aren't designed to be answered!

NOTHING TO THINK ABOUT

One of the functions of these questions, and all deconstructive methods in fact, is to give us nothing to think about. If the delivery of such questions is carefully timed, they can help slow down peoples' thinking and reduce the density of their thoughts. "Thinning out our thoughts" produces an experience of inner peace, within which unconditioned mind can be more easily be recognized. Traditional teachings use the metaphor of clouds and the sun: The clouds don't have to disappear in order for us to see the sun, but they do need to thin out a little.

In nondual approaches to therapy, the thinking process is thinned out by not feeding the interpretative process, not digging for problems, not offering people anything to think about. We stay in communication and in an intimate relationship while gradually reducing the ideas, concepts, and advice we give people to process. I say "gradually" because if we suddenly stop giving input, it can be extremely upsetting and disconcerting for people. The initial responses can range from boredom, listlessness, and sleep to restlessness and agitation. Some people may find it challenging to stay conscious when they have little or nothing to entertain them. It can be challenging to remain aware and awake in the absence of any cognitive stimulation. Others may find the experience frightening or threatening.

Just as fasting can be easier if we gradually eat less and less over a period of time, "thinning out the thoughts" by reducing conceptual input can gradually prepare our minds for thinking about nothing. One way to reduce the density of a person's interpretations is to ask a question such as, "What would be happening now if we weren't doing what we're doing?"

So we need to calibrate the level of cognitive input we provide as we skillfully introduce people to inner peace. There is no need to eliminate thoughts completely and no need to understand what is happening in the present moment.

SEEING THROUGH—THINKING ABOUT NOTHING

When a person's thoughts have slowed down somewhat, we may move their thinking into an inquiry into the nature of unconditioned mind. When we try to think about nothing, not an idea we have about nothing, but absolute nothing itself, we can quickly enter into the experience of the unconditioned. When we think about nothing, we have fewer and fewer thoughts because our thoughts have no content to attach to and so our capacity for conceptual elaboration is seriously undermined. Using Buddhist terminology, this is where the cultivation of serenity *(shamatha)* transforms into the practice of "seeing through" *(vipashyana)*. The practice of not giving ourselves (or someone else) anything to think about simply reduces the topics we can use to stimulate our minds. The practice of "thinking about nothing" becomes untenable—in fact, impossible—because the practice simply doesn't provide a basis for our conceptualization.

The relationship between the practice of serenity and "seeing through" should now be clear. The practice of serenity begins by giving us less to think about. Then, at a certain point, "having nothing to think about" is the same as "thinking about nothing," which is the practice of seeing through all presenting structures *(vipashyana)*. In turn, "thinking about nothing" becomes untenable because there's no foundation for our thoughts, and this naturally slows our thinking down even further. This in turn gives us less thought material with which to identify, which deepens our ability to see through conceptual structures. In this way, serenity and "seeing through" empower each other.

There are many ways in which we can invite someone to think about nothing. If they're relatively open and spacious, we might invite them to think about nothing by asking, "What would you say is happening right now?" They may recognize that there isn't much structure or content to hang on to; what's happening is actually *nothing*. At first, people tend to think about their ideas or images of nothing, but these concepts are progressively seen through, bringing them closer to a direct experience of nothing. Then, at some point, they relate to the experience that has no content, which directly reveals unconditioned mind. The following dialogue will give you some idea about how this might unfold.

Peter:	I'm wondering what this is?
Beth:	Well, we're sitting quietly talking.
Peter:	Yes, but I'm wondering what "this" is?
Beth:	What?
Peter:	This. What's happening now.
Beth:	I don't know what you're talking about.
Peter:	I'm not sure I can describe it. I'm talking about this.
Beth:	You mean this moment?

Peter:	Perhaps. I'm not sure I can't even say if it's this moment, because… Well, it's not this moment in contrast to another one.
Beth:	It's this…. Right?
Peter:	Yes.
Beth:	This—right now?
Peter:	Are we talking about the same thing or not?
Beth:	I don't know. What are you talking about?
Peter:	This. I can't say anything more than that.
Beth:	It's not anything is it?
Peter:	It's certainly not a thing—not a thought or sensation.
Beth:	I know what you're talking about.
Peter:	You do, do you?
Beth:	Yes, it's this. I've got it. There's nothing more to say, is there?

CONTENTLESS CONVERSATIONS: TALKING ABOUT NOTHING

In order to support people in cultivating the experience of "seeing through," or *vipashyana,* we also need to be able to talk about nothing. We need some fluency in a special type of conversation that can look like other conversations except that they have no subject matter. These conversations are used to induce an experience of unconditioned mind. This is the real transmission of nondual therapy: the sharing of no content. Zen speaks about this as mind-to-mind transmission; Dzogchen as "direct introduction" or pointing out instructions.

Since we're speaking from nothing, our communication is ultimately contentless. We're using speech to impart a contentless transmission. The point of such communication is to reveal the unconditioned mind. Sometimes, however, therapists new to the nondual approach may find themselves talking about nothing and begin to feel uncomfortable. Their words don't have the obvious and familiar structure of ordinary therapeutic communication, and they may doubt themselves and stop talking out of embarrassment or confusion.

So we need to develop confidence in the therapeutic value of communicating about nothing. After all, it's the only way, short of teaching practices or techniques, to introduce the client to unconditioned mind in the therapeutic interaction. Inevitably the other person won't be able to understand what we're saying within their normal frame of reference, and they may become confused as they attempt to understand it in their usual ways. At this point we might introduce a question like "What are we talking about now?" If they reply, "I don't know," we may say, "I'm not surprised because I don't know, either. In fact, I can't know, because we're not talking about anything. Even though we're using understandable language, there's no subject matter." Of course, we need to be able to say this with confidence in the nondual experience, or else the other person may think we've lost our sanity or become confused.

In these conversations we distinguish that which can't be distinguished. We point to the unconditioned mind by showing that we can't point to it. We weave our subjectless conversation into the thematic conversation of the person with whom we are in communication. We braid our contentless responses with the other person's communication until their mindstream is brought to the experience of unstructured awareness. The following illustrates how this may happen.

Clive:	I had a whole lot of questions when I came in here but now I just can't formulate them. I haven't experienced this before. Where does this lead?
Peter:	Here.
Clive:	Where is here?
Peter:	Yes. Where is here?
	[Silence]
Clive:	I want to know if this supports creativity.
Peter:	What is creativity?
Clive:	Creating something that hasn't existed before.
Peter:	This would seem to fulfill your criterion. We began a few minutes ago with what you knew, and now we are somewhere that you haven't been before.
Clive:	But what have we created?
Peter:	This.

Clive:	But what is this? I don't know what this is. It doesn't seem to be anything at all.
Peter:	Perhaps we have created nothing.
Clive:	I think so. We have created nothing out of something.
Peter:	Without anything changing at all. Everything is here, exactly as it was when we began.
Clive:	Except that we aren't interpreting our experience.
Peter:	But that is exactly what we are doing right now. [Silence]

THE PARADOXES OF NONDUAL CONVERSATIONS: ARTICULATE CONTRADICTIONS

When we begin to speak from no-mind, it is inevitable that paradoxes and contradictions will creep into our conversations. They arise when we describe unconditioned mind with any real accuracy and precision. One of the most obvious paradoxes is that the unconditioned mind is simultaneously something and nothing. It *is* because it *isn't*.

In the twenty or so years that I have been teaching and facilitating nondual work, I've found that communicating fluently and naturally in paradoxes is the most difficult aspect of this form of therapy for practitioners to acquire. Somehow we need to make a leap of faith and be willing to articulately contradict ourselves in a totally up-front and confident way. If someone says to us that we've just contradicted ourselves, we need to be able to say, "Yes, that's right. I have. Because that is how it is. There's no other way to accurately describe this state."

At a certain point we betray the experience of the unconditioned mind if we aren't willing to say that the unconditioned mind "is" because it "isn't;" that it's totally unrelated to our conditioned existence but indistinguishable from it; that it can't be lost or gained, yet it repeatedly arises and disappears. India's most celebrated and "rational" philosopher, Nagarjuna, had no problem speaking paradoxically. In a verse of praise at the beginning of his famous text, *The Fundamental Verses of on the Middle Way,* he says of the ultimate teaching and the ultimate state that it is:

> Unceasing, unborn, unannihilated, not permanent, not coming not going, without distinction, without identity, and free from conceptual construction.

When our thoughts are born at the point where the conceptual touches the nonconceptual, we are *compelled* to use paradox, negation, and absurdity.

CONCLUDING DIALOGUE

The following dialogue integrates a number of the conversations we've been talking about in this chapter along with other moves that feature in my expression of nondual work in a group setting.[12]

Anne:	I'm feeling bored with what we are doing right now. I want to actually do this work, rather than just describe what is happening for us in this room. I want to get into my fixations. I want to see how I'm fixating, and how to avoid this.
Peter:	Can you see that you are fixating right now? You are creating that this isn't it. Actually you can see from your mood and the way you are holding your body that you are stuck. Given the general mood you are in, whatever you say, it will be an expression of the feeling that this just isn't it.
Anne:	Yes. I can see that. I know that I'd like things to be different, but just wanting it to be different isn't changing anything. And you're right. I do feel stuck with this. [Pause]
Peter:	You seem to be wanting me to do something. It also feels as though you want some attention directed specifically toward you, in the hope that something will then shift.
Anne:	Well yes. I do.
Claude:	I'd like to ask if…
Peter:	Please excuse me interrupting. We will come back to your

query. But I'm just wanting to observe Anne, that you are already poised to interpret whatever Claude is about to say as "more boring description." At this moment you are predisposed to interpret whatever you hear as less than relevant. In other words you are predisposed to create that "this isn't it."

Anne: Hmm, yes. Well, I prefer what you are saying now. This is more like what I've been wanting to do. I find this useful.

Peter: Perhaps. But now you are starting to move in the opposite direction. You're interpreting that this is it, or at least that this is closer to how things should be. Your experience is suddenly lighter. You don't feel particularly stuck at this point. In fact, in the absence of any obstruction this could evolve into an experience of...

Anne: I've got it. I just got it. I've got what this whole process is for.
[Silence]

Henri: What happened? What did you do?

Anne: Nothing.

Henri: But you must have done something. You seem so certain and clear.
[Silence]

Henri: So what is it?

Anne: I don't know. I can't say what it is. I can't describe it, but I've got it.
[Silence]

Henri: But if you can't say what it is, how do you know you've got it?

Anne: But I have got it. I know. There's no need to know what it is. I've just got it. There isn't anything to know.

Henri: But what about the Zen saying Peter sometimes quotes, that "the moment you think you've got, you've lost it."

Anne: You can't take this away from me because in fact there isn't any IT. There's nothing to lose.

Henri: I can see that.

Anne: I'm just thinking. I could lose this. I'm wondering if there is a different experience that is completely invincible.

Peter:	Be careful! [Laughing] You can't afford to think like that.
Maurice:	My understanding is that enlightenment is permanent.
Peter:	You have to be very careful who you listen to right now.
Anne:	What do you mean?
Peter:	If you take Maurice's suggestion seriously and begin to participate in his construction, your present experience will very quickly dissipate.
Anne:	So what should I do? Who should I listen to?
Peter:	I'm just pointing out the consequences of the different interpretations you could take on board.
Anne:	I already feel that something has been taken from me.
Peter:	But you say that as though you have no role in it. If we hang on to something long enough, it is bound to shift at some point. In fact, the moment we judge that it is valuable we have already distorted the original experience which lay beyond any judgment of good or bad, desirable or undesirable.
	However, it is also very easy to become fixated on the idea of observing our fixations. We can think there is some intrinsic value in doing this. In fact, if we think there is some value in doing it, then we will condition ourselves to observe our fixations, even when this is quite unnecessary. If we become attached to the notion of observing our fixations, or any other type of spiritual process for that matter, we condition ourselves to becoming perpetual seekers. This is just to say that balance is required when observing our fixations, so we don't become self-aware in a neurotic or obsessive way.
Michèle:	But it still seems to me that you are saying that this is it, because you like it. Before, when you were feeling frustrated and bored, you said that that wasn't it, and now you are obviously feeling great, so you think that "This is it."
Anne:	This has got nothing to do with what I want. In fact, I don't want this. It just is.
	[Silence]

ENDNOTES

1. I would like to thank the editors of this volume, John Prendergast, Ph.D., and Ken Bradford, Ph.D., for helpful comments on the first draft of this chapter.

2. As a generalization, and purely for the purposes of locating this essay within Indo-Asian traditions, we could say that pure listening is more closely aligned with the Mahati (Dzogchen) and Mahamudra nondual traditions, whereas pure speaking is more closely connected with Madhyamika and Advaita. Soto Zen emphasizes pure listening, whereas Rinzai gives emphasis to pure speech. (Sketches of these traditions and their practices can be found in Peter Fenner, *The Edge of Certainty: Dilemma on the Buddhist Path*, 2000). The approach we are developing here is ideally biased neither toward pure listening nor pure speaking.

3. My work is delivered through the Center for Timeless Wisdom (www.wisdom.org). The core program we offer is a nine-month training called Radiant Mind (www.radiantmind.net). The framework for my work is described more fully in *Radiant Mind: The Effortless Way of Pure Presence*, Sounds True, Louisville, Colorado (forthcoming with CDs in 2007).

4. See Peter Fenner, "Nonduality and Therapy," in *The Sacred Mirror* (ed. John Prendergast, Peter Fenner, and Sheila Krystal), Paragon House, St. Paul, Minnesota (2003) for more specifications of positive and negative listening in terms of nonverbal expressions of these and also how positive and negative listening attempts to add to, or take energy away from, people's constructions.

5. Here I am distinguishing thinking, not thinking, and nonthinking. Thinking is the process of thinking that is accompanied by the belief that we can "go somewhere" or "get somewhere" as a result of our thinking. It's the type of thinking we engage in when we are trying to understand our experience or solve a problem. Not thinking is the cessation of thoughts. This is a very rare occurrence for most people, since even the supposed gap between thoughts is a thought! Nonthinking signifies a natural arising and dissolution of thoughts that is free of goal orientation. In the same way we can distinguish doing, not doing, and nondoing. Nondoing is the *wu wei* of Taoism.

6. Elsewhere I have used the term "deconstructive contemplation" to refer to both the verbal and silent components of this work. The more proactive forms of deconstruction can be called "deconstructive analysis" or "deconstructive inquiry," which is also how I translate *prasanga-vichara*. *Prasanga-vichara* is a form of deconstructive inquiry originally developed by Nagarjuna in the second century. He brought analytical sophistication and precision to the Perfect Wisdom worldview by casting it in a vigorous philosophical dialectic. Nagarjuna's seminal work is the *Root Verses on the Middle Way (Mulamadhyamakakarika)*. There are several English translations. Practitioners of the

Madhyamaka are categorized as Deconstructionists *(Prasangika)* and Constructionists *(Svatantrika)*. The Deconstructionists dismantle all positions or fixations using *reductio ad absurdum* arguments *(prasanga)*. The Constructionists offer an alternative position at the close of their independent arguments *(svatantra)*.

The *Prasangika* or Deconstructive version was refined and systematized by later Indian philosophers such as Chandrakirti and Shantideva. Chandrakirtis wrote an important commentary *(Bhashya)* to Nagarjuna's *Root Verses* and an independent work titled *An Introduction to the Middle Way (Madhyamakavatara)*. See Peter Fenner, *The Ontology of the Middle Way*, Dordrecht: Kluwer Publications (1990), and *Reasoning into Reality: A Systems-Cybernetics and Therapeutic Interpretation of Middle Path Analysis*, Boston: Wisdom Publicaitons (1995). Shantideva's seminal work in this area is the ninth chapter of the *Introduction to the Awakened Lifestyle (Bodhicharyavatara)*, of which there are now several translations in English.

In their turn Tibetan philosophers produced a range of hybrid systems in which they aligned the *Prasangika* system with other Buddhist ontological systems. See Jeffrey Hopkins, *Meditation on Emptiness,* Cumbria: Wisdom Publications, 1983; Robert A. F. Thurman, *Tsong Khapa's Speech of Gold in the* Essence of True Eloquence*: Reason and Enlightenment in the Central Philosophy of Tibet,* Princeton: Princeton University Press, 1984, and José I. Cabezon, *A Dose of Emptiness: An Annotated Translation of the* sTong thun chen mo *of mKhas grub dGe legs dpal bzang,* Albany: State University of New York Press, 1992.

7. In the nine-month Radiant Mind training, I distinguish about eight different types of deconstructive conversations. Students explore these separately and then learn to automatically recognize the optimal inquiry to use and how to seamlessly combine elements of different conversations into an organic whole. In many ways it's just moving from pedagogically defined structure to free-form performance.

8. The term "unfindability conversations" is derived from the Mahayana *vipashyana* practices, which aim to experientially show that everything (thoughts, feelings, and perceptions) are fundamentally unfindable *(na labdha, mi rnyed)*.

9. The use of koans is usually associated with Rinzai Zen as a formalized set of questions or vignettes drawn from encounters between Zen masters and students that are designed to deconstruct the conceptual mind in order to reveal unstructured awareness or "no-mind." But koans are actually timeless.

10. In Korean Zen the main koan is the question "What is this?" The first record of this koan occurs in an exchange between the sixth Zen patriarch Huineng and a young monk named Huaijang, in which Huineng asked Huaijang, "What is this and where did it come from?" Huaijang couldn't answer. But he

took the question away with himself and used it as his sole form of inquiry for several years until he realized what it was pointing to. He then returned to see Huineng, who again asked him, "What is this?" Huaijang replied, "To say it is something misses the point. But still it can be cultivated."

In practicing Korean Zen, one sits in meditation and asks over and over, "What is this?" This leads into the questions, "What is what?" "What is the 'this' that I'm trying to work out?" As Martine Batchelor, *Principles of Zen*, Hammersmith, London,Thorson, (1999, 84) explains, "The question anchors us and brings us back to the present moment. But we are not repeating the question like a mantra…. What is important is that the questioning is alive, that the question is fresh each time we ask it."

11. When and how to pose these questions is discussed in Fenner (2003).

12. I have described the principles and practices of a nondual approach as it applies specifically to group work in a lengthy unpublished essay titled "Deconstructive Contemplation: The Dynamics of Nondual Groupwork."

NONDUALITY

A Spontaneous Movement "To" And "Fro"

Kaisa Puhakka

INTRODUCTION

Nonduality is an idea we can think and talk about. More immediately, it is a state into which we disappear or a state from which we appear. But even to call it a "state" is to grasp at something static and solid in a situation that is essentially fluid and ungraspable. A better way to think and talk about nonduality may be simply as "appearing" or "disappearing." Better yet, of course, is to not think or talk at all, for all such activity sets up a duality between the talker and that which is being talked about.

When one freely gives oneself to the activity of appearing and disappearing, there is no self and no concept of nonduality, but just an effortless flow that does not grasp at any identity or concept and is imbued with a natural sense of well-being. Moments of such flow occur in psychotherapy spontaneously and far more frequently, I suspect, than is generally recognized. They are easily missed because they tend to be subtle and fleeting. Moreover, therapists and clients alike often actively and mostly unconsciously flee from these moments and the impending loss of self that comes with them.

Those who have tasted the natural well-being associated with a momentary disappearance of the self may try to recapture it, and if they are therapists, perhaps set up conditions that could bring it about for their clients as well. Such efforts, however, proceed from the standpoint of a self as a distinct and enduring identity. From that standpoint, the disappearance of the self—nonduality—is something to be attained by some sort of technique or spiritual practice. But paradoxically, any attempt to make itself disappear only affirms the self's existence. Many spiritual practitioners have found themselves dead-ended in this paradox. What happens to them at this dead end? They may quit their spiritual pursuit right then and there, perhaps with a sense of defeat and despair, or with a sense of relief and liberation. Or they may doggedly continue in their pursuit. All of these may happen to the same person at different times. It depends on where the person is "coming from" at the time.

One place the person may be coming from is the viewpoint of the self who experiences nonduality as something distinct from itself even while perhaps intellectually knowing better, and who then seeks to capture or recapture it. Another is the viewpoint—not really a viewpoint at all but perhaps more akin to a boundless "viewspace"— of the boundless and ungraspable flow of reality into which the self naturally and spontaneously disappears and from which it naturally and spontaneously appears. Understanding or *being* this state is the same as *seeing* it. In contrast to the limited viewpoint of a self, a "viewspace" that excludes nothing sees that there is movement into and out of it—a "pendulation," as Lumiere characterizes it.[1] At this fundamental a level, the movement is spontaneous and natural and so needs no explanation. On the other hand, an enduring sense of identity is *not* natural but an artifact, and so cries for understanding: How does it come about? In this chapter I invite the reader to inquire with me into the activity that brings about and maintains the sense of identity of a separate self.

Let us call the activity that creates and maintains the sense of self "fixating," and the resultant self the "fixated self." From the standpoint of the fixated self, nonduality is fixated as well, as a state to be grasped or a concept to be understood—an object for the subject that is the fixated self. But tragically, the object can never be attained by the subject that seeks it. The quest for nonduality or "nondual experience" exposes the root of alienation, of loneliness, of self-doubt, and of the myriad forms of human suffering in ways that no other quest does.

A self that is not fixated naturally disappears and appears, or "goes into" and "comes from" states of nonduality. In the following pages, we will as well explore this natural activity, its manifestation in speech and behavior, how it occurs in the psychotherapeutic encounter, and the qualities of presence and connection associated with it. Finally, we will address the issue of talking about nonduality. Therapists, as much if not more than other people, like to talk and think. And when nonduality or nondual wisdom becomes a concern to us, we can't help but talk about it. Most of the ways we talk and think about nonduality tend to fixate it by turning it into a conceptual object or idea, but there are also ways of talking and thinking about it that tend to unravel the fixation and deliver us from a state of separation to a nondual "coming" and "going."

FIXATING THE SELF

Most psychological theories assume the fixation of the self from the start. They differ widely as to how the self is constituted or when, but most agree that once it has been constituted, it's *there*. It may be subject to modification, even to falsification, but in its basic ontological existence, the self is assumed to be there. In every psychotherapeutic encounter, says the premise, the client's self is there, and the therapist's self is there, and the two interact. It seems, then, that nothing needs to be done to bring the self into existence or to keep it going; all that activity was done in the past. The job of psychotherapy may be to change or transform one or both of these selves, but through it all neither therapist nor client doubt that they will endure without their having to do anything about it.

Questioning this premise seems pointless when one considers that conditioned patterns of fixating the self were laid down early in one's life. They are deeply ingrained in our brains, and so it does indeed seem that nothing needs to be done to maintain and perpetuate the fixated self. But let us look more closely. What are these conditioned patterns and how are they being maintained right now? Notice how, paradoxically, in positing the conditioned patterns as *already there*, the consciousness that does the positing creates a division between itself and those patterns. Notice the activity of fixation in the very resistance to letting go of the assumption of the fixated self.

Can we take a step further and suspend this activity?

You might stop reading for a moment to observe this activity going on in your body and mind right now. Notice the subtle tensions, pushes, and pulls in the body and thoughts and images and other subtle activities like alertness and readiness to look, to reflect, and so on in the mind. You don't have to clearly discern all that's going on there; it's enough to make contact with the feel and texture of it. Then consider this question: If all that activity suddenly stopped and were gone, would *you* still be there?...

The intellectual answer (at least to a good Buddhist) is "no." Yet honest reflection reveals that, contrary to that intellectual position (if that's what yours is), a feeling of subjectivity had accompanied the experience of observing thoughts and sensations. It is very subtle, but perhaps you can discern the *activity* that creates that feeling as an ongoing pulling back and perhaps slightly pulling in to form something like a point of subjectivity. Notice also how this activity creates a space between the point of subjectivity and its object, whatever that may be.

If you have been able to observe the activity of pulling in that forms the point of subjectivity, you will have also noticed that this activity, and the point of subjectivity, are extremely unstable. The pulling in tends to spontaneously relax and flow outward, and with that, the point of subjectivity also tends to spread and dissolve. There is no permanence to this kind of subjectivity. Something else needs to happen for the self to fixate itself as an enduring observer or enjoyer of experience.

✳

The self fixates itself by resisting one or the other of the two spontaneous activities, *pulling in* and *flowing out*. This resistance tends to keep in place the tension and the space that separates the subject of experience from its object. The fixation of the self can happen in one of two ways, depending on which activity—the pulling in or the flowing out—is being resisted. Put differently, the self can fixate itself as either subject or as object.

When the pulling-in activity is fixated, the self takes up a permanent position as a subject or a "bystander" witnessing whatever is going on. The sense of self is preserved by not letting oneself be absorbed in anything. In fixating itself as subject, the self positions itself with the affirmation "I am." This is the way, for example, of some spiritual practitioners who seek liberation or enlightenment by cultivating detachment. The effort to fixate the self as a subject is usually associated with a lot of self-consciousness and of being cut off from the world. In more extreme cases, as in schizoid states, there may be a sense of unreality about everything and an experience of self clinicians call "depersonalization." R. D. Laing (1990) describes a schizoid patient whose existence as a self had become so tenuous that he had to keep constant vigil, day and night *watching himself* lest he cease to exist. In less extreme and more everyday situations, the attempt to "center oneself" is often nothing more than a fixating of the self as a subject. People can fixate the self as subject by taking an attitude or holding an opinion about ideas or practices.

When the flowing-out activity is fixated, the self secures a permanent position as an object. It grasps and holds on to things, persons, ideas, or practices it considers precious or as worthy of striving for. It identifies with these objects and becomes them. For example, I am smart, not a pushover, etc., or I am a spiritual practitioner, a humanistic psychotherapist, a seeker of wisdom, etc. In fixating itself as an object, the self takes on an identity, "I am this, I am that." Some contemporary spiritual seekers fixate the self as object in a rather convoluted way, by denying that their self is their true identity and attributing their true identity to the "higher self" or Brahman or something else.

In reality, fixating the self as subject and fixating the self as object both occur simultaneously, or they can alternate rapidly. But often there is a preponderance of one or the other type of fixation, which confers a particular flavor to the personality. For example, people who tend to fixate as subject are often described as "introverts," while people who tend to fixate as object are described as "extroverts."

As in any encounter between persons, in psychotherapy therapists fixate the self and clients fixate the self. Therapists fixate the self whenever they come from an agenda to control or direct, or even just to "facilitate" what's going on with the client. Fixation of the self is at the heart of clients' troubles. More severely troubled clients fail to fixate a self in a coherent pattern that is acceptable by the standards of the community. But such a failure is *not* the same as not fixating the self. A therapy where the therapist comes from a fixated self—so long as his or her self has a more coherent and successful pattern of fixation--can be helpful to such clients. But a therapy, or a moment in therapy, that embraces the client unconditionally without fixation of self on the part of the therapist can hold the client with a depth of acceptance and love not possible when the therapist is coming from a fixated self.

THE SELF NATURALLY "COMES" AND "GOES"

When examining the feeling of subjectivity in the previous section, we noted the essential instability of the point of subjectivity when it is not fixated. The activity of pulling in that creates the subject-point constantly gives way to the opposite activity of flowing out that dissolves it.

We can witness the natural coming and going of the self in anything we do.

Allow your attention to make direct contact with something, say a candle flame or the flow of sensations in your body. Now if you allow that contact to become deep enough to absorb the observer-you, the distance between you and the object tends to collapse. You find yourself in the flame, or you find the flame in you. Sometimes the space between you and the flame collapses so completely that you are gone, and the flame and everything else is also gone. This "gone" moment typically does not last, and in the next moment, you the observer are there and so is the object. But it is a new-born you, a fresh you, and a fresh object as well. This is probably familiar to you in and out of meditation practice. If it is, then what typically follows is probably also familiar to you. The self fixates by grasping at the object and tries to make the "gone" state (a memory image of what just happened), now become a desired "One" state, happen again. At this point a painful battle may ensue in which the self, divided against itself, tries not to fixate itself, yet the harder it tries, the harder it fixates itself.

Why does the division within consciousness happen in the first place? I know no answer to this question, though, arguably, we can trace the rise of human civilization to that division. I suppose our brains are wired that way. Nothing needs to be done to make it happen. In fact we are not there to make anything happen *until after* consciousness has divided into subject and object. The sense of self and the urge to do something arise with that division. If at that moment we didn't do anything about it, the polarization and division would just as naturally depolarize and dissolve, and with it the sense of self would disappear. And then it would appear. And again disappear, in a natural ebb and flow.

Examples of the natural coming and going of the self abound in everyday life. Whenever you go fully into a relationship or an activity of any kind, your self is gone. You are so absorbed in that activity— for example, sweeping the floor, meditating, or attending to another person—that nothing of you is left to stand back and watch. In such moments you forget yourself. Your self is gone. In the next moment someone calls on you or something else catches your attention, and the self is there, wondering, "Who is calling me?" "What is that?" In the next moment you may be fully engaged in some other activity, or with another person, and the self is again gone. In this way, the self comes and goes, effortlessly appearing and disappearing in the activity we call life. This natural coming and going of the self can be seen in the play of children whose spontaneity has not yet given way to the anxious self-consciousness that comes with the pressure to fixate the self according to the expectations of family and community.

✳

The coming and going of the self is our natural state and so is available at any time. It ceases to be available only when the self is a problem. For spiritual practitioners the self is a problem because it's there when we don't want it to be there or is limited in its capabilities or wisdom when we'd like it to be unlimited. So the self is a problem to be solved either by eradicating it or improving on it. You might sit down to meditate with a goal to solve the problem of your self. In the quiet of the sitting the self may dissolve. But then someone speaks to you, and the self arises and not only arises but immediately fixates: "Hey, you are disturbing *my* meditation, interrupting the attainment of my goal!"

If the self is not a problem and you sit down to meditate, then there is nothing to attain and no disturbance. Someone calls your name, the self arises, you give yourself fully to attending to the person who calls, and, without any goal to attain, the self is gone. You may then decide to return to the meditation or pursue some other activity, and at that moment the self arises again.

In the natural coming and going of the self, the problem of the self is gone—not solved but simply gone. We can see that the self need not be banished or even improved in any way. We can also see that the self really cannot be banished or improved; when it comes to the self's own projects, fixing is the same as fixating. When this understanding reaches deep into our bones, it allows us, as psychotherapists, to manifest a space of acceptance for our clients that is not just a matter of approach or even attitude on our part but is ontological, reaching into the heart of being with a tremendous power to heal.

"COMING FROM" NONDUALITY: ORIGINAL SPEECH

The sense of self arises with the division of consciousness that simultaneously creates subject and object. But where does the self "come from"? In a way, it comes from nothing. But this is not a "nothing" as opposed to "something," not a "lack" of something. Lack has a trace of that which is wanting. A self may be fixated around that something and carry its trace. But the nothing from which a self arises anew has nothing to do with lack and carries no trace of what is wanting. The Sanskrit term *sunyata* refers to this nothing and is usually translated into English as "emptiness." In Mahayana Buddhist literature, however, the "emptiness" of *sunyata* does not refer to a reality that could be "empty" or "full" or even both. Rather, it refers to a realization the hallmark of which is "absence of conceptual construction" (Padmakara Translation Group, 2004,

p. 50). Such a realization negates all platforms for conceptual construction—a point rigorously explicated again and again in the Buddhist literature on *sunyata*. (See, for example, the writings of Nagarjuna and Chandrakirti, Buddhist sages of the second and fifth centuries, respectively). Yet *sunyata* does not negate reality—if anything, the absence of conceptual construction allows reality as such or "suchness" (*tathata*) to shine forth in its immediacy.

Reality absent of conceptual construction is what we have in this chapter called "nondual" reality or awareness. When nondual reality first divides into subject and object in the act of perception or conceptual thought, a space of expression is created between the subject and object poles of consciousness. The self has its first manifestation in this space, thus arising or "coming from" nonduality.

If you have ever watched a person having an insight, a real "aha!" moment, you may have witnessed a self arising. In the actual moment of insight, the person's self disappears, leaving her with vacant eyes staring into space and perhaps a slightly dropped jaw. In the next moment, a smile spontaneously spreads on her face, and an "aha!" accompanying that smile may be the first expression of her newly arising self.

We usually identify "insight" with that expression or, even more likely, with the content of its verbal expression. In grasping at the content to verbalize it, however, the self is fixating itself. But in the prior moment, often signaled by a spontaneous smile, the self arose afresh. And prior to that moment, there was a "nothingness" that was the womb from which the insight and the self expressing it in the smile were born. All expression that is truly original is born from that womb.

✳

After a *sesshin* (an intensive meditation retreat) at a Rinzai Zen monastery, I engaged a fellow practitioner in a conversation. Nearing fifty, he had practiced Zen for twenty-five years and was an internationally known mathematician. I was curious about how his creativity was faring in middle age, as I had heard that mathematicians usually peak in their early to middle twenties. "On the contrary," he said, "I find myself becoming more creative over the years, as I get closer to my real self." He laughed, and added, "You know, I am talking about nothing really." He then described how, sitting in the Zendo, he becomes one with himself and everything is gone including himself, and then, out of the nothingness, mathematical relationships in three-dimensional form spontaneously float up. To me, his description captured the essence of creation—something coming from nothing.

Speech that spontaneously comes from nothing and is the expression of a self arising afresh is creative in this literal sense that it comes from nothing. It is very different from the far more common speech that comes from assumptions of a fixated self and expresses the reactions of a fixated self. "Original speech," as I call the former, has nothing to do with having high novelty value or shock value. The content of what is being said is often not important, but the qualities of saying it always are. Original speech is simple, spacious, and usually sparse. No words are said that are not meant, and nothing that is meant is left unsaid. It is simple because there is no hidden agenda to preserve or validate the existence or esteem of the self.

✴

When I was a child growing up in Finland, my family spent the three summer months of the year in the country. Across a meadow and a patch of woods lived our closest neighbor, an old man named Heinonen who was indigenous to the region. The ritual that started our summer was a visit to Heinonen. My parents had taught my sisters and me to respect the customs of the indigenous folk who were famous for their sparse speech. We sat quietly by the door as Heinonen puffed on his pipe. A grandfather clock against the back wall ticked away time that had slowed to a near halt. Everything was quiet, like a still lake at sunset. "Soooo," said Heinonen. A couple of more puffs, and he continued, "The swallows have come." His words dropped like pebbles onto the surface of the lake, creating circles that rippled outward. The ripples gently rocked us who were immersed in the lake. The clock kept ticking, and eventually one of us dropped a pebble that sent a ripple back, "Yeah, so they have."

Original speech has the qualities of extraordinary clarity and vividness as well. These, and the simplicity, and most of all, the truth of it that "seems to directly touch itself,"[2] confer it tremendous power.

Sometimes original speech takes the form of images.

Some years back I saw a young man in psychotherapy. He was brilliant but extremely inhibited except when he could talk in abstract ideas far removed from his personal life. The sessions had been painfully stilted for months, and often I wondered why he kept coming when I wasn't really helping him. Eventually I threw in the towel but still showed up just because he did. After several more weeks, he began to talk about himself, haltingly, hesitantly, his voice almost choked off. There were long silences in our sessions. In one of those silences, an image came up for me, seemingly from nowhere but compelling in its vividness: a table of feast, decorated with flowers and brimming over with delicacies beyond imagination. The feast was being offered to my client and he stood in front of it, looking at it hungrily, struggling to swallow with a parched throat. "Go ahead, you can do it. You can have it," I found myself whispering to him, surprised at myself, and yet not surprised. He was taken aback as if he had just been found out, but he also looked at me with a new kind of curiosity. Three weeks later, he told me that he had befriended a young woman and that he had just asked her out and she had agreed. This was the beginning of not just the first relationship in his life but of a long journey to a full life in the world.

"GOING INTO" NONDUALITY AND THE FEAR OF DISINTEGRATION

Going into nonduality happens in moments when the self dissolves and is gone. In the earlier example of a person having an "aha" experience, the person is "going into" nonduality in the moment just prior to the smile spreading on her face. In that prior moment, the person's jaw is slack and eyes are vacantly staring in space. As far as her "self" is concerned, it's not there. Prior to being "gone," it was there, engaged in thinking that perhaps came to an impasse, and suddenly the thinking and the structure of the self which the thinking created and maintained were all gone. In everyday experiences of insight, the "gone" moment is infinitesimally short, so short that one is barely aware of a discontinuity in the flow of thinking and experience. Afterward, the discontinuity is filled in by memory, and one typically describes the experience of insight by saying something like "Suddenly something happened" and "I experienced a shift in my consciousness." But when it actually happened, there was no "I" experiencing anything; the self was "gone."

These moments of self being "gone" often become noticeable to practitioners of certain kinds of meditation. This is the case especially in Buddhist meditative practice. The dissolution of the self then becomes the desired goal of practice. The practitioner, hoping to "go into" nonduality, "gets into" trying to dissolve the self instead. But the self cannot dissolve itself. It cannot really even *allow* itself to dissolve, for that, too, sets up a duality between the one doing the allowing and the state that is supposed to be achieved by doing it. Notice how "allowing" can be a mental attitude that fixates the self.

The dissolution of the self happens spontaneously. The good news is that dissolution of the self is absolutely easy, no effort is required. The bad news is that we don't want to give up the effort. It has come to define our identity. We also want to see returns. We have worked hard to end our separate existence, to become "one with nonduality," and when it finally happens we insist on being there to witness and celebrate it. Spiritual practice can be a trap, a way of fixating the self that turns the dissolution of the self into a prized goal. It can become a vicious cycle of fixation: The more difficult the attainment of the goal, the more we value the quest for it and the self that engages in that quest—which intensifies the conflict between the quest and the fear of our own disintegration, thus fixating the self even more.

✳

Some of us work as therapists for clients who have severe disturbances. Such clients sometimes manifest an intense and desperate fear of disintegration. As therapists, we would like to be able to embrace this fear and lovingly hold it for our client, until he or she can tolerate and accept it. But when we fear our own disintegration, we hold our client's fear in an anxious, fearful way, not in a loving and welcoming way. Our severely disturbed clients can take us to the edge. Sometimes love and care overcome fear, and we let ourselves fall off the edge. In such moments, who is to tell what is spiritual practice and what is psychotherapy practice? We can be grateful to our clients, just as we are to our spiritual mentors and teachers.

A client in a psychotic state may manifest not the fear of disintegration of the self, but the actual disintegration. The fear may be there as well, though it is not always. A therapist who works from the premise that one fixated self is encountering another feels compelled to hold onto the fragments of the client's self where the client no longer can—or perhaps just does not care to—do so. In such a situation, the therapist's fixated self enters into the struggle for the survival of the client's self. Sometimes the struggle is won, but often it is not, and in any case there is a great deal of anxiety involved, at least for the therapist if not for the client.

Disintegration of the self is very different from dissolution. In disintegration the fixated self attempts to hold on to fragments of self-identity, and these may or may not be recovered into a reintegrated identity. In dissolution there is no holding on to anything; the tension and frantic grasping at an identity or fragments of identity are gone. Often when working with psychotic clients, I feel grateful for the opportunities, in highly structured meditation situations set up so as to remove any need to hold onto a self, to witness my own disintegration fear and its giving way to dissolution.

✳

Several years back I met a client for the first time at a county jail. He had been picked up by the police and charged with disorderly conduct. He had been in and out of the mental health and prison system for decades, and had been diagnosed with paranoid schizophrenia. On this occasion, I was asked to evaluate him to see if he was competent to stand trial. It became quickly evident that the man was in an acute psychotic state, and his speech was incomprehensible—"word salad" is the technical term for the way he was speaking. I tried to understand him to no avail, and yet he obviously wanted to communicate something. I offered him a piece of paper and a pen so he could write it down, but his sentences were a syntactic jumble. Perhaps because of his urgency, I felt compelled to be truthful rather than humor him, and so wanted him to really get it that I did not understand him no matter how I tried. In the end, naked and spent, I just sat there with him for a few more minutes before I left. Three months later, while walking across the front lawn of the local state hospital, I heard someone calling, "Hi Dr. Puhakka, do you remember me?" It was the same man, now coherent after three months on medication, and he was very happy to see me. How did he recognize me and remember my name, which even people with minds in fine working order usually don't? Somehow, while he and I were both "gone" sitting there in the county jail, we had met somewhere where intact egos (fixated selves) don't set foot.

TALKING ABOUT NONDUALITY: PARADOX

Finally, I want to return to the observation I made early in this chapter, which is that psychotherapists, perhaps more than many other people, like to think and talk. Especially when talking about nondual awareness, we are not "coming from" that awareness. The self is fixated by thinking and talking, and much of the time we express a fixated self in our transactions. Still, the situation is usually somewhat fluid, and a fixated self tends to dissolve—unless it actively engages in an activity that tends to fixate it more. Whenever the self affirms itself as subject vis-à-vis an object, fixation occurs. We discussed this earlier in the chapter. Here I would like to explore possibilities of thinking and talking that do not fixate the self but, on the contrary, tend to dissolve it.

Is it possible to talk about nonduality without turning it into an object? Just the requirements of English grammar seem to rule it out. Yet there is a way of talking that can evoke a direct, intuitive seeing in which the subject-object structure unravels even as it is being created by the talking and staged by the speaking and listening situation. This is the way of paradox, and it begins with the recognition that, when talking about nonduality, talking is not just different from the real thing but actually negates the very thing that is being talked about. What makes a paradox a paradox is an impasse from which there is no way out. Such an impasse is created when one affirms nonduality. In doing so, a duality is set up between that which is affirmed and that which is not (or which is implicitly denied). But in setting up that duality, one is affirming the very thing one did not want to affirm.

Can you feel the impasse? Can you notice how the mind does not want to stay with the impasse but tries to escape as quickly as possible? One way to escape is to space out, to let the mind get all fogged up. Another way to escape is to look for a solution to the paradox—some way of showing that it's not *really* a paradox. For example, we might think, "Ah, but true nonduality affirms everything *and* its opposite. It's the inclusive 'both/and' stance." But if you examine this "solution," you will see that affirming the "both/and" stance" just creates another dualism (between it and what it is not). There really is no escape from a genuine paradox. Staying with a paradox is much like koan practice, of which Lin Chi, the founder of Rinzai Zen, said, it's like having a red-hot iron ball stuck in your throat: You can't swallow it and you can't spit it out (Watson, 1993).

✳

Nondual wisdom traditions all recognize paradox at the heart of their own talk and walk. Their teaching devices often employ paradox, though not all of them are as brutal as koan practice in Rinzai Zen can be. When we stay with paradox and don't space out or run to solutions, the structure of consciousness that's caught up in the paradox becomes transparent and starts to soften. We begin to see— not just believe, but actually and immediately see—how a stance or position about anything sets up a dualism. We no longer feel we need to take positions or beliefs, our own or anybody else's, very seriously.

This lack of seriousness expresses the loosening of the fixated self. It is spacious and light, and very different from the inflated buoyancy of someone who dismisses everything because he knows it all. It is also different from the subtle superiority of someone who is keen on pointing out the paradox in other people's positions and how they are caught up in it, and finally, it is different from the deflated cynicism of one who is disillusioned and doesn't care anymore.

There is nothing wrong with positions as such. Taking them seriously is the problem. Whenever we feel that we need to hold a position, or that we need to dismiss a position, we get serious. And when we are serious, the self is fixated. On the other hand, when the need to take positions is gone, we can be more spacious, holding whatever positions are put forth lightly and playfully. Our clients come in with all sorts of positions that burden them and make them serious. Therapists sometimes add their own positions to the mix, which creates heaviness, anxiety, and often confusion. At other times, therapists take their client's position seriously and find themselves as disempowered as the client is by it, unable to offer much help. Not taking positions seriously frees up in the therapist a knowing that has nothing to do with thinking. It is a direct, intuitive knowing that simply sees what is there. This "seeing" can just as well be called "feeling." It is very intimate and touches what it sees/feels directly. Empathy is intrinsic to it. Not taking positions opens up space for this knowing to spontaneously arise. The self that affirms no positions but "comes from" nonduality expresses it.

✳

Thinking and talking are kinds of doing. But there is another kind of doing that, as therapists, we feel even more compelled to do, and that is helping our clients. As "nondual therapists," we understand that nondual presence cannot be made to happen, that clients cannot be made to "go into" it. But if we cannot at least facilitate its happening, if we cannot at least gently invite our clients to join us in "going into" nondual presence, what good are we as therapists? Especially, what good are we as practitioners of "nondual psychotherapy"? These are compelling questions, and writers on the topic seem to fall on one or the other side of a divide in answering them.

Some say yes, we can do something to facilitate nondual awareness and presence in our clients. Others say "no," there is nothing that can or need be done because nondual awareness is always present, and doing something to bring it about only sets up a duality. This controversy is as old as the spiritual traditions that first introduced nonduality as an idea and a practice. In the context of those traditions, the controversy typically centers round the question of whether awakening is spontaneous and unconditional and thus not dependent on practice, or whether awakening is a matter of gradual attainment and thus something that can be cultivated by practice. *The Sacred Mirror* (Prendergast et al., 2003), to which the present volume is a sequel, offered compelling takes on this issue on both sides. On the "practice" side, for example, John Prendergast suggested that clients can be engaged in a kind of eye-gazing he calls "sacred mirroring," which "tends to welcome presence into the foreground of awareness for both client and therapist" (p. 90). On the same side, Sheila Krystal offered that EMDR reprocessing can "naturally recondition the client around the universal themes of impermanence," etc. which increases the possibility for the emergence of nondual awareness. (pp. 122–23) Finally, Stephen Bodian suggested that forms of spiritual inquiry can be, and have been, used as teaching techniques in nondual wisdom traditions (pp. 233–43).

Others in the volume side with "no practice." For example, Dorothy Hunt states, "What is awake and aware does not require years on the meditation cushion… In fact, it cannot be acquired and it cannot be lost. It does not come and go with states of mind" (p. 167). In a therapy that expresses nondual awareness, Dan Berkow says, "there is no demand that a client change, stay the same, move to a different psychological space, nor retain the present sense of one's place and image" (p. 193). Adyashanti in the same volume appeared to side with "no practice." He was asked repeatedly (pp. 79, 86) what if anything therapists can do to help facilitate people to awaken, and his answer was that it is not the job of the therapist (or anyone else, including himself) to wake people up. The job (his and perhaps ours as well), he said, is to be oneself (pp. 79, 89–87).

Who is right? Let's say, everybody is, and nobody is (and I am not sure even this is right!). The interesting thing about this controversy is that no matter how the dividing line is drawn, for example between the "gradual enlightenment" schools of Buddhism (e.g., Soto Zen or Theravada) and the "sudden enlightenment" schools (e.g., Rinzai Zen and some schools of Tibetan Buddhism), the lines of the controversy are redrawn within each side of the divide, and the debate continues unabated. Those who believe that awakening is guaranteed by doing the practice correctly and patiently may find that their efforts come to naught. Yet those who believe that no practice or "facilitating" is necessary or even possible cannot help but practice and "facilitate." My Rinzai Zen fellow practitioners did not believe that practice can "get them to" enlightenment; nevertheless, they kept practicing. And the Roshi taught us even as he kept telling us that he had nothing to teach. After a grueling *sesshin*, we sometimes mused about this paradox. At some point, it seems wiser to call what we did nonpractice (an option favored by Fenner in *The Sacred Mirror*). But to talk about nonpractice or nontherapy does nothing to ease the discomfort of the paradox, the red-hot iron ball that one can neither swallow nor spit out.

There seems to be no solution to this controversy, and I must confess that I am not unhappy about this state of affairs. As a final remark, let me simply say that paradox is an antidote to seriousness, and so a gateway to openness and humility. Awareness of paradox can be a powerful cure for the therapist's professional countertransference—his or her seriousness about him or herself as a therapist. As therapists, we often cannot help but "try to do something" for our clients, cannot help but facilitate nondual awareness in them. But if we recognize what we are doing with full awareness of the red-hot iron ball stuck in our throats, we may just burst out in laughter.

ENDNOTES

1.   Please see *The Sacred Mirror*, p. 255.

2.   See Hunt, in *The Sacred Mirror,* p. 181.

EXPERIENCING THE UNIVERSE AS YOURSELF

THE NONDUALITY OF SELF AND SOCIETY

David Loy

There is a line a famous Zen master wrote at the time he became enlightened which reads: "When I heard the temple bell ring, suddenly there was no bell and no I, just sound." In other words, he no longer was aware of a distinction between himself, the bell, the sound, and the universe. This is the state you have to reach....

Stated negatively, it is the realization that the universe is not external to you. Positively, it is experiencing the universe as yourself.

—Yasuntani Haku-un[1]

THE NONDUALITY OF SELF AND OTHER

If the sense of self is a construct, so is the external world, for each implies the other and they are results of the same mental discrimination. When there is no inside, there is no outside. In the *Sokushinzebutsu* ("Our mind is the Buddha") fascicle of the *Shobogenzo*, Dogen described his own experience by quoting the Chinese master Yang-shan (d. 916): "I came to realize clearly that mind is nothing other than mountains, rivers and the great wide earth, the sun, the moon and the stars." If our usual sense of separation from mountains, etc., is a delusion, then our nonduality with them is not something that needs to be attained. There has never been a discrete self. That delusion merely needs to be dispelled, and one way to do that is to concentrate on something so wholeheartedly that the sense of a separate "I" that is *doing it* evaporates. This approach is implied by Dogen in *Genjo-koan,* the first fascicle of his *Shobogenzo:*[2]

> To study the buddha way is to study the self. To study the self is
> to forget the self. To forget the self is to be actualized by myriad
> things. When actualized by myriad things, your body and mind
> as well as the bodies and minds of others drop away. No trace of
> realization remains, and this no-trace continues endlessly.

"Forgetting oneself" is how we lose our sense of separation
and realize that we are not other than the world. Meditation (e.g.,
zazen) is learning to forget the sense-of-self, which happens when
"I" become absorbed into "my" meditation-exercise. If sense-of-self
is a result of consciousness reflecting back upon itself in an attempt
to grasp itself, such meditation practice makes sense as an exercise in
de-reflection. Consciousness *un*learns trying to grasp itself, real-ize
itself, objectify itself. Awakening occurs when the usually automa-
tized reflexivity of consciousness ceases, which is experienced as a
letting-go and falling into the void. "Men are afraid to forget their
minds, fearing to fall through the Void with nothing to stay their
fall. They do not know that the Void is not really void, but the realm
of the real Dharma."[3] When I no longer strive to make myself real
through things, I find myself "actualized" by them: awakened to the
possibilities they provide.

Such a nondual experience does not transcend the world except
in the sense that it reveals what that world is when there is no attachment to particular things—especially myself—within it. If mind is
"mountains, rivers, earth, the sun, the moon and the stars," this mind
is nothing other than your mind and my mind insofar as they are absolute in the original etymology of the term: un-conditioned. Meditative techniques decondition the mind from its tendency to secure
itself by circling in familiar ruts (recurring thoughts, feelings, dispo-
sitions, etc.), thus freeing it to become anything. The most-quoted
line from the *Diamond Sutra* encapsulates this in one phrase: "Let
mind come forth without fixing it anywhere."

An example of Zen koan practice is helpful here. In the Zen lineage I am most familiar with, a first koan such as Joshu's Mu is treated

somewhat like a mantram. Putting all one's attention into "muuu…" (repeated silently during breath exhalations) undermines the sense-of-self by letting-go of the reflective mental processes that sustain it. At the beginning of such practice, one attempts to concentrate on "muuu…" but inevitably distractions arise such as thoughts, feelings, memories, desires, etc. A later, more focused stage is when one can concentrate on "muuu…" without losing it: "muuu…" effectively keeps other thoughts, etc., away. The stage when "both inside and outside naturally fuse" occurs when there is no longer the sense of an "I" that is repeating an objective sound; there is only "muuu…" This stage is sometimes described by saying that now "muuu…" is doing "muuu…": it is "muuu…" that sits, walks, eats, and so forth. At this point the teacher may help by cutting the last thread: an unexpected action, such as a blow or shout or even a few quiet words, may startle the student into letting-go. "All of a sudden he finds his mind and body wiped out of existence, together with the koan. This is what is known as 'letting go your hold.'"[4] One classical Chan story tells how Kuei-shan Ling-yu (771–853) was awakened by the sound of a pebble striking bamboo. When the practice is ripe, the shock of an unexpected sensation can help it penetrate to the very core of one's empty sense of being—that is, it can be experienced nondually.[5]

The primary ethical implication of this deconstruction is the realization that my life and destiny cannot be extricated from that of "others" in the world. Responsibility for others arises naturally as the expression of genuine awakening. Contrary to popular belief, bodhisattvas do not postpone their own enlightenment; helping others is how they perfect their enlightenment. To help others is to help myself, for no one is really saved until we are all saved. Liberation means forgetting one's own *dukkha* ("suffering, dis-ease") only to wake up in, or *one with*, a world full of *dukkha*. This experience is not sympathy or empathy but com-passion, "suffering with." What will the meaning of life be for such a person, freed from our usual narcissistic self-preoccupation? The career of the bodhisattva is helping others, not because one "ought to," but because one is not separate from one's situation and through oneself that situation draws forth a response to meet its needs.

THE NONDUALITY OF SELF AND LACK

That the sense-of-self is a construct has many other psychological implications. Although psychotherapy has achieved much insight into the dynamics of our mental *dukkha* (repression, transference, etc.), the Buddhist denial of self arguably points more directly at the root of the problem: not dread of death, finally—a fear still keeps the feared thing at a distance by projecting it into the future—but the more immediate and terrifying (because quite valid) suspicion that *"I" am not real right now*. If the self is a delusive construct, there is a subtle yet significant distinction between fear of death and fear of the void: Our deepest anxiety is our own groundlessness, which we become aware of as a sense of *lack* that motivates our compulsive attempts to ground ourselves, in one way or another. This gets at what is most distinctive about the Buddhist path: At the heart of our *dukkha* is our *anatta* (selflessness).

Dukkha is usually translated as "suffering," but everything we usually identify as suffering—including being separated from those we want to be with, and stuck with those we don't want to be with—is included in the first type of *dukkha*, and there are two other types. The second type is the *dukkha* due to impermanence: the realization that, although I might be enjoying this ice cream cone right now, it will soon be finished. The best example, of course, is our awareness of inevitable death, which often haunts our appreciation of life.

The third type of *dukkha* is more difficult to understand. It is the *dukkha* due to "conditioned states" *(sankhara)*, which refers to the lack of a self, the fact that my sense of self is a construction and therefore ungrounded. This ungroundedness is like a hole at the core of my being. It is usually experienced as a sense of lack that tends to be a source of continual frustration because it can never be filled up. No matter how hard I try, my sense-of-self never becomes a real self.

Sakyamuni Buddha did not use psychoanalytic terms, but our understanding of *anatta* can benefit from the concept of repression and what Freud described as the return of the repressed in symbolic form. If something (a mental wish, according to Freud) makes me uncomfortable and I do not want to cope with it consciously, I can choose to ignore or "forget" it. This allows me to concentrate on something else, yet what has been repressed tends to return to consciousness, irrupting in obsessive ways as symptoms. Existential psychologists have argued that our primary repression is the awareness that we are going to die. *Anatta* implies a slightly different perspective.

Buddhist doctrines analyze the sense-of-self into sets of impersonal mental and physical processes, whose interaction creates the illusion of self-consciousness—i.e., that consciousness is the attribute of a self. Yet our consciousness is more like the surface of the sea, dependent on unfathomable depths that it can never grasp because it is a manifestation of them. The problem is that this conditioned consciousness wants to ground itself, to make itself (feel) more real.

The consequence of its perpetual failure to do so is that the sense-of-self is always shadowed by a sense-of-lack, which it always tries to escape. The return of the repressed in the distorted form of a symptom shows us how to link this basic yet hopeless project with the symbolic ways we usually try to make ourselves real in the world. We experience our sense of lack as the feeling that "there is something wrong with me," but that feeling manifests, and we respond to it, in many different ways. The tragedy of all our objectifications, however, is that no amount of X can ever be enough if it is not really X that we want. When we do not understand what is actually motivating us—because what we think we need is only a symptom of something else—we end up compulsive.

Then the neurotic's anguish and despair are not the result of his symptoms, but their source. Those symptoms are necessary to shield him from the tragedies that the rest of us are better at repressing: death, meaninglessness, groundlessness. "The irony of man's condition is that the deepest need is to be free of the anxiety of death and annihilation [read lack]; but it is life itself which awakens it, and so we must shrink from being fully alive."[6] If the autonomy of self-consciousness is a delusion that can never quite shake off its shadow-feeling that "something is wrong with me," it will need to rationalize that sense of inadequacy somehow.

The *lack* of *anatta* shifts our focus from the terror of future annihilation to the anguish of a groundlessness experienced here and now. On this account, even fear of death and desire for immortality symbolize something else, becoming symptomatic of our vague intuition that the ego-self is not a hard core of consciousness but a mental construction, the axis of a web spun to hide the void.

Developmentally, the sense of self is internalized in childhood largely from others' views of us, and we remain acutely vulnerable to the opinions of others. This means that our quest to become real usually takes the form of attempts to gain others' approval or submission: the desire to show off one's money and possessions, or become famous, or gain power over others, etc. To be famous is not just to be loved by many anonymous people, as Freud put it; it is to (hope to) feel more real because our existence is acknowledged by so many others. The same applies to "status symbols." Many of the people who own a Lexus car want one not just because it is such a fine car; they want to be recognized as the kind of person who drives a Lexus. In this way consumerist desires feed on our basic insecurity, which according to Buddhism is susceptible only to a spiritual solution, because it ultimately derives from an uncomfortable intuition of our ungroundedness.

Since for Buddhism there was no original sin and no divine expulsion from a prelapsarian paradise, this situation turns out to be paradoxical: Our worst problem is the deeply repressed fear that our groundlessness/no-thing-ness is a problem. When I stop trying to fill up that hole at my core by vindicating or real-izing myself in some symbolic way, something can happen to it, as in the earlier example of working on the *mu* koan.

The sense-of-self cannot eliminate the sense-of-lack that inevitably haunts it, but from an awakened point of view I am already grounded in the totality. Buddhism implies that I am groundless and ungroundable insofar as delusively feeling myself to be separate from the world; yet I have always been fully grounded insofar as I am interdependent with the world. With that conflation, the no-thing at my core is transformed from a sense of lack into a serenity that is imperturbable because there is no-thing to be perturbed. A mind that seeks to ground itself by fixating on something dooms itself to perpetual dissatisfaction, for the impermanence of all things means no such perch can be found. But since it is our sense of lack that compels us to seek such a perch, the end of our lack allows a change of perspective. The alienation of a reflexive sense-of-self always trying to fixate itself turns into the freedom of an absolute mind that can become anything insofar as it does not need to become something.[7]

THE NONDUALITY OF SELF AND SOCIETY

What, if anything, does the spiritual process described above have to do with social issues? Doesn't it imply that social problems are just projections of our own dissatisfaction? Unfortunately, it's not so simple. Since most of us haven't realized our true nature, we are preoccupied with our *dukkha*/lack, and even as we tend to form collective selves, we also tend to "group" our sense of lack.

In fact, many of our social problems can be traced back to a deluded sense of collective self, a "we-ego" or "wego" such as one's own race, class, gender, nation (the primary secular god of the modern world), religion, or some combination thereof. In each case, a collective identity is created by discriminating one's own group from another group. And with these wegos, like the ego, the "inside" is opposed to the other "outside," which makes conflict inevitable, not only because of competition with other groups, but because the socially constructed nature of all group identity means that one's own group can never feel secure enough. For example, our GNP is not big enough; our nation is not powerful ("secure") enough; we are not technologically developed enough. If these are instances of group-lack, however, our GNP can never be big enough, our military can never be powerful enough, and we can never have enough technology. This means, therefore, that trying to solve our economic, political, and ecological problems with more of the same is a deluded response.

It is ironic that institutionalized religion often tends to reinforce this sense of group self, because religion at its best encourages us to understand and subvert the destructive dualism between self and other, between collective self and collective other. This kind of nondual universalism—or, better, nondiscrimination—which does not involve privileging us over them, provides the basis for Buddhist social action. Yet in some ways our situation today is quite different from that of Shakyamuni Buddha. Today we have not only more powerful scientific technologies but also much more powerful institutions.

The problem with such institutions is that they *tend to take on a life of their own as new types of wego*. Consider, for example, how a big corporation works. To survive in a competitive market, it must adapt to the constraints built into that market. Even if the CEO of a multinational company wants to be socially responsible, he or she is limited by the expectations of stockholders and Wall Street analysts; if profits are threatened by his sensitivity to social concerns, he is likely to lose his job. Such corporations are new forms of *impersonal* collective self, which are very good at preserving themselves and increasing their power, quite apart from the personal motivations of the individuals who serve them. This suggests that the response of a socially engaged Buddhism must become somewhat different, too. We are challenged to find new ways to address the institutionalized forms of *dukkha* they now create and reinforce.

There is another Buddhist principle that can help us explain this connection between *dukkha* and collective selves: the *three roots of evil*, also known as the three poisons. Instead of emphasizing the duality between good and evil, Buddhism distinguishes between wholesome and unwholesome (*kusala/akusalamula*) tendencies. The main sources of unwholesome behavior—the three roots of evil— are greed, ill will, and delusion. To end *dukkha*, these three need to be transformed into their positive counterparts: greed into generosity, ill will into loving-kindness, delusion into wisdom.

The important question for engaged Buddhism is: Do the three roots of evil also work impersonally and structurally, in modern institutions?

It seems to me that our economic system institutionalizes greed in at least two ways: corporations are never profitable enough, and people never consume enough. To increase profits, we must be conditioned into finding the meaning of our lives in buying and consuming. Such an economic system is based on a historically conditioned worldview that views the earth as resources, human beings as labor, and money as capital to be used for producing more capital. This process has become circular: It is self-reinforcing, and it has, it can have, no end except more and more of the same thing. Everything else, including the environment, employment, and quality of life, tends to become subordinated to this anonymous demand for ever more profit and growth, a goal-that-is-never-satisfied.

I think the best example of institutionalized ill will is militarism. If we include all the military expenses hidden in nonmilitary budgets, the United States now spends as much on its military as the rest of the world combined, and while social expenditures are being cut, the military budget continues to grow each year. Imperialist adventures such as the second Iraq War, based on lies and propaganda, quickly became disastrous, while the "war on terror" has made us less secure, because every "terrorist" killed or tortured leaves many grieving relatives and friends who have reason to hate the U.S.

Each of us lives inside an individual bubble of delusions, which distorts our perceptions and expectations. We also dwell together within a much bigger bubble that determines the ways we collectively understand the world and ourselves. If we understand the third collective problem as *institutionalized ignore-ance*, it helps us see that modern life in all developed (or "economized") nations is organized in a way that works to conceal the *dukkha* it causes. The system inflicts *dukkha* on all of us, but most of all on people whom we do not perceive and therefore do not need to think about. Thanks to clever advertising and peer pressure, my son can learn to crave Nike shoes and Gap shirts without ever wondering about how they are made. I can satisfy my coffee and chocolate cravings without any awareness of the social conditions and environmental situation of the farmers who grow those commodities for me. In fact, without some serious effort on my part, I may never face the relationship between my addictions and the often destructive monocultural agriculture that makes them possible. My son and I are encouraged to live in a self-enclosed cocoon of hedonistic consumption.

Realizing the nature of these institutional poisons is just as important as any personal realization one might have as a result of spiritual practice. In fact, any individual awakening we may have remains incomplete until it is supplemented by such a "social awakening." In both cases, what is needed is a greater awareness that goes beyond the limitations of ego- and wego-consciousness. Usually we think of expanded consciousness in individual terms, but today we must penetrate through the veils of collective delusion to attain greater understanding of dualistic social, economic, and ecological realities.

If this parallel between individual ego-lack and group wego-lack holds, it is difficult to avoid the conclusion that the great social, economic, and ecological crises of our day are also *spiritual* challenges, which therefore call for a response that is (at least in part) also spiritual. This is a challenge that cannot be evaded: Can we find or create therapies that address these larger collective forms of suffering and delusion?

ENDNOTES

1. *The Three Pillars of Zen,* ed. Philip Kapleau (Tokyo: Weatherhill, 1966), pp. 107, 137.

2. *Moon in a Dewdrop,* ed. Kazuaki Tanahashi (San Francisco: North Point Press, 1985), p. 70.

3. Huang-po, in *The Zen Teaching of Huang Po,* trans. John Blofeld (London: Buddhist Society, 1958), p. 41.

4. Hakuin, quoted in D. T. Suzuki, *Zen Buddhism* (New York: Anchor, 1956), p. 148. For more on this process, see Yasutani's "Commentary on the Koan Mu," in *The Three Pillars of Zen,* pp. 71–82.

5. For more on this process, see David Loy, "A Zen Cloud? Comparing Zen Koan Practice with The Cloud of Unknowing," *Buddhist-Christian Studies* 9 (January 1990).

6. Ernest Becker, *The Denial of Death* (New York: Free Press, 1973), p. 66.

7. For more on this, see David Loy, *Lack and Transcendence: The Problem of Death and Life in Psychotherapy, Existentialism, and Buddhism* (Atlantic Highlands, NJ: Humanities Press, 1996).

WALKING THE TALK

THE PRINCIPLES AND PRACTICES OF EMBODIED SPIRITUALITY

Mariana Caplan

There is no question that there is an unseen world. The problem is how far is it from midtown and how late is it open?

—Woody Allen

I was twenty-four years old when I arrived in India for the first time. I had only a one-way ticket, a change of clothes, my journal, and a small handful of cash. Not an Indian rupee nor a guidebook to my name. My sole intention for that trip was to learn to listen to, and follow, the true voice of the heart. Even at that time I had done enough spiritual practice and psychological work to understand that not every voice that came from within was the voice of the heart. That there were, as Russian mystic G. I. Gurdjieff taught, multiple "I's" within each of us. I knew the true voice of the heart had near-doubles, imitations, and even outright sabotaging impostors as well as sincere but unobjective aspects of the self that did their best to provide spiritual guidance from within but whose voice still did not represent the innermost voice of the heart.

Yet even armed with that awareness, what I could not have appreciated so early in my spiritual search was the immensity of the task before me—that I must learn not only to access the true voice of the heart, but to then integrate that understanding into the body on a cellular level, into the deep grooves of psychological conditioning, into all aspects of daily life. To integrate that nondual source of wisdom into every microfiber of dualistic expression. I could not have imagined then that the mere insight into nondual reality—as awe-inspiring and life-changing as it is—was merely the beginning of the spiritual journey rather than its completion. That I could not and would not be satisfied until I could find a way to integrate that nondual wisdom such that it would gradually transmute all aspects of my experience—from intimate relationships and friendships, to sexuality, to child raising, to my relationship with the environment. I simply could not have known what such an integration would require. How potent and stubborn our mental habits and repetitive thought-forms are; how deeply the conditioning of karma, psychology, and a society based on ignorance, scarcity, and fear had worked its way into the cellular structure of the body. To *embody* my nondual insight and experience would be no small task.

Since that first trip to India, a great deal has transpired. I have engaged over a decade of discipleship with my own spiritual teacher, Lee Lozowick, who is a master at revealing the countless forms of self-deception we encounter on the spiritual path, ranging from spiritual narcissism to erroneous notions of enlightenment, to a collectively mistaken notion of the goal of spiritual life itself (Caplan, 1999). I have done extensive research into the movement of contemporary spirituality in the Western world, and interviewed many of the greatest teachers, mystics, and scholars in the field, as well as countless spiritual aspirants. As a result of my research and of working as a spiritual counselor with clients and teaching at several spiritually oriented universities in the U.S., I have found myself privy to an uncommon body of spiritual data—what we might call "the underbelly of enlightenment." The kind of spiritual gossip that would make any serious aspirant of the path quiver in their shoes if they took it seriously and realized that absolutely nobody, including themselves, is exempt from such spiritual shortcomings, and that anyone, including themselves, can fall.

I have heard harrowing tales of how some of the most admired, "enlightened" teachers of our time have abandoned their children in their pursuit of spirituality; how they have used spiritual practice to avoid human intimacy and mistreat their intimate partners, often using spiritual terminology itself to justify this dismissal (Caplan, 2002b). Scandals of sex, money, and power pervade the contemporary spiritual scene like a lewd virus that spreads undetected until it has caused irreparable damage. Nearly every time I give a public presentation, somebody approaches me and begins, "I've got a story the likes of which you have never heard...," at which time they proceed to tell me a relatively common story about how "X" teacher, a self-professed celibate, slept with countless students, claiming they were providing a "tantric initiation"; or how they cheated on their wife and had sexual relationships with the young women and men in the community; or how they forbid women in the community to have children, telling them it would cause too much attachment, or that it was impossible to raise a healthy child before one was enlightened oneself. They tell me stories of how self-proclaimed enlightened teachers manipulated their students to give them large quantities of money, or how their narcissism ran rampant and they ended up lying, cheating, and abusing their students and loved ones—whether the abuse occurred on a physical, psychological/emotional, or spiritual level. As Theravadan Buddhist teacher Jack Kornfield is fond of saying, "If you want to know how enlightened somebody is, ask their husband/wife."

So what is the real nature of the problem we are facing here? How can human beings experience great satoris, momentous breakthroughs into the nondual nature of experience, and mind-shattering mystical visions while continuing to express themselves with the same, if not greater, ignorance, arrogance, aggression, and violence that is the hallmark of Western civilization? How is it, as John Welwood wrote in *The Sacred Mirror* (2003), that "all the great attainments in the area of spiritual practice and realization, wonderful as they are, have hardly begun to transform the overall quality of human relationships on this planet, which are still driven by the most primitive of motivations and emotions" (p. 161)? Whereas mystical and nondual experiences may have a profound impact on us—perhaps the greatest of which is to initiate us into a lifelong commitment to the spiritual path—it is clear that for most people, if not everyone, accessing nondual states of consciousness is not equal to integrating them.

Therefore, instead of misinterpreting the shortcomings of spiritual teachers and spiritual practitioners either to self-righteously separate ourselves from the "spiritual sinners" who fall so low (do we know what we would *really* do if given that power?) or to justify our own disillusionment, laziness, and failure to take responsibility for our own deepest spiritual possibilities, why don't we instead engage a deep collective inquiry into the subject? Why not become passionately curious about our own personal blind spots in relationship to our own spiritual development, as well as about the shortcomings of the spiritual movement in general, so that we can work toward a new spiritual integration that will allow us to truly listen to the voice of the embodied heart? Why not dare to be part of a movement toward spiritual integration that has rarely been achieved either in ancient or modern culture? I believe that one of the greatest challenges of modern spirituality is to find a way, both individually and collectively, to integrate our spiritual insight and experience into all aspects of our daily lives, a principle and practice referred to in this essay as *embodied spirituality.*

The principle of embodiment refers to the integration within the body of all levels of mental, emotional, and spiritual development. "A fully embodied spirituality," writes Jorge Ferrer, "emerges from the creative interplay of both immanent and transcendent spiritual energies in complete individuals who embrace the fullness of human experience while remaining firmly grounded in body and earth" (Tikkun, 2006).

The Bauls of Bengal, an obscure sect of practitioners from India, describe their practice of embodied spirituality as *kaya sadhana,* which means "the practice of ultimate realization in the body in this lifetime." They say that God dwells within the body of human beings, and that the most effective way to know God is through one's own embodied experience. The call of embodied spirituality is to learn to access the truth of our own divinity, and to infuse all aspects of reality with this awakened attention—beginning with our own bodies, and extending into the greater bodies of family, community, culture, country, humanity, the earth, and the cosmos itself. Our embodiment begins with ourselves and gradually extends outward to heal the world.

Although such embodiment sounds great (who could argue with it?), for those who have given such integration an earnest attempt, or for those spiritual aspirants who have been brutally self-honest with themselves regarding how effectively they have integrated their spiritual insight into their moment-to-moment experience (the easiest place for a self-check is one's relationship with one's intimate partners and children), we see that the practice of embodiment is much easier said than done! Wouldn't it be more convenient to use the vast array of spiritual technologies available to us to transcend dualistic experience and leave our bodies? To find a way to rest in the eternal now such that we would never again have to face our past trauma? To meditate our way through the illusion of psychology and personal history?

It certainly seems that it would be simpler if such transcendence were an option, yet for most people it does not prove to be possible in any lasting way. That is why people often emerge from an extended meditation retreat feeling full of peace and serenity only to find themselves almost immediately reacting with great emotion to their partner, cursing other drivers on the highway, or regressing into familiar, self-sabotaging mental and emotional habits. Unfortunately (from ego's perspective), and fortunately (from the perspective of the need to integrate our spiritual wisdom), the areas where we have not integrated our spiritual wisdom seem to catch up with us sooner if not later.

NONDUAL INSIGHT AND THE DANGER OF SPIRITUAL BYPASSING

"Spiritual bypassing," a term coined by John Welwood, refers to the phenomenon of using spiritual ideas and practices to bypass or avoid dealing with certain personal or emotional "unfinished business," to shore up a shaky sense of self, or to belittle basic needs, feelings, and developmental tasks, all in the name of enlightenment (Welwood, 2000).

The primary arenas in which most spiritual aspirants fall unconscious, regardless of their degree of insight, boil down to money, power, and sexuality, the realm in which the fruits of our spiritual integration are expressed...or not. Jack Kornfield tells the story of returning from Asia in his late twenties as a young monk dressed in robes, finding himself in an intimate relationship, and quite shocked to see how easily his inner peace could be destabilized by the psychological challenges of human intimacy. Most spiritual teachers, if they are willing to be honest, could share a similar story, whether it relates to sexuality and intimacy, money, power, or spiritual bypassing.

Contemporary schools of body-centered psychotherapy, including Peter Levine's Somatic Experiencing and Staci Hane's Somatic and Trauma work, suggest that psychological trauma is stored in the body on a cellular level. The "trauma" they speak about applies to almost everyone in modern times, whether or not we remember any single event as the cause of our wounding. When this trauma is unhealed, it eventually catches up with us in spiritual life.

It is important to recognize that most contemporary spiritual traditions—particularly those that developed in the East, where the psychological and cultural context is entirely different—simply were not designed to penetrate the cellular, psychological wounding caused by the type of trauma that is so prevalent in Western culture. Particularly when engaging with Eastern-based spiritual technologies, as transcultural and objective as their wisdom appears to be, it is our job to see to it that this wisdom becomes integrated with the particular types of spiritual bypassing and psychological unconsciousness that we are prone to as Westerners. It is only recently that new psychotherapeutic approaches (see Lynn Marie Lumiere's essay "Healing Trauma in the Eternal Now" in *The Sacred Mirror*) have begun applying nondual spiritual approaches to the healing of trauma.

Many of the contemporary schools of Advaita Vedanta work from a "top-down" approach in which nondual states are accessed, often on the level of mind or spirit. Ideally, those insights integrate into the bodily, psychic, and psychological levels of the student's experience. Yet all too often this challenging integration does not occur. Because many of these schools offer a path of "instant enlightenment" rather than a more gradual approach, there is a tendency to presume enlightenment at the first hint of awakening (Caplan, 1999). In addition, many do not educate their students on the importance of formal spiritual and psychological practices to prepare the body and psyche to integrate the tremendous energetic "voltage" that such states bring with them. Consequently, the body is unprepared to assimilate and integrate the experience. There will always be "fast-food" seekers of spirituality who want a quick fix, and "half-baked" teachers (most of whom are well meaning) who are all too eager to give it to them. The powerful spiritual "technologies," such as many of the popular neo-Advaita approaches offer, easily lend themselves to this fast-food approach.

Furthermore, when an individual experiences a nondual state, the illusory nature of psychological constructs and relative reality is temporarily apparent. However, because such states are highly transitory, what is often left of the experience is a memory of the realization. This memory can be useful, or an impediment. If the memory serves as a reminder that most of our "problems" are largely a misperception of the mind based on conditioned constructs, rather than something true and real, or if the memory inspires us to continually open to a greater reality that exists within us, it is likely to be useful. However, what often occurs, particularly if there is not adequate awareness of the dangers of self-deception and spiritual bypassing, is that the egoic, dualistic mind co-opts the nondual insight—"adopting" its realizations of ultimate, nondual reality—and uses this knowledge to avoid dealing with the gritty, murkier aspects of relative reality.

Of course such misconceptions are not inherent in nondual wisdom itself, nor to any specific school of nondual wisdom, but arise in the context of ego's relationship to nondual perception. It is therefore critical to remain alert to the danger of spiritual bypassing in which the enlightened aspects of the individual remain blind to that which remains unillumined within them.

As a playful example, I will excerpt here part of a chapter from my forthcoming book, *Pandora's Secret* (this was also published in *Radical Spirit*, 2002). The passage is based on a satire written about my experience with spiritual men—whom I referred to as "Zen boyfriends"—I met in my early twenties. A Zen boyfriend, in this context, is defined as "a man who skillfully uses spiritual practices and ideals as an excuse for his terror of, and refusal to be in, any type of real relationship with a woman."

By the time he got back from two years of satsang in India, Jake thought he had become enlightened, though he wouldn't have dared to say as much. He had become a student of one of those Indian teachers who skillfully create mystical experiences in their groupies by temporarily cutting through their psychological blocks to union and then declaring them enlightened. The master gets a swollen head and an immense reputation for being able to enlighten people, and thousands of Western hippies who haven't begun to face their own darkness believe they have risen above it and then proceed without solicitation to try to bestow the same boon upon others. Jake was a living example.

The first night was all right, as far as Zen boyfriends went. I enjoyed hearing of his adventures over a cappuccino, only occasionally irritated by his references to having "seen through the nature of reality" or having "become one with everything." Of course, by early evening he needed space, which meant that his new unity with everything precluded union with me. It was a hauntingly familiar story.

The next day, as we walked in Muir Woods in meditative silence at his request, my patience with his spiritual game ran out. I tried the direct approach. "Jake, if we're going to hang out together I need to feel like you're really here with me and not always so detached."

"But who is the 'you' who wants to hang out with the 'me'?" he queried in response, refusing my invitation to descend from the nondual universe he had convinced himself he was inhabiting to a place where we might have a real conversation.

"*I* am the me and *you* are the you!"

"There is no difference, so we can never really be apart or together it's all the same."

"You're full of shit."

"But who do you think is the 'me' that is full of shit?"

"I think it's YOU!"

"Who's getting angry?"

"*I'm* getting angry."

"Look into my eyes, what do you see?"

"You."

"Look more deeply. Now what do you see?"

"I see a lonely man who thinks he's enlightened." Frustrated and teary-eyed, I walked away and sat on a log by the stream trying to figure out why I kept attracting these men.

He followed, and sat down beside me, oblivious to having discounted my plea for relationship in the name of spirituality. "Why did you come all the way over here to cry?"

I give him an end-of-the-relationship look. "Because there was no one there to hold me if I cry, and I'd just as soon cry alone than cry with nobody."

Access to spiritual truth, when not integrated, is a very dangerous weapon. We cannot assume that simply because we have had profound spiritual illumination, the darkness within us—however illusory we have perceived it to be from our state of realization—has dissipated. If we do not learn to manage our psychology, our psychology will continue to manage us. I believe that the primary value of nondual insight is discovered when that perception is integrated into the dualistic world. Why? Because duality—the world of manifestation and form—is simply one expression of the nondual.

THE INSEPARABILITY OF NONDUALITY AND DUALITY

Ngakpa Chogyam, a Tibetan Buddhist teacher from Wales, explains that nonduality, or emptiness, has two facets: One is the empty, or nondual, and the other is form, or duality. Therefore, duality is not illusory, but rather one *aspect* of nonduality. Like the two sides of a coin, the formless reality has two aspects—one is form, the other is formless (personal interview, 2002). When we perceive duality as separate from nonduality (or nonduality as separate from duality), we do not engage the world of manifestation from a perspective of clarity, and thereby we fall into an erroneous relationship with it. From this perspective it is not "life" that is *maya,* or illusion; rather it is our relationship to the world that is illusory.

The teachings of the inseparability between nonduality and duality are found in many traditions. The *Heart Sutra,* the most well-known sutra of Mahayana Buddhism, states that "matter is not different from emptiness, and emptiness is not different from matter. Matter is emptiness and emptiness is matter."

Similarly, the *Pratyabhijnahridayam,* one of the doctrines of Kashmir Shaivism, states, "The Lord has the universe for a body." In Hindu tradition, the *lingam* is a phallic symbol that represents Lord Shiva, or the masculine principle of formless truth. It sits at the base of a *yoni,* which is roughly shaped like a vagina and represents Shakti, or the feminine principle of manifestation. Together they represent the point of enlightenment.

Therefore, the great nondual insight of oneness is, in its optimal expression, simultaneously the insight of oneness that pervades all duality. In *Wearing the Body of Visions,* Ngakgpa Chogyam writes, "The limitless multiplicity of the world of form is seen as providing limitless opportunities for the realization of non-duality: emptiness is presented *through* form" (p. 172). In *The Sacred Mirror* (2003), John Welwood affirms:

> Letting the relative be as it is, then, reveals the absolute. Thus there is no need to give absolute being a special status apart from the relative process of form evolving in time, for these are inseparable. Realizing this frees us up to move fluidly between engaging with our experience and discovering its spacious indefinable nature, without regarding either side as more real than the other. There is no need to set up any divide between duality and nonduality. (p.154)

In contemporary times, when human beings are collectively manifesting a world dominated by greed, violence, and the capacity for self-destruction, we can no longer afford to keep our spiritual insight on the transcendental mountaintop, but are instead called to penetrate and transmute the dualistic world of form and manifestation with the diamond perception of nonduality.

THE QUESTION OF INTEGRATION

There is no one formula for how integration occurs. Every human being has distinct karma and an inimitable psychospiritual composition. Therefore, whereas there may be general patterns through which integration occurs, the precise process through which any given human being becomes spiritually integrated is necessarily unique. The truly integrated human being—who has assimilated and embodied a profound level of spiritual realization such that it penetrates all aspects of her life—is the rarest among human beings, and of the few who have neared this goal, each has had his or her own unique unfolding. Still, I believe that such integration marks the evolution of spiritual culture that awaits us, and thus it is important to engage a collective inquiry to explore various approaches and theories of psychospiritual integration.

Many of the new schools of nondual wisdom advocate what they call a "waking down" approach. Through various techniques, the spiritual teacher, or therapist, aids the student or client to perceive nondual awareness. Through this help, the student or client accesses a distinct vantage point from which he may perceive important aspects of spiritual truth, including: 1) the empty, or nonexistent, nature of the "I" who believes himself to have difficulties; 2) the nature of the conditioned mind that creates stories and histories that are, in essence, highly subjective; 3) the transitory nature of all experience. The benefits of this powerful, ancient approach—particularly in its new application to Western psychotherapies—are numerous and well documented throughout this book and its accompanying volume, *The Sacred Mirror*. Its primary danger, as discussed earlier, involves often subtle and undetected forms of spiritual bypassing that easily arise in individuals who are not well grounded, who have a tendency to dissociate from their bodies, and who do not have a reliable, external source of spiritual guidance and feedback.

On the far other end of the spectrum we find most of the more common forms of psychotherapy: therapies that focus strictly on the "stuff" of life, the contents of consciousness. These therapies boldly take on the great mire of the mind, the labyrinth of personal history, the land mines of trauma, the endless wounds of confusion and pain that mark our personal past. Such therapies endeavor to unwind the knots of the deep psyche one by one, or at best in small groupings.

The dangers inherent in these types of therapies are numerous, and quite familiar to many of us who have experienced them. One can remain forever mired in the contents of mind and psyche—endlessly seeking to disentangle a dualistic universe that has at its essence no substance. To attempt to work with the contents of consciousness, especially to try to "heal" them without having any experiential knowledge of what consciousness is, will necessarily lend itself to countless errors and misperceptions. Similar to the medicines that treat symptoms only without understanding or addressing the underlying causes of the illness itself, traditional psychotherapies often fail to address the core issues of consciousness itself and are therefore limited by their very nature.

My personal approach—both in my own transformational process as well as in my work with clients—lies somewhere between these diverse perspectives and is characterized by a principle that my spiritual teacher, Lee Lozowick, termed *enlightened duality,* defined as "the realization of nonduality as expressed in and through the body and the full expression of all of life, experiencing and enjoying it as it is, without identification." The *context* of enlightened duality is nondual awareness, while its *content* is duality.

From the perspective of enlightened duality, the key to effectively working with all the "stuff" of this world without getting caught in the mire of it is an abiding awareness of the nondual nature of all manifest phenomena. Whereas perhaps the nondual perspective is not available to the practitioner at all times, it has been glimpsed powerfully enough so that the individual's *context* of enlightened perception becomes increasingly grounded and stabilized. Thus, while the practitioner of enlightened duality goes about her day, the world of duality and manifestation is engaged fully, including whatever emotion, neurosis, effort, struggle, or joy arises. Nothing is denied as illusory, prematurely transcended, or "spiritualized" away; yet, bringing nondual awareness to the moment has an enormous impact on the clarity that the individual can express in any given situation.

Enlightened duality works with all the gritty, neurotic, profane, and imagined "unspiritual" aspects of our experience, yet views all experience from the context of oneness. Thus it is similar to the "top-down" approaches of contemporary schools of nondual wisdom in its adherence in nondual truth. It differs from these approaches in that it does not directly evoke nondual experience through teaching or technique, but instead this awareness serves as a silent, prevalent context from which the ordinary stuff of life is considered. When enlightened duality is applied to therapy, the nondual perspective is transmitted to the client through the energy or awareness of the therapist such that spiritual insight arises naturally within the client's own awareness, even though spiritual theory and technique may never be mentioned.

The primary danger of enlightened duality is that by focusing so much on duality and manifestation one can fall into the trap of presuming he or she is abiding in a nondualistic context when in fact he or she has fallen prey to a divided perception of reality. Whereas all practitioners of spirituality are subject to the dangers of spiritual bypassing, I believe that enlightened duality is less prone to this danger than many of the popular schools of neo-Advaita Vedanta.

THE PRACTICE OF ACCEPTANCE

The practice of *acceptance* is perhaps the most potent tool with which to unfold an embodied, passionate, bright, truthful relationship to ourselves and all of life. "To accept is the most powerful weapon. There is no weapon indeed for having the realization of truth that is more powerful than this: to accept oneself," said Swami Prajnanpad (unpublished transcript). John Welwood's article "Double Vision," in *The Sacred Mirror,* refers to this great Indian master, now deceased, who recontextualized the psychological vision put forth by Sigmund Freud in the 1920s within the context of nonduality.

Swami Prajnanpad taught that enlightenment is not separate from anything else that is. Therefore, to abide in oneness one does not leave the world of duality to hang out in a transcendental universe of bliss and detachment, but instead he becomes "at one" with absolutely everything that arises, on every level, within oneself and outside oneself. In ceasing to separate oneself from anyone or anything, he is in complete union with everything, and thus his experience is nondual, or not two. "When you have taken everything, expanded everywhere," he writes, "then you are one" (unpublished manuscript). And then:

> Face, face, face what appears to be real, see its real nature. When you feel, it is real with you. No tricks of escaping: Have the courage to face the fact. Accept, accept, what is, never try to deny, to disown. Accept and be.

Learning to fully accept and become one with all aspects of experience—to become fully conscious of *everything*—is so vital that when somebody asked the late Tibetan Buddhist master Chogyam Trungpa Rinpoche what he did when he found himself in the hell realm, he said he tried to stay there as long as he could. To be able to stay awake, aware, and at-one-with all the dark, hidden, and unconscious aspects of oneself and of all experience is a great power and freedom. It is the power to live in truth, honesty, authenticity, and integrity in any and all circumstances, including the transition into death.

The perspective that Swami Prajnanpad offers represents an evolution in psychology. To contextualize the dynamics of the human mind from the perspective of nondual experience is the beginning of the creation of an enlightened psychology. The psychology of mind becomes transformed into the psychology of truth. I believe that modern psychology will reach its peak when it becomes one with spirituality. When it teaches us how to open up to, and become one with, all aspects of experience.

WALKING THE TALK

To fully embody and integrate spiritual wisdom, we literally have to turn toward everything in order to learn to like, but also eventually love—everything. In the most practical way, the call is to open to everything, especially that which hurts us and especially when we want to close. One of the primary purposes of spiritual life—far from our fantasies of the eternal Disneyland—is simply to learn to feel and to accept. To feel means to open toward all that is unconscious with us. This includes our denied suffering as well as the great source of hidden love that dwells within us. As we deepen our capacity to dwell within the totality of our own embodied experience, we will feel *everything* more deeply—the "dark" as well as the "light"—and we will learn to be at one with everything. This is an aspiration of great magnitude, but practiced first on the laboratory of the body, which, since we are not separate from divinity, is a precious and sacred laboratory. This practice of learning to feel, which would seem so obvious, so basic—is also totally uncommon: simply learning to feel, and then broadening that skill to heal the world.

Just prior to his enlightenment, Gautama Buddha approached the famous Bodhi Tree, circumnambulated it seven times, and sat down to meditate, resolving that "even if my blood should run dry I will not leave this seat until truth has been realized!" Renouncing the needs of his body and resisting the lures of the demon Mara—who attempted to seduce him with all that is beautiful, alluring, and pleasant as well as that which is terrifying and monstrous—he stayed in place until the clarity of enlightenment emerged from within.

In contemporary times, extended tree-sitting is not what most people need to realize the truth of their own nature. Our task is different. We have already renounced the needs of our body and repressed its wisdom. We've done so for all the wrong reasons and through very different means, including overindulgence in superficial pleasure, comfort, and food, countless mental and emotional distractions, and a pervasive disassociation from the organic rhythms, cycles, and wisdom of our bodies. In this way, we have numbed ourselves and disconnected ourselves from our deeper nature. In contemporary times, when alienation and dissociation pervade, our own body *is* the sacred Bodhi Tree that calls to us, inviting us to dwell deeply within its sanctuary, to stand unwavering in the face of the demons of self-hatred, self-denial, self-abandonment, shame, unworthiness, helplessness, and neediness until the essence of our own embodiment reveals itself and we reinhabit our bodies as our rightful home. When this happens, our blood, rather than running dry, will run hot to boiling, our bones will be infused with strength, our skin will emanate a natural radiance, and a wellspring of unshakable solidity and contentment will arise from our own source. The deep waters of our embodiment will swell and ebb with great life force, and some hint of the great Divinity will be revealed from within.

In its ultimate integration, the realization of nonduality should be no different than the realization of embodiment. If we are truly able to express our spirituality in such a way that it is no different from our daily experience, our bodies will eventually become the transmuted expression of our own integrated consciousness. The more deeply we embody our ephemeral, relative reality, the more deeply we dwell in the absolute truth of our experience.

HEALING FROM THE HEART

Embodying Nondual Wisdom

Penny Fenner

INTRODUCTION

This chapter is particularly inspired by my understanding and experience with Dzogchen, or Complete Perfection teachings in Tibetan Buddhism. It is geared for the nondual therapist, client, or practitioner seeking to more deeply embody such wisdom into their life.

The nondual traditions like Zen, Advaita Vedanta, Mahamudra, and Dzogchen point to the fact that our true nature is whole and complete, exactly as it is. The nondual experience goes beyond preference, and in its inclusiveness embraces the full breadth of feeling, thought, need, response, belief, interpretation, and sensation. Over millennia, tens of thousands of words have been written to describe what is ultimately an indescribable state of complete fulfillment. Volumes of poetry have pointed to a longing within the core of our being when there is yearning for at-one-ment with all, to be merged as One in the infinite vastness of our true being.

Even a mere glimpse of nondual reality leaves a profound imprint in one's mind and heart stream. In the moment of realizing that who and where we are is perfect, just as it is, the mind is liberated from habitual, conditioned clinging, creating healing and blissful fulfillment. This glimpse can become the porthole for a lifetime of longing to reactivate that moment of complete fulfillment. Whether this was experienced as a foretaste, or more pervasive enduring experience, we still need to know how to navigate the rapids of daily living; pay bills, manage interpersonal relationships, respond to requests and demands, and deal with the inevitable conflicts and challenges life brings.

The nondual therapist needs to be acutely aware of pitfalls on the spiritual path, staying alert to potential, personal blindness by adopting and promoting radical self-honesty. None of us can pretend to be engaged in any sort of spiritual work if we don't have a strong basis of loving-kindness rooted in our inner being. Without this often-missing dimension, our neurotic, conditioned aspects either remain suppressed or are conceptually deconstructed in the name of spiritual awareness. The embodiment of nondual wisdom requires this foundation of self-love so as to integrate the relative and absolute aspects of reality, as so clearly distinguished in Buddhism.

RELATIVE AND ABSOLUTE REALITY

The relative reality corresponds to the world that is known through our body and mind. It refers to the tangible, ordinary, everyday experience of going about our business in the phenomenal world where things have the appearance of solidity and form. The absolute or transcendent reality corresponds to the open, unmarked, and insubstantial reality that underlies the existence of everything. This nondual reality points to the essential nature of how things really are, absent of inherent substance, meaning, or form. Absolute reality is not something we can contrive or make up. It has nothing to do with our beliefs or preferences, nor is it something we can gain, acquire, or learn.

From a relative, conditioned viewpoint, we typically feel separate not only from each other but from the interdependence of all arising phenomena. When we are habitually caught in perceiving relative reality as solid, real, and absolute, we unconsciously grasp onto our preferences—be these beliefs, people, emotions, or places, to try and control our experience. Or we try to reject, escape from, that which we don't like! Whether we're holding on to or rejecting experience, suffering is the result. Instead of seeing our preferences as impermanent, arbitrary manifestations of an uneasy mind seeking solidity and control, they feel real. This constant push-pull in terms of what is happening sees us manipulate our experience in order to "get it right" in an unending search for happiness beyond the present moment.

To embody the nondual we must integrate the relative and absolute so that the clarity and spaciousness of the absolute can blend seamlessly with the complexities of living in a conditioned world. In traditional Buddhist practice this is done in two ways. When meditating we place our focus on the nature of reality in relation to the absolute by closely observing our thoughts, feelings, and perceptions as arising from spacelike awareness. We then transpose this experience in everyday life by cultivating our perceptions so as to see everything as though it is illusory. We bring our expanded meditative experience into every waking moment. As the two merge over time, we experience the spaciousness of all experience, irrespective of its content or nature. As the great Tibetan sage, Longchenpa, points out:

> *Whatever mental states and thought processes arise*
> *Never become what they seem to be.*
> *If you know that this is the situation*
> *You are free from all notions about striving.*[1]

As we look directly into the nature of what is arising to observe how it manifests and from where, we inevitably collide with the slippery paradox that what we are seeking cannot be grasped, as it seems to be arising from nothing, from nowhere. We may realize that not even this recognition can be held on to, for there is nothing solid upon which we can cling! As Tsoknyi Rinpoche instructs:

> *Don't get caught up in perceiving.*
> *Yet experience is present.*
> *While still being empty we perceive;*
> *While perceiving this perceiving is empty in essence.*
> *It is not confined to one or the other;*[2]

When we truly see how things are, shorn of imposed preference, there is nothing to do. However for as long as we avoid, suppress, or deny *any* aspect of our experience, there is work to be done.

ERRING TO AN EXTREME

If we become fixated in either the relative or the absolute, we are still trapped in dualism where one viewpoint is rejected for the other.

If we cultivate only an experience of the absolute and fail to appreciate how our thoughts, speech, feelings, and physical behavior influence our actions and future, we can lose touch with relative reality. This can leave us disillusioned or frustrated, spaced out or disconnected from others or, worse still, disassociated, potentially losing our capacity to be effective or safe in the physical world. The therapist needs to be solidly grounded in their own spaciousness, alert to pitfalls on this seductive path. If absolute reality is interpreted to mean nonexistence, it can seem like an easy way to avoid the pain of relative reality if we don't "like" the reality we are in. This can lead to irresponsibility or carelessness with others and profound self-deception.

On the other hand, if we err to the extreme of thinking that everything we perceive is real and solid, we can be stuck in such ignorance,[3] thereby blocking access to the transcendent that can liberate our conditioning.

Preferring either extreme presents a distorted view of reality as either real and solid, or empty and meaningless. From the absolute perspective, whatever we're seeking is actually empty of all existence; it is nonsolid, fleeting, a mirage or dream to which we have become attached. Only through truly meeting *whatever* is arising can we see its ultimately empty nature and so be liberated from conditioned clinging. When the ego's usual defenses and boundaries naturally dissolve, our true nature, which is none other than wisdom love, is revealed.

Without loving-kindness we typically become defensive against the pain of relative reality, keeping us deluded and trapped.

STRONG FOUNDATION

Being human grants us the capacity to experience deep emotions and feelings. Recognizing the absolute nature of reality does not preclude or remove this. In fact, being open to all that is, can have us feel *even more deeply* because nothing is closed or blocked from our awareness. We connect with a broad spectrum of experience, emotionally, mentally, physically, and spiritually, such that nothing is barred.

To be this open demands full presence in our being, such that we are unable to ignore anything in our feelings, past, stories, hopes, fears, or memories. We meet whatever is arising, not fixated or stuck in any one experience, but real and present with "what is," here and now. Trusting, letting go, resting in the unknown with a clear, spacious mind and open heart sees us awaken to what is and always has been right here. This level of openness demands a tremendously strong foundation of self-love, courage, and strength in order to endure the vicissitudes of life without flinching. As we embrace all of who we are, we recognize the coemergence of the substantial (relative truth) and insubstantial (absolute truth). Connecting with the vast unknown of the transcendent the power of conditioned ego loses its force replaced by unconditional nonegoistic self-love that is not dependent upon outer circumstance or any condition. This wisdom love is our true nature that has always been, right here.

In the interplay between the relative and absolute resides one of many ungraspable paradoxes. For as long as the two realities are seen as being separate we are missing the point, for they are interdependent, arising within each other.

> *But before the sun entered me,*
> *the sun was in me—*
> *and also the cloud and the river.*
> *Before I entered the river,*
> *I was already in it.*
> *There has not been a moment*
> *When we have not inter-been.*[4]

SPIRITUAL MATERIALISM

During the past decade the notion of "spiritual materialism"[5] has been of continued relevance given the easy availability of nondual teachings, which appear to offer an immediate balm from suffering in the form of "instant enlightenment!" On many occasions I have seen practitioners speak of the absence and nonexistence of self in ways that reflect a misappropriation of profound concepts. For a start, enlightenment is not something we can acquire, or for that matter, lose. What's more, how can anyone attain enlightenment if there is no one, no self, going anywhere, doing anything?

Another understandable but misguided perception involves the belief that if the self does not exist, then there should only be an experience of pure bliss, signaling the ending of all suffering! If we are "resting in the spaciousness of mind" not going anywhere, what seems like "resting" may in fact simply be a preferred option to dealing with emotions stirring beneath a calm surface. This clear preference can stimulate an unconscious disconnection from the fullness of the present moment, when it is not the preferred reality.

At a subtle level, we may fear there is nothing upon which to rest if we truly let go. "It is generally fear of space, a fear that we will not be able to anchor ourselves to any solid ground, that we will lose our identity as a fixed and solid and definite thing. This can be very threatening."[6]

Some practitioners blindly strive to eradicate all negative emotions like fear, or any aspects of the ego, in the name of spiritual freedom. This misguided conception inevitably leads to the suppression, distortion, or denial of what is true. Embracing the entirety of all that we are—positive, negative, and neutral—demands an inscrutable capacity to be present to whatever arises, including fear. Radical self-honesty becomes our ally, a torch shedding light on any arising emotions that are a natural aspect of being human.

Cultivating such honesty demands that we foster heartfelt compassion toward all relative arising phenomena, be these conflicting thoughts, feelings, or emotions, as well as develop an appreciation of their inherent emptiness. If we ignore, deny, or judge any aspect of our experience, we are still trapped in dualistic thinking!

ABSENCE OF ATTACHMENT TO PREFERENCE

When we are present to things just as they are, neither suppressing our pain nor indulging it, our attachment to preferences simply dissolves. Perhaps realizing that there is no inherent form to which we can cling will shock us into the recognition that absolutely nothing is missing, broken, or needs to be fixed. And so we may be propelled out of the fundamentally dreamlike state into reality.

> *In the moment of looking we immediately see that it is empty,*
> *That there is no thing to see.*
> *There is no center and no circumference.*
> *It is wide open,*
> *A moment of being totally wide open.*
> *It is totally clear,*
> *Without even a single speck of dust.*
> *There is nothing to fix the attention on.*
> *This is called empty essence.*[7]

In this all-encompassing seeing, there is real aliveness. We are completely connected and grounded in our body, with no fixation on any one aspect of our experience. Nothing is avoided, all is felt, and there is no preference for anything to continue or stop. It simply is as it is. How things are is fundamentally perfect, flaws included. Herein we find the embodiment of the nondual.

MISGUIDED OPENNESS

Nondual therapists or practitioners need to be alert to misguided signals of openness. A practitioner's mind may seem clear when he expresses nonattachment to any particular outcome or situation. Provided he is grounded in his body and responsive to the outer world, this may not be a problem. However, signs of disconnecting from problems or difficulties, being ungrounded, will reveal itself in the way a practitioner manages emotions.

> *…we have not become vacant;*
> *Neither absentminded not spaced out—*
> *Experience or perception is not blocked.*[8]

Clear preference or overconceptualization for the absolute, coupled with a lack of bodily grounding, can show up as avoidance or disidentification with emotions. When excessive, this can stimulate varying degrees of disconnection or even disassociation. This is more common when someone has been exposed to the language and practice of the nondual, yet lacks sufficient self-love or connectedness with their body and its attendant feelings. Ignoring one's responsibilities, or displaying high levels of self-centeredness or lack of compassion for others, are classic examples where the transcendent viewpoint has been misused to justify an essentially egoistic view of the absolute! In extreme cases a practitioner may become disassociative, potentially experiencing symptoms like:

- Feeling like one is in a daze—going into a trance
- Feelings of confusion and/or disorientation
- Difficulty understanding or connecting with others
- Inability to understand others' suffering
- Depression
- Severe anxiety attacks
- Struggle to hold down work or study

These symptoms may occur when it is just too challenging to work with intense feelings like pain, grief, anger, shame, or fear; in cases of unhealed trauma, "hanging out in the absolute" can appear to be an easy "solution." I have worked with several clients who have been exposed to nondual teachings and come to me confused and upset because they feel cheated. Unable to sustain the reality of the absolute because strong emotions are manifesting, they fall into the language of the nondual in an attempt to deal with their pain. They might say: "I am not here. No one is here. There is no past. There was no abuse." While such statements may well be consistent with the language of nondual teachings when pointing to the inherent emptiness of all phenomena, self included, engaging such thoughts when there *is* pain simply offers a bypass from the challenge of being in the relative world. If there is no natural outflow of loving-kindness holding the person, then what is thought to be absolute reality risks being purely conceptual! You cannot transcend the relative if it has been bypassed!

Spiritual language may be nothing more than "mind-made concepts which they are just repeating."[9] Thinking that "there is no one here" or "there is nothing to integrate" misses the point if such words are not accompanied by wholehearted consistency in action. There is a risk of nondual language becoming a trigger in fostering irresponsibility, mental gymnastics, a distorted viewpoint, or indiscriminate awareness in the spiritual seeker.

Alert to this risk, nondual therapists and practitioners must have highly developed levels of resonating concern or compassion[10] such that our hearts are "on line." The depth of our own capacity and experience is measurable in terms of our own degree of openness to admit to how we are truly feeling, from the core of our being, whether or not we like it or think it is spiritually or socially acceptable. Only when we are open to the full spectrum of experience can we skillfully respond to *whatever* is arising, not conditioned by concepts or theories.

CASE STUDY: RACHEL

Rachel was thirty years old and prior to meeting me had been in therapy on and off since she was thirteen. The yoga teacher who referred her was unsure how to help her integrate what had become a profoundly disassociated way of being. Rachel had been sexually abused by her father and spent much of her life in orphanages and foster homes. She was highly intelligent, had begun but never finished a law degree.

For five years Rachel had received teachings in Advaita Vedanta, during which time she experienced extreme states of sheer bliss where she no longer felt that "she," her problems, or her history existed. For five years she was so blissed out she felt unable to share her experience with anyone, including her teacher; she thought her experience to be a totally sacred, private experience between her and God.

During those five years she became increasingly unable to function in the real world. She had not maintained a job or lived in the same accommodation for more than a few weeks at a time. A year before we met she had been hospitalized, unable to even feed herself.

Most therapists seemed to have given up on her, or so she said. She was extremely angry, and terrified of "losing her mind" again. She was highly mistrustful that *anyone* could help. Her nondual experience had left her ill equipped to be in the world.

It seemed to me that for Rachel, the *nonexistence of self* had provided a wonderful platform on which to disconnect from the pain of life. If she didn't exist, then none of her past or associated problems existed. For five years this way of thinking seemed to have successfully anaesthetized her from the pain of relative reality, until she lost all ability to manage this reality and ended up hospitalized.

In recent months before meeting me she had discovered orthodox Judaism, its structure and form giving her a community and a much needed sense of security. However she was still terrified of life and paralyzed by tremendous anger. She was resistant to most traditional therapy.

Knowing she had recently moved into new, shared accommodations, I focused on deepening her connection with relative reality. I suggested she create a garden to tend over the next few months. As well as this practical exercise, I led her through a simple meditation to stimulate a feeling of being stabilized and rooted to the earth like a huge old oak tree. The tree meditation helped her connect breath and body in a simple, positive way. She was guided to place her attention on simple, easily accessible feelings, images, and sensations.

Very gradually, healing began to happen. The relative world became less frightening and as a result less to be avoided. As she began to feel a deeper connection with herself, self-trust began to grow. This was a slow, cumulative process that occurred over several weeks. Small, incremental, solid steps were important.

I gave her an additional practice for cultivating loving-kindness that helped deepen the development of trust in her own basic goodness. Self-love grew. Without this self-loving foundation, what had been understood as transcendent seems to have been none other than a highly disassociated state of nonbeing.

ACCEPTING "WHAT IS"

> *The hurt you embrace becomes joy.*
> Call it to your arms where it can change. A silkworm eating
> leaves makes a cocoon. Each of us weaves a chamber of leaves
> and sticks....[11]

We cannot meet and dissolve conditioned patterns of pain, loss, fear, anger, and grief without self-love. Without loving-kindness, meeting one's pain can become masochistic, addictive, or self-destructive. We can become so lost in the relative that our pain seems more than real, our patterns solid and permanent. Instead of experiencing ego death, we become ensconced in the relative intensity of our patterns, unable to see their ultimately illusory nature.

THE ELIXIR OF LOVING-KINDNESS

In Buddhism, relative *bodhicitta* refers to the manifestation of a heartfelt desire to unselfishly avail oneself to do whatever is needed in order to remove the causes for suffering. Absolute *bodhicitta* refers to the powerful, unmitigated, direct understanding of openness, or *sunyata*, where we see things exactly as they are, thus liberating us from the trappings of conditioned preferences. When we open ourselves to the heart of *bodhicitta*, deep gentleness permeates every breath of our experience.

> *Sometimes go outside and sit*
> *In the evening at sunset,*
> *When there's a slight breeze that touches your body,*
> *And makes the leaves and the trees move gently.*
>
> *You're not trying to do anything really.*
> *You're simply allowing yourself to be,*
> *Very open from deep within,*
> *Without holding onto anything whatsoever.*
> *Don't bring something back from the past, from a memory.*
> *Don't plan that something should happen.*

Don't hold onto anything in the present.
Nothing you perceive needs to be nailed down.
Simply let experience take place, very freely,
So that your empty, open heart
Is suffused with the tenderness of true compassion.[12]

CASE STUDY: EMMANUEL

Emmanuel contacted me due to his ongoing struggle to regain the peaceful clarity of an initial "awakening" during which he had "an epiphany of experiencing pure awareness during a retreat" several years earlier and then "lost it, by grasping for it…I kept looking for that same, wonderful clear state in which nothing is lacking, to repeat itself. It did not do so."

Emmanuel's life has been consumed by the acquisition of knowledge and learning. His initial, profound experience gave him a potent taste of the transcendent leading him to subsequently read extensively in the hope that he would understand and reactivate that which cannot be grasped intellectually. The essence of two conversations by e-mail and phone follow.

First Conversation

Emmanuel: I feel so slow in learning this stuff, not because I am retarded but possibly because I overly intellectualize. It's so hard for me to let this go. I have read so much Dzogchen and Zen and attended a variety of teachings, but this has not put me back in that magical state of presence you describe in your book.[13]

Penny: The paradox here is that letting go is not something we can do! The intellect has an important part to play, but you seem to overemphasize its value rather than letting it rest so you can "simply be" with what is.

E: I know! I seem to be so far from that simple state too much of the time. I really don't think I want to be present to "what is"!

P: Do you know that what you just said presents a valuable

opportunity, if you can become present to your resistance and any upset attached to that?

E: (pause) I understand this conceptually, but if I try to do what you suggest, I still secretly want things to be other than how they are! I am thinking about my anger. How do I apply what you, and all the teachers, are saying to my anger? This is a condition I have suffered from much of my life. It is so damaging to me with all my relationships. Should I simply stop and say: "I am angry; that's just how it is." Do I just ignore the fact that my spouse then becomes angry as a result?

P: No Emmanuel, not at all. This would be a classic misconstruction of the teachings. Being with what is does not mean being indifferent, or saying "whatever" when anger arises! That would be irresponsible, showing a lack of real compassion because in truth, our actions *do* impact others; we mustn't ignore that we live in a world of relationship and interrelationship. This is where we have to go right back to basics and employ loving-kindness. Invoking loving-kindness is the key here. We need to combine the "not knowing" state you talked of before with the warmth and tenderness of loving-kindness, directing this to those parts that feel negative, hurt, angry, etc. We need discriminating wisdom to know when and how to act.

E: Okay! But I don't understand how you "do" this. Isn't the heart of nondual therapy to do nothing and just rest in uncontrived awareness? There seems to be a gap between the words you and all the others speak, and me getting it!

P: First, I think it's important to point out that nondual wisdom does not mean standing by mute or paralyzed. It is highly responsive, loving, open, and unconditional. Plus you can't have discriminating wisdom when the heart is not on line. What you end up with is simply a conceptual preference.

E: I hear you and there is still something missing! I feel frustrated.

P: Would you like to explore this more directly? In my experience such emotions and feelings can be a doorway.

E: Okay! If you think that would be helpful.

P: Let's take a moment to check in to your experience. You might like to close your eyes to focus you more directly on your emotions, your current frustration included; take some long deep breaths. (Breathes deeply several times) Where in your body are you feeling frustration? Can you use the breath as an instrument of awareness, and observe what your body feels? Let's do this together.

E: Okay. (long pause) There is an ache, around my chest. It hurts. I don't like it.

P: Can you allow yourself to stay present to that ache, without attaching any story to it?

E: It is very intense.

P: Ah, yes. By breathing gently and consciously, can you imagine surrounding this intense feeling with warmth? Like you are holding a small child.

E: (silence)

P: Can you tell me how old is this feeling? Can you attribute an age to it?

E: Yes, I feel very young—maybe six or seven.

P: Can you see the little boy who was feeling this, the little Emmanuel?

E: This is weird, but yes, I can. (Long silence. Voice quavers.) I feel so sad.

P: Yes.

E: This has been inside me for so long. I can't believe I am in tears. (long silence)

P: Does this feeling "need anything"? Does it have a voice, so to speak?

E: Kind of. It wants me to stay here, and not go away.

P: Yes. Perhaps in staying with it, you could softly soothe it by breathing warmth and loving-kindness into it, from your heart to the heart of the little boy?

E: (long silence) Hmm. It's changing. I don't know what I am feeling now. It's different.

P: Can you just be with this, just as it is?

E: Yes. It feels sweet. (long silence)

Thank you so much.

Second Conversation

E: Your thoughts and way of working have brought out another side of the awareness that, in my experience, is seldom emphasized. I recall quarreling with teachers at retreats because in my mind the idea of "naked awareness" or "one taste" sounded so hideous to me, so detestable. It sounded like I would just sit there if an intruder were raping my wife.

P: Certainly not! Can you now see that when we cultivate "discriminating wisdom," we don't become mute blobs?

E: You're right. It is different.

P: So, tell me, how are you doing?

E: I am amazed at the impact of our last conversation. I admire your expertise in knowing what buttons to push and how to do it.

P: What do you mean?

E: Well, over the years when I heard the lamas talk about compassion or opening the heart, I mostly rejected this as artificial. What you did seems to have been most helpful.

P: What are you noticing in your body and emotions right now?

E: A kind of excitement, like that of the newly converted! I probably need to be careful, right? Otherwise I may think I have arrived somewhere!

(Laughter)

E: But with that qualifier, I do think I am truly more open and can better access the truth of what is really happening! It's now obvious why I contacted you! I needed to seek psychological help all along; I just sought out the wrong people!

P: Maybe. Or perhaps they were perfect at the time! Who knows? What I feel is that something has really softened and opened for you. That is all that I know. Anything more is interpretive and can't be substantiated!

E: Indeed! (silence)

Thank you.

P: And you. Let's end our session by singing together the prayer of the Four Immeasurables.[14]

> May all beings be well and happy,
> May all beings be free from strife,
> May all beings return to love,
> Peace be with you for evermore.

FOSTERING LOVING-KINDNESS

Emmanuel rediscovered the peace he had craved. By opening his heart and connecting with his emotions, he managed to empty his typically full mind of conceptual proliferation. As Krishnamurti said: "Only when you put away the things of the mind, only when your hearts are empty of the things of the mind, is there love. Then you will know what it is to love without separation, without distance, without time, without fear—and that is not reserved to the few."[15]

Loving-kindness practice[16] is a powerful way to awaken the heart of compassion, providing a transformational antidote to typically aversive emotions like fear, anger, jealousy, pride, or arrogance. Sometimes when we do this practice, we feel nothing. At other times the practice may be accompanied by physical sensations of warmth and receptivity. Or we may contact feelings like anger or fear that seem to be the root of our inner harshness, emotional agitation, or discomfort. Without a deeply resonant pool of inner loving-kindness, we typically analyze or reject unwanted feelings, just as Emmanuel had done for many years.

With loving-kindness we can be more available to each moment, however it arises. This affords a capacity to attend to painful, tight aspects that occlude our true nature from shining forth! By directing loving-kindness toward such feelings, we develop inner robustness. Instead of trying to talk ourselves into or out of what we are feeling, we are open to the full play of human experience. Dualistic fixations melt away and we find that our "empty, open heart is suffused with the tenderness of true compassion."[17]

INTEGRATION WITH THE BODY

By fostering a kindhearted disposition toward negative feelings, they lose their edge. In meeting the relative experience directly, we go beyond it and thus realize the absolute. Paradoxically, instead of trying to transcend our shortcomings, they dissolve in the face of utter openness.

Ignoring somatic impulses or overanalyzing the manifestation of pain or difficulty does not free us up. It simply conditions us to avoid what is arising by employing sophisticated self-justifying stories.

With loving-kindness we learn to nonjudgmentally work with the bodily sensations related to our judgments or preferences. Once aware of the issue or emotion, we consciously direct our awareness, using the breath as the awareness tool, into the body to feel whatever is arising. This manifests as energy underscoring our thoughts. At times the feeling will have associated images and memories, like Emmanuel's six-year-old residing within his memory bank. Instead of analyzing or interpreting this, we direct our attention to lovingly meeting the feelings and sensations, as though they are being held in nonjudgmental acceptance. This simple method has the capacity to untie the very knots that hold fixations in place. The more deeply we reside in loving-kindness, the more nonpreferentially intimate we become with the flux and flow of experience.

TRUE EMBODIMENT

As we equally embrace whatever is arising, we are neither driven by hope and fear nor ignoring such feelings. We function from the raw truth of who we really are. This state is fully inclusive and non-preferential. Along with a clear spacious mind is a heart open to feel the richness of human experience, and a body attuned to the flow of emotional, sensory receptivity. When the bhakti[18] heart is filled with love, and the wisdom mind is calmly all-seeing, a sense of fulfillment and generosity flow into and through us. Gratitude fills our heart. The deeper our absorption in the marriage of the relative and transcendent, the more pervasive is our nondual experience.

This in no way guarantees that another wave of past conditioning will not arise to meet us. Old woundings from childhood, difficulties in current intimate relationships, career challenges, financial and health crises are grist for the mill in life. No matter how spiritual or evolved we are, the true task in embodiment lies in our willingness to be courageously honest and lovingly present to whatever arises. The real wisdom lies not in seeking to hang out in the absolute, but in uncompromisingly embracing the entirety of being in the relative world.

As we progressively integrate nondual wisdom into everything, the gap between relative and absolute narrows, dissolving the boundary between all dualistic concepts including enlightenment and suffering. Within the natural freedom of being, we are enveloped in ever deepening acceptance, humility, and love. Alongside humility comes tremendous relief in letting go conditioned or newly acquired concepts and theories, preferences, hopes, and fears, such that we can peacefully abide in "not knowing," grateful for the presence of each moment to be just as it is.

ACKNOWLEDGMENTS

I would like to thank John Prendergast, Gidi Ifergan, and Joyce Harris for their valuable feedback when this chapter was being finalized. And to my daughter Brooke I offer gratitude for being the joy bubble you are!

Readers may send their comments and feedback to me at: penny@fenner.org, or visit my website for current details and upcoming events: www.skillfulaction.com. In Australia I can be reached at +61 3 9885 0119, at or 23a Britten Street, Glen Iris, Victoria, 3146.

ENDNOTES

1. Longchenpa, *You Are the Eyes of the World,* trans. Kennard Lipman and Merrill Peterson under the inspiration of Namkhai Norbu, Novato, CA: Lotsawa, 1987, p. 37.

2. Tsoknyi Rinpoche, *Carefree Dignity,* Rangjung Yeshe Publications, 1998, p. 71.

3. *Avidya*, Sanskrit word meaning delusion or ignorance as to the true nature of our Being. In Advaita Vedanta, eradicating ignorance leads to the realization

of the Self, and the ultimate freedom from deluded thinking. In Buddhism, *avidya* is recognized to be the root of all clinging or grasping which mires us in suffering.

4. Thich Nhat Hanh, *Interbeing*—poem in *call me by my true names,* collected poems of Thich Nhat Hanh, Parallax Press, 1999, p. 150.

5. Chogyam Trungpa Rinpoche, 1940–87, the great Tibetan teacher of the Kagyu school in Tibetan Buddhism, famous for his radical teachings that were integral in bringing Buddhism to the West. *Cutting through Spiritual Materialism* was first published in 1973.

6. Chogyam Trungpa Rinpoche, *Cutting through Spiritual Materialism,* Shambhala, 1973, p. 22.

7. Tsoknyi Rinpoche, *Carefree Dignity,* p. 71.

8. Ibid.

9. The great master Patrul Rinpoche, quoted in Sogyal Rinpoche's *Dzogchen and Padmasambhava,* Rigpa, 1990, p. 15.

10. Translation of the Tibetan word *snying rje*; *snying* meaning heart, and *rje* king or lord.

11. Rumi, *The Glance,* trans. Coleman Barks, Penguin Putnam, 1999, p. 66.

12. Tsoknyi Rinpoche, *Carefree Dignity,* p.160.

13. Referring to *Essential Wisdom Teachings: The Way to Inner Peace.* Nicholas Hays, 2001 (with Peter Fenner).

14. The Four Immeasurables, also known as the *Brahma Viharas* (Sanskrit) refer to love, compassion, joy, and equanimity.

15. *Sayings of J. Krishnamurti,* compiled by Susanaga Weeraperuma, New Dehli, Motilal Banarsidass, 1998, p. 107.

16. Examples of loving-kindness practice can be found in *Being Zen,* by Ezra Bayda, Shambhala, 2003, and *The Healing Power of Mind,* by Tulku Thondup, Shambhala, 1996.

17. Tsoknyi Rinpoche, *Carefree Dignity.*

18. A Sanskrit word that means intense devotion and supreme love for the divine. The *bhakti* heart is filled with divine love, for no reason other than the knowledge "we are love."

NONDUAL WISDOM AND BODY-BASED THERAPY

Sheila Krystal

If you live on the breath,
you won't be tortured by hunger and thirst,
or the longing to touch.

The purpose of being born is fulfilled in the state between "I am"
and "That."

—*Lalla*

For many years I have been interested in the role of nonverbal, body-based (or somatic) therapies in healing and awakening. Combined with self-inquiry, they offer an opportunity to breathe and be quiet and ultimately realize that the mind does not hold the answer to life's deepest questions. With this realization may come a glimpse of our true nature, an alive yet empty silence arising as Presence. Breathing deeply and physically letting go allows people to become comfortable with the undivided vastness, where the mind or ego is not in control. Body-based therapy can help people relax completely, surrender to the experience of this vastness, and receive it fully. When the body is deeply relaxed, attention can more easily move beyond the body. Ironically, the ultimate body-based therapy leads to the realization that "I am not only the body."

In any psychotherapy from the nondual perspective, there is no separate therapist and no client, no one doing and no one being done to. Ideally, there is just love and an impulse to be of service to That which is beyond the mind. As soon as the therapist takes herself to be a therapist and the client takes himself to be a patient, however, both can be thrust back into the socially induced trance that says we really are the collection of memories, history, preferences, attitudes, and beliefs we've been conditioned to take to be the self.

The body is an appearance within consciousness but also a beautiful expression of Oneness.

—*Adyashanti*

Recently I had an interesting conversation with a spiritual teacher in the nondual tradition, Hui Neng,[1] who has personally experienced a variety of body-based therapies. I include his comments here because I think they clearly articulate both the value and the limitations of somatic therapies from a nondual perspective. He said:

I have had my share of body-based therapies and have had very positive experiences, as the movement of stuck energies brought obscure areas into conscious recognition and energized the perceptual world, inner and outer. Yet bodywork in and of itself doesn't bring about a breaking free from the bubble of the personal "I" consciousness. The result depends on the context in which the healing work is done, on the mind-set and expectations (conscious and unconscious) of both therapist and client, and on what is communicated between them, both overtly and telepathically. Even in potent modalities that use breath, body-opening-awareness, and subtle energy awakening, there's usually the implication that there's a substantive "I" that's separate, that's on a journey, that goes through a process, that's making progress (or not), and that has to fit into a system. If the therapeutic modality doesn't imply this, usually the healer or therapist does, merely by thinking they're a "doer"—or even an "enlightened non-doer"! In reality, Presence does all the work. To the degree that awakening happens, everything else is merely the pretext that allows what never was to stop imagining it exists!

When I asked him what really heals, he replied:

Ultimately, awakening is what heals, not the shuffling around of elements in the dream or hypnotic trance. Awakening heals when it becomes apparent that Consciousness is already healed!

Awakening is irresistible and brings all into Itself, where it always has been. For example, laying on of hands, and its Eastern variation known as shaktipat, bring about a sense of energetic enlivening or relaxation and may result in physical healing, kundalini experiences, and dramatic chakra openings. But what is the result? You have a profound healing or an explosion into incredible joy, bliss, and Light, and you end up taking on the beliefs of the person who transmitted these experiences to you, be they a Christian, a Muslim, or a Hindu. You've been imprinted with a new set of cues about how to behave, think, feel, move, and the concept of "transmission" is used to foster the idea of someone who gets a transmission—and then, after getting it, is "special"—and of another someone who gives transmission and is even more special. In reality, there is no difference between the guru/teacher/healer/therapist and the disciple/student/patient/client. Any system that implies a separation of any kind, especially one born of specialness or elitism, has nothing to do with true freedom or healing.

In my own experience, when the body-based psychotherapist is inspired to work from no-mind, not taking herself to be anything special or different from the person she is sitting with and not doing anything out of the ordinary, somatic therapy can result in the reduction of suffering, the realization that we are not just the body, and a glimpse of nondual reality.

Make your mind and body express the real which is all and beyond all.

—*Nisargadatta Maharaj*

OVERVIEW OF CLINICAL APPROACH

I would like to describe my own approach to somatic psychotherapy, with a particular focus on my work with a client recovering from heroin addiction. As I mention earlier, I have found that nonverbal body-based therapy that gently focuses only on the breath and energy moving through the body can be an excellent way to sidestep the mind and the client's story or hypnotic trance, especially when clients live primarily in their head and take themselves to be their thoughts. The strong hold of the conditioned mind can be loosened as clients attend to the breath and are encouraged to make sounds but not to verbalize any arising thoughts. Sounds can express and discharge preverbal emotion, helping to remove energy blocks in the throat and upper chest.

I am trained in Reichian bodywork, deep tissue massage, and Trager work, and I've been rolfed and taught by Ida Rolf, initiated into Reiki, and instructed in a tantric Hindu method of healing and a Navajo form of laying on of hands. I have also worked with yoga, *pranayama,* kundalini, chakras, subtle energy, and meditation for many years.

Since 1973 the body-based aspect of my clinical practice has consisted primarily of *pranayama* (deep yogic breathing used to restore health and balance) and the laying on of hands. I don't make any mental distinction among the different modalities I use and don't think about what my hands are doing when I'm intuitively touching someone, other than observing standard ethical guidelines. I call it laying on of hands, or sacred touch to my clients. Since training in EMDR more than a dozen years ago, I have been adding bilateral stimulation to the mix during bodywork to intensify the experience, move energy, and process trauma.[2] (See Krystal, *The Sacred Mirror.*) Interestingly, Reich and his students used a penlight to induce bilateral eye movements in his clients, which he believed loosened energy blockages associated with resistance and armoring in the eye segment of the body.

When I practice bodywork from a nondual perspective, I hold to the following principles: that we and everything else in the world are manifestations of a unified whole or conscious field in which human beings are inextricably interconnected; that there is an innate healing principle waiting to awaken within us all; and that seemingly separate people can support each other and exchange the energy of love and kindness.

Body-based therapy from this perspective becomes a mostly nonverbal inquiry into the psychological and physical patterns of trauma and conditioning and the holding of that conditioning in the tissues of the body. Such patterns are evoked as the client attends to the felt sense of awareness in the body and focuses on accelerated deep breathing methods and on the roused energy moving through the body. While recognizing and resting in the silent, seamless vastness of oneness, the therapist holds the empty space for the client with her own attention, breathing deeply, and at times touching the client in various ways, which can facilitate the flow of energy, occasionally giving breathing, movement, or vocalization instructions. The therapist can also synchronize her breath with the client's, which further blurs any perceived separation between the two. As the breath deepens and increases in tempo, the body becomes super-oxygenated, the pH of the blood changes, and an altered state of conscious excitation is induced. In this altered state, old conditioning, traumatic memories, and attendant emotions surface to consciousness and are experienced and resolved as the body lives through them fully and then releases the tension and armor that had guarded against them out of fear of the trauma recurring. The release of the energy charge can be accomplished through various means, such as making noises, kicking, hitting pillows, stretching, and touch. In combination with bilateral stimulation, this process of excitation and energy discharge can be very evocative and helpful in letting go of old, rigid habits of defense. No two sessions are the same, and all are guided by intuition, the inner voice of oneness.

When the practitioner is fully present, silent, and resting in empty awareness, therapeutic resonance can occur (see Prendergast, Peter Fenner, this volume). Through therapeutic resonance, clients may catch a glimpse of nondual reality as they come to realize that there's no problem to be solved. Therapeutic resonance is synergistic and helps uncover and activate the client's own awareness and intuition while guiding the therapist in creative ways. For example, during the bodywork process, the therapist may find her hands touching the client in ways that can help release tension and blocks, reveal tracks for energy to flow, reassure the client during strong abreaction, and balance chakras or energy centers in the subtle body. When the therapist is herself in no-mind, empty and present, she is directed from within about where, when, and whether to touch the client's body. Sometimes she senses tension or pain in her own body in a kind of clairsentience, or sympathetic resonance with the client's body, which signals her where to touch the client. Physical touch is not always necessary, and the therapist may sometimes just sit with the client. The essence of the bodywork is the client's own focus on living in the moment, on the breath and body, and on the movement of energy through the body as memories, emotions, and experiences arise. Sessions are usually nonverbal, with most conversation reserved for the end or for the beginning of the following session.

CASE STUDY

As an example of how body-based therapy occurs in my private practice, I will describe the case of a forty-eight-year-old woman referred by a family friend who presented herself as a heroin and opiate addict in recovery for the ninth time. She had been sexually abused at a young age by a family member, had started using heroin at thirteen, and had lived on the street and in jail before cleaning up the first time and moving to a halfway house after a drug treatment program. Later she moved to Los Angeles and worked in the film industry for many years while struggling with her addiction. In an effort to quit her habit, she had tried inpatient and outpatient recovery programs, twelve-step programs, and various kinds of psychotherapy and meditation and had lived in halfway houses and drug treatment communities. She had been clean off and on, once for as long as sixteen years.

Recently she had returned to the Bay Area to live with a parent and get clean again after leaving her stressful career in the entertainment industry. This time, she said, she was determined to sustain her recovery. She had already tried various types of meditation, was familiar with several spiritual traditions, and was open to using self-soothing techniques, EMDR, and bodywork in her therapy sessions. She complained of long-standing upper back and neck pain as the result of a bicycle accident in which she broke her collarbone, shoulder, and many ribs, and punctured her lung. Her heroin habit and addiction to other painkillers had helped her handle the pain for 10 years. She reported suffering from anxiety and depression, was unable to maintain love relationships, and had given up on finding a lover.

Our first bodywork session followed several sessions of work with meditation and EMDR, during which she strengthened her recovery by clarifying her goals: to live and surrender to life and its emotion instead of craving for escape; to not always look for problems to avoid or solve; and to let go of her self-concept as addict. With EMDR and meditation she began to work through her many childhood and young adult traumas and finally began to let go of the self-perpetuating and fear-based concept that she's a heroin addict. Wishing to "get out of [her] head," she asked to do Reichian breathwork.

After she had reported briefly about her week, we quieted down and dedicated the bodywork session to the highest good and greatest growth for us both. I asked her to lie on her back, fully clothed, with her arms to her sides palms up and her legs up and bent at the knees with her knees a few inches apart and eyes closed. I covered her with a blanket and darkened the room. As preparation for this first session, I had already demonstrated the two kinds of breathing styles that I would ask her to switch between from time to time during the session. In the first type of breathing, called chest-belly-out, the client takes a deep breath through the nostrils into the chest and then into the belly in one fluid movement, holds the breath in, and then exhales slowly. In the second type of breathing, called panting, the client takes six short pants in and out through the mouth, followed by a long exhalation through the mouth, then repeats the pattern of six short breaths and a long exhalation continuously thereafter until told to stop panting. After she became comfortable with the technique, we spent about ninety minutes cycling through the two types of breathing. She was definitely in a state of excitation—she made some noise during the panting, and her hands showed temporary signs of tetany (minor muscular cramping and curling). While she was breathing, I silently worked with my hands on her left side first, starting with her left foot, loosening up her shoulder blade and arm, doing deep tissue work along her back with the weight of her body on my hand and then on her neck, face, and eyes. I asked her to notice the difference between the two sides of her body and suggested that she see if she could make them equally relaxed. After she had tried this experiment, I proceeded to work on her right side, reserving plenty of time for her neck and face. I had her kick and pound on cushions until she had discharged the energy several times, and I invited her to allow her knees to splay out and rest on the floor with each exhalation after panting. Lastly I asked her to rest, legs stretched out on the floor, while I touched her subtle body chakra areas in the manner of Brugh Joy and an old Navajo healing method involving trembling motions of the hands.

Most of the time during the session I kept my eyes closed as I moved around her on the floor while remaining empty and as free as possible of any thought about what, if anything, was going on. I allowed my hands to go wherever intuition instructed them and to do whatever seemed obvious to me at the time. Needless to say, the touch never enters the breast or genital area, and clients are always fully clothed and usually covered with a blanket, as the excitation tends to make them feel cold. The therapist can use whatever touch, massage, or healing techniques that they feel drawn to and proficient in as they close down the session while the client breathes naturally.

When we were done and the client had rested for a few minutes, she reported, "My thoughts about using (drugs) fade into the background of my mind now. *The background is what I take myself to be.*" Later she said, "Peace of mind is my natural birthright." I asked her to sit in the garden surrounding my office for a while to digest and rest before driving home.

The next week she reported with great surprise and delight that after our session she had noticed "right away" that her back pain had disappeared and not returned. It remains absent now, many months later. But she also reported that her cravings had increased, and she found herself looking for her mother's Vicodin. We talked about how the bodywork was bringing into awareness some of the old conditioned patterns of thought and emotion born of trauma and the attendant desire to avoid or assuage her pain with drugs, which her experience had convinced her "worked." We also talked about how all movement happens in spirals, and thus resurgences of craving during therapy do not necessarily indicate regression.

Each of the following bodywork sessions were similar in form yet totally different in terms of specific instructions and when and where I touched the client, since each session occurred in the moment and was responsive to changes in the moment. When she returned for her third session a week later, she reported that she still had cravings for heroin but now understood how to "distract herself from her mind" and felt empowered enough not to "give into the cravings" or to the temptation to look for her mother's pain medication. "The craving wasn't as strong, and I tried looking around for drugs and then stopped. I just went off and started thinking about something else after a few minutes. No, it wasn't even that long. I felt grungy and fluey for a few days, but now I feel better. It must have been detoxification. Now I'm more relaxed, even emotionally."

Between the third and fourth bodywork sessions she attended a *satsang* with a visiting Advaita master from India. At the beginning of the fourth session. she reported: "The craving isn't as intense. It came to mind but didn't really get any further than that, and I didn't look around for drugs. I thought maybe I don't want to do this [look around for drugs], and I didn't. Now I know what you've been saying to me all this time—the same thing we heard in satsang!" Although living life "in recovery" was no longer seen as a problem, the concept of being "in recovery" was next to dissolve, during the breathwork and touch of the fourth session. After she reported that *"living is just living, and there is no recovery from anything, just old habits and programming falling away.* I no longer need them. I know now that life doesn't give me more than I can handle, so I no longer need to escape from my experience, even painful emotion. I just breathe deep. I'm looking now for how 'high' shows up naturally in my life. Instead of tightening up and holding the emotion in, I breathe now, the emotion releases itself, and I feel relieved." In my experience, this disidentification with the addiction recovery process as taught by the twelve-step programs is, ironically, the key to true recovery.

After yet another session of bodywork, which focused more

on her pelvic segment, the client reported that she was losing her boundaries like she used to do when drugged. But now she realized she had been creating a second mental reality with heroin that she had to detach from or see through just as she was seeing through the nondrugged state. She was recognizing that mental states come and go, but what was real was her awareness of the states. Her cravings were less frequent, and the urge to look for drugs rarely distracted her. After describing a disagreement with her mother during which she was observing her own reactions, she reported: "I didn't go through the whole mind-set of what I did wrong. The first thing I used to look at was what did I do wrong—that old programming [I got from her]. That doesn't happen the way it used to anymore when I'm with her."

Several sessions later, musing about a low period in the past and the changes she had experienced since then and attributed to the bodywork, she said, "For three weeks before the first bodywork session, I was desolate and had no spiritual connection. That ended after the first session. I realized that I lose my spiritual connection when I use drugs and am no longer psychic. That's not reality. I had no interaction with others when I was using and didn't get fed. Now I can recognize what I need [to do for myself instead of using drugs] before I get into a state of discontent and dissatisfaction. *And I breathe and get quiet and remember the truth* [about who I really am]. I can't be dishonest [with myself and avoid my negative experience with drugs] anymore."

At our ninth session, she came in complaining of new tension in her neck and shoulders. She also described two nightmares from the preceding week, one from the night before her session. In both dreams she was extremely angry at her mother and was yelling and screaming at her, "Why did you want to treat me like you did? You're so miserable!" She interpreted the dreams to mean that she was "dealing with her mother's unconsciousness programming of her." During the bodywork session she cried and kicked her legs early on and then settled into peaceful deep breathing. At the end of the session she commented that her neck and shoulders were no longer tense and that she could use that temporary tension in the future as a signal to look within at her relationship with her mother.

In the next session she began by saying, "Thoughts of using arise, but now they just pass, and I don't have them very often. The burning pain in my back never came back. I have more self-value and less underlying anxiety, expression of rage and release. My mom and dad ostracized me for being alive and a female, and there was always an undercurrent of 'There's something wrong with me, I'm not a valuable person, I have nothing to offer anybody else or myself.' I'm sure that came from the abuse, but I've forgiven him now. He was drunk and ignorant and didn't know what he was doing much of the time. He's doing his best now."

The next week she began the session with the statement, "For the first time in my life, when I get anxiety, I have a sense of calm within me that I've never had before. I had blamed myself all these years. How ridiculous! I sometimes still have craving, and the seduction of the memory of warmth and calmness [from the experience of being high] comes up. The craving causes the anxiety, and so does wanting to please people and knowing I can't. But [the anxiety] went away in a minute because I stopped thinking." She also realized that when she was craving her opiates, her memory was distorted in favor of what was positive. Painful memories had faded with time and things in the past, like using opiates, looked more rosy again. The fact that she forgot the bad and remembered the good was a warning not to trust her memory when it came to craving drugs. She felt that this was an important insight into maintaining her recovery. Between sessions she had tripped and fallen down stairs and had hurt her upper back and tailbone, "but the original pain is gone from that first session."

As this client became more and more confident in her recovery, we began to meet every other week and then, after nine months of weekly or biweekly sessions, less frequently. Finally she decided to try her new wings and check in whenever she felt she needed a tune-up. As I write this chapter a year later, I continue to work with her occasionally, and she checks in now and then to let me know that her new awareness is still deepening and stabilizing on its own. During our work together she felt ready to leave her mother's home and strong enough to continue staying off heroin. Currently she is looking for a job and her own apartment. There is no guarantee that she will not use again. The difference now, however, is that she has had an epiphany and, as she says, knows who she is. In a famous letter to Bill W, one of the founders of AA, Carl Jung wrote that recovery from addiction is possible only when the addict has a spiritual awakening, a genuine experience of the numinous. This is the potential of body-based therapy done from a nondual perspective.

In my practice I've seen similar positive and lasting results with body-based therapy in combination with EMDR and meditation by clients plagued with anxiety and panic, depression, compulsive behaviors and obsessive thinking, eating disorders, and other symptoms of suffering. I chose this case as an illustration because addiction is so recalcitrant and causes extraordinary suffering for so many.

CONCLUSION

The essence of body-based therapy from a nondual perspective is attention, relaxation, and inquiry into memory and habits of mind, behavior, and body. As they breathe and their bodies relax deeply, clients begin to wonder how many times they can persist in thinking the same thought while still believing that it is significant. They question their relationship with thought and the emotions associated with it and begin to ask the deeper question of who is thinking and feeling. Their attachment to thoughts and beliefs can loosen as they directly experience a deeper essence that is beyond thought and emotion. This essence itself creates the healing in therapy as people wake up from the cultural trance and examine their circumstances. They realize that situations are simply what they are and that the mind creates problems through its interpretations of those situations. Eventually, out of this deeper awareness arises whatever experience the client ultimately needs in order to see through his or her perceived separation from essence and to be free of suffering once and for all. Essence ultimately realizes itself as all that is and readies itself to blossom into contentment with what is.

ENDNOTES

1. Also known as Krishna or Jeff Perlmutter.

2. Please see my chapter entitled "A Nondual Approach to EMDR," in *The Sacred Mirror: Nondual Wisdom and Psychotherapy.*

NONDUAL AWAKENING

Its Source And Applications

Timothy Conway

HISTORICAL INDIAN SOURCES OF NONDUAL REALIZATION

In this astonishing dream of life, a growing current of *nondual spiritual realization* is enlightening various circles of religion, spirituality, and psychotherapy. What, historically speaking, is the source of such nondual realization?[1] The first known articulation of nondual awareness in human history emerged over three thousand years ago in northwest India, within the Aryan people's *Rg Veda* oral "scripture" of sacrificial hymns and spells. The *Rg's* later compositional layers (1100 B.C.E.?) occasionally express *a surprising nondual intuition of the One Reality*. This Divinity transcends any monolatrous, anthropomorphic God like Egypt's Akhenaten or the Hebrews' YHWH.

In the famously paradoxical *Nasadiya* "There was not" Creation-Hymn (*Rg Veda*, x.129), we hear the *rishi* poet-seers sing of the deep, formless Reality. Prior to being or nonbeing, darkness or light, life or death, and prior to the gods, this undifferentiated One somehow mysteriously generates via "creative heat" the life force, and from this force emanates a differentiated world of earth and heavens. Elsewhere we hear high praise of "That which is earlier than earth and heaven, before the gods had being... that One wherein abide all things existing" (x.82). "The One manifests as all this" (x.2; viii.58).[2] Incipient Vedic theology thus points to an unborn *(aja)* One Truth *(ekam satyam)* mysteriously, wondrously expressing ItSelf as multiplicity. This is *panen*theism, no mere pantheism or theism, for this Divine Source/Substance is both transcendent and immanent—God *beyond* all and God *within* all. Over time this nondual *theology* would

231

be "owned" and internalized for India's sages as a nondual *psycho-spirituality* of the One Self/Awareness, realized right Here, right Now within the heart/mind of male and female sages.

Several ancient Vedic *Brahmana* commentaries arose. The *Satapatha Brahmana* (c. 1000 B.C.E.), attributed to sage Yajnavalkya, apparent "father of nonduality," speaks of a pure absorption in Self, *Brahmabhava*, "the *Brahman* state/mood." This key term *Brahman* denotes the infinite, nondual, *trans*personal (not "impersonal") Reality, Power, or Awareness. By this point in time, the "thought-surpassing mystery" of *Brahman*[3] was considered identical with the One Truth, *ekam satyam*. A new stage of Vedic prose commentaries, the *Aryanyaka* "forest" literature, emphasized the *Brahmanas*' inner trend and pointed to an even deeper, intuitive meaning of Vedic rituals—*pure identity with the Absolute.* "What I am, that He is; what He is, that am I." Thus speaks the *Aitareya Aranyaka* (ii.2.4.6), one of only three extant *Aranyakas*.

Then, around 800 B.C.E., nondual awareness began to be even more boldly, consistently affirmed in a new class of oral teachings, the *Upanishads*, "works of monumental significance in the history of India and of the world."[4] This lore—the planet's oldest substantial wisdom literature, filled with introspective psychology and metaphysics, reverential awe, benign humor, and sharp-witted paradoxes—affirms a panentheist theology of *Brahman* and spiritual realization of the Divine *Atman*/Self, identical to *Brahman*. The *Upanishads* hugely amplify this era's trend toward an interiorized wisdom-knowledge *(jnana)*, a keen-eyed contemplative mysticism, in place of the liturgical, action-oriented *(karma-kanda)* Vedic religion of the upper-castes, the Aryans. The *Upanishads* signal a rationalist and deeply spiritual revolt against an encroaching cult of *brahman*-caste priests and their extravagant Vedic ritualism and symbolism.

This was not a mass movement. *"Upanishad"* means "secret doctrine," and the wisdom was indeed kept secret for a few centuries, available only to select, mature disciples of certain gurus. Significantly, neither the Buddha, his disciples, nor their diverse visitors in north India of the sixth/fifth century B.C.E. ever speak of the panentheist mysticism based on *Brahman-Atman*. There is talk of the celestial god *Brahma* (masc.), but not the Absolute, transpersonal *Brahman* (neuter). Had the Buddha and his many followers known how the *Brahman/Atman* was discussed in a nonreifying way by the *Upanishad-gurus*, his "not self" *(anatta / anatman)* doctrine of disidentification might have taken a more nuanced connotation and precluded twenty-five hundred years of Buddhist-Hindu alienation on this crucial point.[5]

The two earliest and largest *Upanishads* were the *Brhadaranyaka* (the *Satapatha Brahmana*'s long appendix) followed by the *Chandogya Upanishad*. Both came from the Ganga-Yamuna river valley in north-central India. Other *Upanishads* were composed from the eighth century B.C.E. to the first century C.E.—the *Taittiriya, Aitareya, Kaushitaki, Kena, Katha, Mundaka, Svetasvatara, Isa, Narayana, Prasna, Mandukya, Maitri, Jabala,* and *Paingala*. The last five evidently come after the Buddha's time; the middle six are roughly contemporary with Siddhartha; the rest originate before him. These *Upanishads* together comprise the *Vedanta*, the *Vedas'* "end" or "conclusion." In addition to these major, classical *Upanishads*, there emerged over the centuries nearly one hundred minor *Upanishads*.[6]

The early *Upanishads* tell of sages Yajnavalkya et al., teaching a profound wisdom of disidentification—*neti, neti,* "not-this, not-this"—from all mentality-materiality *(nama-rupa);* and realization of one's actual identity as Divine *Atman*-Self. This true Self, prior/interior to body-mind-soul-ego, is, again, none other than *Brahman*, the Absolute Being-Awareness-Bliss *(Sat-Cit-Ananda)*, the timeless, spaceless, changeless, colorless, partless, speckless Fullness *(Purnam)*, the Source/Witness/Substance of the multileveled Cosmos.

Hence the Advaita ("not-two," nondual) "secret doctrine" of the *Upanishads*: *The awesome Divine Source of the world appearance is not remote or distant, but is, in most intimate fact, our true Identity, our real Being.* This Self/Reality is invisible, imperceptible, not an "other," a thing or entity, and thus is not seeable or knowable as an object. However, Self/Reality is eminently *be*-able when ignorance *(avidya, ajnana)* has suddenly or gradually given way to innate Divine Self-Knowing *(vidya, jnana, prajna)*. Moreover, this Self is *Trans*-personal, infinitely greater than the merely "personal," and certainly not "impersonal" as too many scholars and clergy have mis-leadingly called THIS Supreme Reality that transcends yet includes all beings.

To awaken listeners from the egocentric, hypnotic trance unto this stupendous Divine Truth, these Vedanta sages issued potent *mahavakya*s, "Great Sayings," like "I am *Brahman*" (*Aham Brahmasmi*), "That Thou Art" *(Tat Tvam Asi),* "This Self is *Brahman*" (*Ayam Atma Brahma),* "Pure Knowing is *Brahman*" (*Prajnanam Brahma),* and "All this is indeed *Brahman*" (*Sarvam Khalvidam Brahma).*[7] Throughout the early *Upanishads* we hear riveting aphorisms:[8]

> "It is the notion of 'otherness' that results in fear [elsewhere, lust, confusion and mortality are mentioned as a result of this dualistic felt-sense of otherness]." (BrU i.4.2)

> Knowing the all-pervading *Brahman,* "subtler than the subtlest, farther than the far, yet right here" (MuU iii.1.5), "without earlier or later, inside or outside" (BrU ii.5.19), one finds OneSelf as the unborn-undying *Brahman,* "independent (*svaraj,* self-ruled), with unlimited freedom in all worlds." (ChU vii.25.2)

> One "knows everything" (BrU iii.1.1), realizing the Essential Self of all gods, humans, animals, beings, worlds. "This is the Seer Itself unseen, the Perceiver Itself unperceived." (BrU iii.8.11) "There's no other seer but He, no other hearer, perceiver, thinker but He." (BrU iii.7.23)

> "When there is some other thing, one can see the other, smell... greet... hear... ponder... the other. [But in dreamless sleep or in fully awake *Brahman*-realization] one becomes the single ocean, the nondual Seer. This is the *Brahman* domain... the highest goal, highest treasure, greatest bliss." (BrU iv.3.31–32)

> "It moves and moves not; It is far and near, within all this and beyond all this." (IsaU 5)

> "This un-showable, constant Being can be realized as One only.

Let a wise aspirant directly realize this insight, not just reflect on tiresome words." (BrU iv.4.10–21)

The calm, self-controlled, interiorized, patient, and collected sage, who has banished all desires, cut all fetters, and thereby undone the heart's "knots," knows that "He who is here in a person and yonder in the sun—is the same One." (TU iii.10.4) "Know: *He is my Self.*" (KsU iii.8)

"It isn't understood by those who [think they] understand It; It's understood by those who do *not* "understand" It. When known via awakening in every state, It is rightly known…" (KeU ii.3)

"The sage relinquishes joy and sorrow, having realized by Self-contemplation (*adhyatma-yoga*)… that primal Divine… The knowing Self isn't born, doesn't die, hasn't sprung from anywhere, hasn't become anyone." (KaU i.2.12,18)

"There the sun doesn't shine, nor moon, stars or lightning—much less ordinary fire. Him alone shining, all else shines as His reflection; the worlds radiate His Light." (KaU ii.2.15) "No one can see Him with sight. By heart, insight and intuition is He contemplated…." (KaU ii.3.9)

"The wise sage has filled all; he is radiant, bodiless, invulnerable, pure, untouched by evil. He, the Seer, Thinker, all-pervading, Self-existent…" (IsaU 8) "His heart the world *(hrdayam visvam)*, He is the Self of all beings." (MuU ii.1.4)

This *Atman*, "brilliant and full of light," isn't realized by sight, speech, senses, austerities or rites. "But when the attention/ intelligence is purified by wisdom's light, one realizes Him who is partless/whole." (MuU iii.1.5,8)

"The sages realize Him who is present in all, and enter into that all…. As flowing rivers disappear into the ocean, giving up their name and shape, so the knower, freed from name-and-form *(nama-rupa)*, realizes the higher-than-high Divine. Verily, one who knows the Supreme *Brahman* becomes *Brahman*." (MuU iii.2.5,8)

"This highest mystery in the Vedanta… is not to be given to one whose passions aren't subdued." (SvU vi.22)

The *Svetasvatara Upanishad*, foreshadowing a rich twenty-five-hundred-year-old tradition of nondual Hindu *bhakti*-devotionalism, emphasizes a panentheist focus on *Siva*, the "Benign One," who is:

"the immense *Atman*, always residing in people's hearts…. The one God, Self of all, ordainer of deeds, the witness *(sakshi)*, the only one *(kevalo)*, devoid of qualities *(nirguna)*… He is the Intelligent among intelligences, the One among many…. the all-knowing One, Lord of both primal nature and individual souls, Lord of the governing qualities (three *gunas: sattva*/harmony, *rajas*/agitation and *tamas*/inertia), cause of bondage, existence and also liberation *(moksha)* from rebirths *(samsara)*." (vi.11,13,16)

For contemplative Vedantins, all these and many other *Upanishad* aphorisms support the essential "triple method" of awakening from the reincarnational/*samsara* dream of "me": namely, *hearing, pondering,* and *meditating (sravana, manana, nidhidhyasana)* upon this revealed Truth until lucidity dawns in an unshakable Self-realizing intuition that one is none other than Infinite Unborn-Undying-Unchanging Awareness. Centuries later, the great "father of Mahayana Buddhism," sage Nagarjuna (second century C.E.), encouraged his listeners to use the same triple method for aphorisms concerning Openness/Emptiness *(Sunyata)* or transcendent-immanent Suchness *(Tathata)*.[9]

Besides the major *Upanishads*, two other ancient works arose to form a threefold *prasthana-traya* Vedanta scriptural canon: first, the 550-line *Brahma-Sutras (Vedanta-Sutras)*, composed by Badarayana (post-200 B.C.E.), and likely our first known Indian author of a consistent Advaita (nonduality) or *abheda* (no difference) viewpoint.[10] His is the only work extant among several compositions by ancient sages who tersely systematized the oldest *Upanishads'* teachings. Among its many Vedanta truths: *Brahman*'s appearance-as-world isn't motivated by need but happens merely as Divine play-ful pastime, *lila,* a central notion for later Hinduism (ii.1.32–33). The individual soul, a mere appearance of *Brahman,* is neither born nor created (ii.3.16–17). *Brahman* might seem twofold—unqualified formless *(nirguna)* Reality, and qualified with attributes/forms/world *(saguna)*—but truly *Brahman* is formless only, without differences (iii.2.11–14). It is pure spiritual Intelligence, but just as the sun seems distorted, decreased, and trembling in its reflection(s) in water, so also *Brahman* appears to decrease and suffer through the body-mind adjuncts (iii.2.16–20). There's no difference between *Brahman* and its manifestation in activity (iii.2.25). One need not work to gain wisdom, yet one must be calm and controlled. For the scriptures prohibit licentiousness (iii.4.27,30).

Second, the 700-verse *Bhagavad Gita* (c. 300 B.C.E.), the "Lord's Song," Krishna's memorable instruction to friend-disciple Arjuna, features an eclectic wealth of nondual wisdom and devotion. The *Gita* reveals how the Divine "I AM"-Self/*Atma* is not only the Cosmic Source and Witness, but the only Reality, the One Actor playing all souls/roles in creation. Krishna's repeated confession as *Avatara,* Divine Incarnation, shows that *Atman/Brahman* is not opposed to a vital, physical manifestation and can be fully, immanently lived within the human drama, not just in some transcendent state. And Krishna's four *marga*s or spiritual paths—*karma, yoga, jnana,* and *bhakti*—are each articulated along nondual lines, meaning that one can live nondual spirituality, full of equanimity and free of dualistic perception or doership-sense, regardless of one's temperament.

The *Bhagavad Gita* forms part of the long epic-poem *Mahab-harata,* which in its developmental history came to include a few far-less-read *"Gitas"* of nondual instruction, the *Sanatsujatiya* and the *Anugita,* containing Krishna's "further instruction." Other *Gitas* independently arose, crucial for Hindu nondual/Advaita tradition, like the *Ashtavakra, Avadhuta,* and *Ribhu Gitas,* chock-full of ecstatic confessions of nondual self-realization.

Meanwhile, key aspects of nonduality—equanimious freedom, emptiness of all phenomena, and awakening to the unborn/undying *advaya* peace and bliss of *nibbana/nirvana*—were being expressed in the Pali-Canon teachings of the Buddha, and then grandly elaborated in early Mahayana Buddhist *sutras* (*Prajna-Paramita*-group, *Ratnakuta*-group, *Samadhi*-group, *Vimalakirti-nirdesa, Sandhinirmocana, Lankavatara, Avatamsaka*), and in the writings of Madhyamika philosopher-giant Nagarjuna, and of Yogacara Buddhists Asanga and Vasubandhu (fourth century). The subsequent Buddhist *tantra* movement featured no-nonsense sages like Saraha (eighth/ninth centuries), Tilopa (989–1069), Naropa (1016-1100) and other nondually-oriented *mahasiddhas*.

Further Hindu expression of nonduality occurred theologically in the motley, encyclopedic *Puranas* (fourth century C.E. onward)—by far the most beautiful and charming among which is the *Bhagavatam Purana* (eighth/ninth centuries C.E.). Its Book 11 (chapters 7–29) contains the "Uddhava Gita" by Krishna, a gem of nonduality. The noted grammarian Bhartrihari (fifth-sixth centuries) expressed clear nondual themes in his *Vakyapadiya* and a more dynamic-vibrational notion of *Brahman* and Its *Sakti*-power.

But it was the nondual commentary on the *Mandukya Upanishad* by sage Gaudapada (fifth-sixth centuries) and, a few generations later, the many works by the towering philosopher-sage Sankara (seventh-eighth centuries), reinforced by the aforementioned nondual *Gitas* and contemporary nondual works like the 29,000-verse (!) *Yoga Vasishtha*, that gave rise to the prominent Advaita Vedanta school in India, still tremendously influential today.

Gaudapada and Sankara distill and give renewed emphasis to the profound psychospirituality of the *Upanishads*. *Atma* is never bound, doesn't transmigrate, and is always liberated. Thus, echoing Mahayana Buddhism, there are no "bound souls" and no "liberated ones," either—the sense of bondage *(bandha)* comes from temporary ignorance. There's nothing to "do" to realize *Brahman* other than hear/ponder/meditate on revealed Truth, for one is always already only THIS. And the phenomenal world has never really been created (the *ajata-vada*, "no-creation view"). World *(jagat),* self *(jiva),* and personal Lord *(Isvara)* are wondrous forms of this Formless Spiritual Reality, products of a mysterious "super-imposition" *(adhyasa)* (a term equivalent to the old terms *maya*/illusion or *vikalpa*/false discrimination). The world and a self-sense appear, sustained by ignorance *(avidya)*, just as a rope can appear as a snake to someone not yet seeing clearly (Gaudapada's famous illustration).

With the dawn of true knowledge, *vidya* or *vijnana*, comes the realization, expressed in Sankara's well-known verse: "*Brahman* alone is real, the world is appearance, the self is nothing but ["disguised"] *Brahman*" (*Brahma satyam jagan mithya, jivo brahmaiva na parah*). The experience of a world of multiplicity is "subrated" or "contradicted" *(badha)* by realizing *there's only Brahman*.[11] In Realization, it is clear that the ordinary world and "*jiva*"-self, are misperceived—the Truth is *Siva*, God. The soul's Real Identity is Divine: "*jiva* is *Siva*." Everyone and every phenomenon in the cosmos is none other than *Brahman*.

Awakened sages serenely know This as direct experience, *anubhava*, not mere speculation or concept. The dreamlike world doesn't literally disappear for a sage, except in dreamless sleep and formless *nirvikalpa samadhi*. Sankara clarifies: "World as world is false/unreal. World as [appearance of] *Brahman* is real." In the "natural absorption" or *sahaja samadhi* recommended by Advaita tradition, it doesn't matter whether a world appears or not. *Brahman* or spiritual Reality alone IS.

Within several centuries, Advaita blended with a deeply devotional, lyrical "love mysticism" in the gorgeous and striking panentheist poetry of Kashmir Saivism's Utpaladeva (c. 900–950) and Abhinavagupta (c. 950–1015); the Marathi Varkari movement's leaders Jnanesvar (1275–96), Namdev (d. 1350?), Eknath (c. 1535–99), and Tukaram (1607–49); and the *nirguni* "formless God" *sants* led by Kabir, Ravidas (both fifteenth-century), Nanak (1469–1539), and the Sikh Gurus.[12] A lovely blend of head and heart. Jnanesvar and the Kashmir Saivas, for instance, assert that the universe arises, not as any "mistake," but as the eternal dynamic love-play of Siva and Sakti, who are mysteriously not two but One.

India's spiritual history sees a dialectic between the deconstructive and constructive, with some nondual teachings more imbalanced toward the transcendent pole of pure *via negativa* realization at the expense of Divine immanence, whereas other nondual teachings—*tantra* and certain forms of "extreme" *bhakti*, for instance—come down the other way into a colorful, complicated *via positiva* mysticism. Space constraints prevent conveying any further historical details, let alone coverage of stellar modern-era figures including Shirdi Sai Baba, Narayana Guru, Ramana Maharshi, Gnanananda, Nityananda, Sivananda, Meher Baba, Nisargadatta Maharaj, Anandamayi Ma, Anasuya Devi, Amma Amritanandamayi et al., who have so impressively lived the nondual dharma they teach—and what wonderful teachings! The interested reader may explore all these profound and delightful expressions of Indian Advaita/*advaya* Awakening, past and present, in two forthcoming publications.[13]

THERAPEUTIC APPLICATIONS OF NONDUALITY

We turn from this all-too-brief history of nonduality, only hinting at its tremendous treasures, to its therapeutic applications. Amusing paradoxes await anyone who winds up being an instrument, a teaching voice, a sagely presence for nondual tradition. For starters, this is a tradition that is never old, always new, and NOW. So "Now," in fact, that many of its sages declare the "tradition" doesn't even exist. *Nothing has ever really happened!* There is only *Brahman/Buddhata/Sunyata*—no world, beings, words, scriptures. "All phenomena are like a dream, an illusion, a mirage, a fairy city," as Nagarjuna, Gaudapada, and Sankara often declare. Advaita reveals that every apparently distinct person encountered in this Divine Dream is, in Truth, *none other than an appearance of the Divine Dreamer,* and *this Awareness has no problems,* hence, there's nothing to teach, no one taught, and no teacher. No guidance, no help of any kind is actually needed for the Infinite/Open/Empty/Full Reality of Self-Shining Spirit.

Ah! but as the same sages affirm, two truths pertain to our situation: the Absolute Truth or Higher Knowledge of true Identity *(paramartha-satya, para-vidya),* and Conventional Truth or Knowledge *(samvriti- or vyavaharika-satya, apara-vidya)* pertaining to the relative world of relationships, each domain to be honored appropriately. And the sages say, Woe unto anyone who mixes up these two levels. For example, rationalizing nonvirtuous, selfish behavior as the Self's *"lila"*-

play to avoid personal accountability; or mistaking dissociated, depersonalized apathy and avoidance of helpful service to sentient beings as "spiritual transcendence." Nisargadatta Maharaj (1897–1981) gets the balance right: "Wisdom says I am nobody, Love says I am everybody."[14] The ancient Buddhist *Prajna-Paramita Vajracchedika* (Diamond-Cutter) *Sutra* puts it: "One must sincerely, tirelessly help save all sentient beings. Yet no sentient beings really exist."

So: in conventional therapy-*satsang* situations, a person comes for relief from some "dis-ease." Most therapists and counselors, unaware of Absolute Reality, presume this person really has a problem and somehow has to be rescued, shifted, or changed from problematic state *A* (which usually has other problematic states *B, C,* underlying *A*) and brought into the desired goal state *X, Y,* or *Z*.

Yet for Absolute Awareness there are no problems. On the level of Conventional Truth, yes, the *personality* has psychic-mental-emotional-physical issues to work through, but one's fundamental, utterly *trans*personal nature has no dilemma whatsoever, no lack, flaw, complication, or suffering. The sagely therapist *recognizes the friend-client in/as the ever-free Self,* the unborn Infinite Awareness characterized by perfect freedom, blissful peace, and radiant vastness.

Also: this friend-client is not an "other." While certainly wearing a distinctive, unique personality with its own history, needs, feelings, and conditioning, his/her transpersonal Awareness is intimately right HERE, not separate from or other than "one's own" Awareness. The many selves inhere in the one Self.

Hence the lovely poignancy of any nondual therapy-*satsang* situation: Divine Awareness in the form of the client "approaches" Awareness in the form of the therapist/facilitator, saying, on the personality-level, "I have a problem." In the inclusive "two-truth" spiritual logic of Absolute-and-Relative, *Awareness compassionately, empathetically shares this client's pain. The drama of the Divine playing the noble role of a struggling human being is so utterly full of dignity and pathos!* Yet, Awareness also knows that this Divine-appearing-as-person basically has no real troubles. All that's "needed" is for Awareness to somehow invite or encourage ItSelf to snap out of the hypnotic trance that one is a limited and problem-prone person, and authentically awaken from the "me"-dream—"I am this, I am that"—to the original, unborn-undying, non-conceptual *I Am That Am.*

From this context of true Identity and enlightened Freedom, any personal issues, now "deproblematized," can then be therapeutically explored, worked through (played through!), and to some extent healed or resolved. A reassuring announcement from many of the most esteemed nondual sages is that *everyone awakens to Awareness because there is only Awareness.* Thus, throughout the therapeutic process, we know that Right HERE is the Divine Heart of existence—Pure Solid Being-Awareness-Bliss—the profound Truth of whatever experience arises.

Therefore, when people come to *satsang* or therapy with a felt-sense of a dilemma or impasse, the *satsang*-facilitator or psycho-spiritual counselor need not further problematize the situation with heavy messages about the person's poor karma, bad tendencies, weak energy, or abusive parenting (even if these are big factors on the relative-conventional level of the personality). We can always be careful in our *satsang*-therapy talk about hyping this sense of the problematic—however well it might play into any of our own self-inflating tendencies as the "helper-rescuer-savior-liberator." Some spiritual groups, now including many spiritually-oriented psychotherapy groups, hype "enlightenment" as the Great Goal and denigrate "unenlightened thought" or "the ego-mind" as a big problem. There is, in truth, no bogeyman. There's only God, playing all parts, destined to awaken from the personal to transpersonal, and on "perfect Divine schedule."

In this respect, the simple, natural Advaita way from the *Upanishads* through Nagarjuna and Sankara and medieval sages down to the illustrious Bhagavan Ramana Maharshi (1879–1950) seems far healthier and more gracious than the "I'm-enlightened/are-you-enlightened?" carnival surrounding certain teachers. *Context here is all-important.* If the native presumption is Divine Freedom, that this entire Kosmos is *God God-ing God,* the One Awareness zestfully playing all the parts/roles, adventuring with highs and lows, pleasures and pains, losses and gains—then any therapeutic work/play happens as part of Freedom Freeing Itself… Perfection Perfecting Itself.

But if, by contrast, one presumes the conventional view that the person is this vulnerable, pathetic package of protoplasm with a mental voiceover (the usual materialist-"scientistic" presumption), or that the person is some kind of "soul in trouble" (the usual religious or psychic presumption), then one will have no end of problems and futile attempts to resolve them. I say "futile" because there is no real resolution within the me-dream. The only ultimate and pragmatic solution to all problems is waking up from the assumption of false identity. Then one is *fully Divine*, consciously playing at being *fully human*.[15]

FOUR MODES OF AWAKENING

Just how Awareness awakens from the me-dream is wondrously mysterious. Beyond the *hearing-pondering-meditating* on Spiritual Truth, Awareness evidently uses any of *four modes* to awaken from its own Divine Comedy or Playful Game of apparent (not actual) "Self-forgetfulness." Competent therapists / *satsang* facilitators simply encourage any of these to occur.

- Completely *stopping/dropping/letting go* the illusion of being merely a separate, personal self. There's no sense of movement, direction, or shift in this radical stopping/dropping, only the cessation of me-and-mine via the realization of "Be Still." In this inner stillness, the obsessive dream of myself/my-world simply falls off and Divine Freedom remains as a pristine, Self-luminous *No-thing* amidst the *Everything* of spontaneous body-mind activity.

- The way a lens suddenly shifts from being blurry to clearly focused, one *Re-cognizes* or "Knows again" that one's real Identity or true Nature is the infinite Openness-Emptiness-Fullness that never moves, changes, shifts, goes anywhere, diminishes, or improves.

- A third mode that Awareness deploys to awaken ItSelf to

ItSelf is *returning Home*, "coming back from" the changeable sense of personal selfhood, usually through the inquiry that asks, "Who am I?" and doesn't settle for or identify with any image, concept, felt-sense, or storyline that might arise. This *Who/What am I?* self-inquiry has a way of "pulling" the Self out of its outward-turned mind, the *pravritti marga* or "outward path" of involvement with worldly objects or one's own thoughts or emotions "back into" one's native, natural condition of ego-free Awareness right HERE. Many folks actually report that, upon awakening, they suddenly feel like they abide in this mysteriously "placeless" place *behind* their old sense of self; they feel spontaneously, immediately *Here*, whereas before they felt identified with a superficial entity or process "out there." Medieval German mystic Meister Eckhart eloquently put it: "God is at Home, man abroad."

- A fourth way that Awareness awakens itself from feeling identified with dream-circumstances and the dream-*persona* seems opposite to mode #3. Awareness, so to say, suddenly *"penetrates"* or *"bursts forth beyond"*—and thereby annihilates the dream of limited identity, the apparently solid world of me-and-my-objects. This "feels like" a forward movement, a blasting through an old, actually flimsy veil of ignorance, grasping, fear, and any sense of egotism defining itself through this separative ignorance and attachment-aversion. Awareness explodes whatever apparently limiting self-concepts or world-concepts and all binding likes and dislikes *(samskaras)* that have arisen as old conditioning. Nothing can bind or limit anymore. One is free, floating, flying, frolicking as the One Alone. Any arising appearances-events are transparent forms or energy-vibrations of this Formless Reality.

In some cases, this awakening happens quite abruptly and "dramatically," a bright light suddenly switched on, whereas in others it occurs gradually, like sunlight slowly, inevitably dawning. In final Awakening, all selfish "seeking" ceases, yet a natural, non-egoic "healing aspiration" continues, a thorough establishing of Awareness-Freedom-Love-Compassion in all aspects of living, spontaneously clearing out much old shadow-material and habitual body-mind tendencies.

Therapeutically, one is simply available as intelligent/compassionate "space" for this to happen. Skilled therapists-guides will come to have, through their own inner guidance, an intuitive sense of how best to serve the client. It starts with clearly knowing by *being* the One, Free Awareness that we are.

I've seen over the many years that excessive use of absolute-level speech by teachers is not fruitful for most individuals. Indeed, "Advaita talk" can too often be abused in a contrarian one-upping manner that is merely a disguised power trip on the part of the wise guy/gal. A client or student asks about, say, some personal or social justice issue, to which the "wise one" retorts, "That is just a dream—nothing is really happening." Such use of absolute-level parlance may look and sound impressive, but is actually corrupt at the core, because it often serves as a subtle put-down rather than loving empowerment. A blend of compassionate, conventional-level psychospiritual counsel along with Absolute-level teachings seems to work best for most folks.

Spontaneous silence can allow our intrinsically *mind-free* Identity to abide unto ItSelf. Partners or groups relax back into their primordial *sahaja* ("inborn"/intrinsic) Awareness-Openness. Yet silence done as a "method" can also become ignorant posturing when there is attachment to physical silence and any aversion toward "disrupting" sounds or useful conversation. Nisargadatta Maharaj, faced with people who claimed they only wanted to "meditate with him in silence," would insist, "Words first, then silence. You must be ripe for silence." Anyway, in genuine awakening, it doesn't matter whether the Silence of the Self occasions physical sounds (i.e., words) or their absence. An active mind is no problem for the sage, just as an active body is no problem—indeed, both are dreamlike instruments for spontaneous expression and service.

COMMON QUESTIONS ABOUT AWAKENING

Certain questions often arise for those in the awakening process. For example:

Q: *I cannot seem to find, know, or perceive the Self or Awareness. I get a vague sense of the Self, but I can't seem to bring it clearly into focus.*

An oft-heard complaint. The Self is not an *object* to be rendered "clearer" or "more focused." The clarity of focus is in realizing that one's true nature as Awareness is *not any kind of object, thing, or entity at all.* Awareness need only rest or abide as ItSelf, sheer Isness-Aliveness-Sentience-Intelligence, the basic roomy Capacity for experience.[16] Invisible and imperceptible, Awareness need not go in search of ItSelf or try to make an object out of ItSelf, just as a fingertip is not "designed" to touch itself and will only convolute or dislocate itself in trying to do so. If you want to perceive the Self, behold the world and all its beautiful beings—Divine Forms of the Formless.

Q: *What basic attitude should be maintained?*

Just be *capacious no-thingness*, with a simple, keen curiosity or affectionate amusement over *Who/What am I? And what the hell/heaven is going on here?* What is the true nature of this arising pain or pleasure, this discomfort or comfort, this confusion or clarity? What is the real nature or underlying reality of this "me"-subject and "my" objects of experience? In general, one inquires *"What is this? What is this particular saliently-arising state (fear, lust, anger, shame, envy, euphoria, pride, numbness, tightness, nervousness, body sensations, thoughts, memories, images, psychic impulses…)? And for Whom does it arise?"*

Awareness being the only Reality, when Awareness investigates Its own emanations-productions, It deconstructs them and knows *neti, neti,* "I'm not this, not this." The Buddha often put it, "This [whatever aggregate or state] is not mine; this I am not; this is not my self." This is Buddhist mindfulness, Hindu witnessing, Christian-Sufi watchfulness. No need to get heavy or obsessive with it. There's nothing to "do" and nobody to "become." *Just be,* just remain as you are, in the relaxed "natural state," lucidly dreaming the life-dream, freely noticing-enjoying the basic fact of Awareness and Its objects. And plainly know that

You are both this Formless Awareness *and* these "Form-full" objects. Thus, you can be fully *engaged* while freely *unengaged*, compassionately *involved* while transcendentally *uninvolved*.

Q: *Why are we here in the first place?*

This, along with many other similar "why" questions, can, of course, be "answered"—e.g., "to love and serve and to enjoy the adventure of being the Formless playing the dance of Form." Yet *"why"* is more usefully redirected to *How* is it that there is an arising sense of self and world at all?

A related "why"-question is *"Why did the Divine Self dream up this painful illusory world and self-sense?"* This, too, can be therapeutically shifted to "Precisely *how* is it that I identify with and problematize any painful situations and self-sense?"

Q: [One is often then asked:] *"So, 'how' come there is suffering?"*

One can always point the questioner back to classic Advaitin/ Buddhist self-inquiry, "Who or What is aware of 'suffering'?" The knowing Awareness, after all, must be quite different in kind from its object. This Changeless Principle Right Here recognizes various changing emotional, mental, psychic, and physical states like suffering, ennui, loss, desire. The Changeless Awareness is not part of or tied to those changeful aspects of experience. If the person further responds, "Well, it feels like my suffering is changelessly part of my life," one can reply, "Where is it, then, in deep, dreamless sleep?" as evidence that suffering comes and goes and is not always, changelessly part of oneself.

But it is also therapeutically useful to sometimes speak on a more conventional, psychological level by distinguishing between *intensity, pain,* and *suffering.* Basically, any form of physical or emotional *pain* is a form of *intense energy* that one does not know how to process psychophysiologically. There is an ancient, evolutionary programming within different species to perceive and judge certain intense stimuli: "Owww! Painful!" Without this discrimination, most animal species never would have survived, lacking incentive to run away from predators chomping on one's limbs. So *pain* is a useful alarm signal. *Suffering* comes in with neurotically self-obsessing thoughts like "Why is God always doing this to *me?*"

One can drop the "suffering" of certain painful situations by letting go inner judgments, resentments, regrets, expectations, and the sense of being the hapless target-entity afflicted by cruel outside forces, and instead simply *notice pain,* along with intelligently making any changes needed (e.g., pulling the hand away from the fire or moving beyond a chronically abusive relationship). This shift from conflicted suffering to fully experiencing pain is well-known to many professionals working in pain-management clinics, where the emergent wisdom has been to teach clients how to meditatively *be-the-pain.* Studies indicate that many people's felt-sense of even physical pain actually diminishes considerably, by up to 80 percent, by focusing upon pain's raw sensations and not getting entangled in self-obsessing thoughts *about* the pain and its relation to "me."

Marathon runners, swimmers, cyclers, weight-lifters et al., routinely take on extremely painful situations while training. Their muscles and entire physiology painfully "scream" as these athletes repeatedly go beyond their normal felt-sense of physical and mental limits, stretching into greater excellence. Most persons suddenly placed into this stressful situation of athletic training would complain of being put into hell. But athletes seek out this situation—they know they can "become the pain" and realize it as *passionately-intense energy.* It's not just that the body-mind starts releasing endorphins and other natural pain-managing chemistry. No, these aware athletes often feel they've been released into nondual aliveness, pure intensity—no more subject of experience, object of experience, or dualistic process of experiencing. Just *pure experiencing.* This is, notably, one of the very definitions of *Brahman* in *Yoga Vasishtha.*

Likewise, we "become one with" any painful physical or emotional situation upon losing the dualistic sense of subject and object(s) and realizing we are really this *Formless Awareness* nondually *being* various *forms of intensity.* This is *Siva* experiencing ItSelf as *Sakti,* Awareness experiencing ItSelf as the sacred world of intense energy.

Q: *I feel emptiness, but it feels like a dead, disconnected, nonblissful, meaningless emptiness.*

Classic self-inquiry, again, would have one inquire "*Who* recognizes this emptiness as such?" Alternately, the individual is invited to explore the precise nature of this dead emptiness—or *any* body-mind state of suffering or dis-ease (e.g., anger, fear). It is Guest—You are nonseparate Host. What are its dynamics? How, precisely, does it manifest for each of the senses and the emotions? How, specifically, is it that the Infinite Being-Awareness-Bliss has packaged ItSelf in such an interesting masquerade? One explores the dead emptiness with that intense curiosity and "lurking suspicion" that it is really an opaque window onto the Divine Reality. So one *makes this dead emptiness the object of an informal, ongoing mindfulness or witnessing meditation* and, through the clarifying and dissolving power of Awareness, one witnesses it unravel and reveal itself as the Divine temporarily appearing in phenomenal form. As Advaita says, whatever is, is *Brahman*. There's no other Reality than this. When Awareness focuses on any object/state, it will eventually dissolve it, like sunlight melts a hard solid ice cube into water then vapor. Awareness ultimately dissolves everything back into pure Aliveness-energy.

It helps here to know that such "dead emptiness" states of feeling hapless, helpless, and hopeless are an almost standard crisis (Self-intended!) to render the "me-dream" so intolerable that one ceases to invest or cathect any more energy in "normal" living and instead awakens to Vastness. In other words, when the dream becomes stultifyingly banal or painfully nightmarish, there's motive to wake up altogether from dreaming. The me-syndrome becomes so "insufferable" that one melts, transcends, or simply pulls back from or snaps out of it by resuming one's real Identity.

Q: *I feel lots of energy coming through me and certain powers. How can I become a "cocreator" with God?*

This question arises when one believes that there are two Selves, God's and "mine." But there is only the nondual Self. Sagely tradition argues here for total humility, clarity, and transparency to preempt narcissism, pride, and megalomania. All that is meant to appear will spontaneously happen in and through the various selves as the Self's play. One need not push the river or add legs to a snake, as Zen says.

Q: *I feel an expanded sense of Awareness in meditation and espe-cially here in satsang/therapy, but then I lose it at other times, like at work. I feel I'm only aware of being Awareness some of the time, not all of the time. How to have more consistency?*

This very common concern presumes that Awareness is a special state of mind coming and going in time and can somehow be made "constant" by some special discipline, when in fact Awareness is time-lessly/always the Constant Substratum of the dream or movie of life. Our Real Nature is this Self-evident, Obvious ISNESS, the only non-changing aspect of our life. All else changes but THIS. And, as Ramana Maharshi frequently pointed out, people already know they are con-stantly the Self and really don't doubt it. Otherwise, if they were only their changing mind-states with no continuity, they would be inces-santly shocked, over and over, moment by moment, by the sudden reappearance of discrete, discontinuous body-mind states.

So we all know, deep down, subconsciously, that we are the One Self-Awareness. All that's "needed" is to stop consciously presuming that we are the changing, limited states of the body-mind and stop searching for some special new body-mind state called "enlighten-ment." The only way we miss Spiritual Truth is by searching for it on the "object"-ive level of body, mind, or psychic-soul.

The fact is that the God-Self—Infinite, Unborn Awareness—is equally present in human confusion and clarity, struggle and ease, failure and success, misery and joy, just as present as when one is on the meditation-seat, the car-seat or toilet-seat. Where else could God be but right HERE? When could God be but right NOW?

The wisdom-knowing of this grand yet simple Truth is what allows for deep relaxation, real freedom, blissful peace, and all-embracing love.

ACKNOWLEDGMENT

Pranams to the Absolute, to the nondual sages, and to John Prendergast, friend and early-1980s housemate, for the invitation to contribute to this growing literature; Elliott Isenberg, for pointing me to Nisargadatta Maharaj's *I Am That* dialogues in 1979; Stephen Quong, for the introduction to Annamalai Swami (a spiritual son of Ramana Maharshi) before my first India trip (1980–81); and Dan McClure, who, in my eighteenth year, two years after a life-changing nondual realization, alerted me to radical "Who am I?" inquiry and "dropping the personality," and urged: "Read everything you can on Ramana Maharshi and Zen."

ENDNOTES

1. I have been asked by the editors to focus on the Indian origins of nonduality, specifically within Hinduism, so I only gloss over nonduality in Buddhism (see other contributors' chapters), I ignore nonduality in India's Jaina tradition (e.g., sage Kundakunda), and I don't at all discuss it outside India within: 1) the ancient pre-Socratic Greek sages in Italy/Sicily—Parmenides (c. 515–450 B.C.E.) and Empedocles (c. 492-32), those "founders of the Western rationalist tradition," who were actually nondual-mystic healers, priests, and masters of trance and stillness *(hesychia)* devoted to Apollo Oulios (see Peter Kingsley's revisionist works); 2) Chinese contemplative Taoism (*Tao-chiao*), taught by sages Lao-tzu (c. fifth-fourth centuries B.C.E.?), Chuang-tzu (c. 369–286 B.C.E.) et al., or; 3) among Western neoplatonic, Christian, Muslim-Sufi, and Jewish-Kabbalist mystics (Plotinus, John Scottus Erigena, Meister Eckhart, Bayazid Bistami, Mansur al-Hallaj, Sanai, Rumi, Moshe Cordovero et al.). One is encouraged to sample, if not deeply explore, all these expressions of nonduality.

2. Wendy Doniger O'Flaherty (tr.), *The Rig Veda: An Anthology*, Penguin, 1981.

3. *Rg Veda,* i.152.5

4. William Mahony, "*Upanishads*," in Mircea Eliade (gen. ed.), *The Encyclopedia of Religion*, NY: Macmillan, 1987, vol. 15, pp. 148–52.

5. Pratap Chandra, "Was Early Buddhism Influenced by the Upanisads?" *Philosophy East & West*, vol. 21, no. 3 (July 1971) pp. 317–24. Two further points: 1) I accept the traditional earlier dating for the Buddha (c. 566–486 B.C.E.), persuasively reargued by Alex Wayman, E. Bruce Brooks, A. K. Narain et al., against the revisionist attempt by Heinz Bechert et al. in the 1980s to argue for

a later date for the Buddha (e.g., that he died in 368 B.C.E.). The dating of not just many Buddhist events but also the *Upanishads, Bhagavad Gita*, etc., and other ancient Indian historical developments all crucially depend on where we temporally situate the Buddha. 2) The Buddhist idea of *anatta/anatman*, "no-self," is better translated as "not-self" and viewed as a disidentification strategy, not an ontology bordering on the nihilistic. See insightful articles by Thanisssaro Bhikkhu (Geoffrey DeGraff), "No-self or Not-self" and "The Not-self Strategy," at www.accesstoinsight.org.

6.   All sixteen major *Upanishads* were fully translated by Sarvapelli Radhakrishnan, *The Principal Upanisads*, Harper & Brothers, 1953. For translations of fewer numbers, see Patrick Olivelle, Swami Nikhilananda et al. Most of the minor *Upanishads* and all major ones can finally be read in English translations, albeit without Sanskrit text or commentary, at www.celextel.org. The minor *Upanishads* adhere either to 1) the pure Vedanta of early *Upanishads*, or else lean toward 2) the rival Yoga-Samkhya system of practices and dualistic views, 3) strict renunciation/*sannyas*, 4) *mantra*-recitation, or 5–7) emerging new sectarian theist cults devoted to Vishnu, Siva, or Divine Mother (*Devi, Sakti*, etc.). Hence, the seven groupings of minor *Upanishads* are known as *Vedanta, Yoga, Sannyasa, Mantra, Vaisnava, Saiva,* and *Sakta Upanishads.* Some minor *Upanishads* have elements from a few or all these categories.

Note that most of the *Upanishads* contain material bearing on creation myths, Vedic rituals, exotica, esoterica, food, sex, gifts, wealth, the body, the afterlife, etc. These *Upanishads* are not "purely spiritual," by any means, but reflect the concerns of the colorful, feisty, and very vital Aryan society in which they arose.

7.   These five *mahavakyas* come from BrU i.4.10, ChU vi.8.7, MaU i.2, AU iii.3, and ChU iii.14.1.

8.   In a forthcoming work, *India's Sages Sourcebook* (Santa Barbara, CA: Wake Up Press, 2007), I give several hundred full quotes, with references, from the sixteen major *Upanishads* and several minor *Upanishads*, as well as a few thousand quotes from many other sages and texts only briefly mentioned in this article.

9.   In several of his works, Nagarjuna uses the equivalent terms *sruti, cinta,* and *bhavana* as the threefold *prajna*/wisdom bringing *Jnana* or *Bodhi*, full Awakening to the intrinsic Buddha-nature, the truth of oneself and all appearance. See Lindtner (1997) for Nagarjuna's additional authentic works beyond his famous *Madhyamika-karika* philosophy treatise (these other works yield a much broader, more balanced view of the sage).

Note: this contemplative method is first emphasized in the *Brhadaranyaka Upanishad* ("See and hear, reflect and concentrate on the Self," iv.5.6), then more succinctly stated as the triple method in the *Paingala Upanishad* (iii.2) and *Brahma-sutras* (iv.1.1) and subsequent works, especially in the treatises by Sankara.

10. Some scholars have tried to argue that the *Brahma-sutras* are more "qualified nondualist" than purely nondualist; other scholars and sages contest this. For translations, see Swami Vireswarananda, George Thibaut, S. Radhakrishnan. For a synopsis of this and many other works of this tradition, see Potter (1981), *Advaita Vedanta up to Samkara and His Pupils*.

11. "*Reality* is that which cannot be *subrated* [disvalued, contradicted] by any other experience…. The only experience, or state of being, whose content cannot be subrated in fact and in principle by any other experience—which no other experience can conceivably contradict—is the experience of pure spiritual identity… wherein the separation of self and non-self, of ego and world, is transcended, and pure oneness alone remains." Eliot Deutsch (1973), *Advaita Vedanta: A Philosophic Reconstruction*, p. 18.

12. On these important sages, see, for starters (and for works not already mentioned), Sankara's most authentically attributable independent work, *Upadesa Sahasri* (various translations; and see Bradley Malkovsky on the probable authenticity of Sankara's devotional hymns); Utpaladeva's *Sivastotravali* nondual mystical-love verses (two English translations exist) and his sagely Advaita work *Isvarapratyabhijna-karika;* Abhinavagupta's *Paramarthasara;* Jnanesvar's *Amritanubhava* and *Changdeva Pasashti,* etc., and other works of the Marathi poet-saints as translated and discussed by R. D. Ranade; and work by Charlotte Vaudeville, John Stratton Hawley, and other scholars on the *Nirguni Sant* and *Sikh* poet-saints. One can also delve further into medieval Advaita/*advaya* developments within Buddhist and Hindu tantra; e.g., see David Snellgrove and Alex Wayman on Indian Buddhist tantra and the *mahasiddhas,* and George Weston Briggs on the quasi-Hindu Natha sect of Saiva *tantrikas* (Gorakhnath et al.).

13. See the author's forthcoming two-volume work, *India's Sages Sourcebook: Nondual Wisdom from Hindus, Buddhists, Jainas, Tantrics, Sants, Sikhs & Sufis,* featuring over 120 sages and texts, and, covering the modern era, *India's Sages: Nondual Wisdom from the Heart of Freedom* (Wake Up Press, 2007), with biographical sketches and ample spiritual teachings of more than thirty sages.

14. Personal communication, Bombay, January, 1981. A version of this same idea is also found in the modern-era "nondual bible" of Maharaj's discussions with aspirants, *I Am That: Conversations with Sri Nisargadatta Maharaj* (Maurice Frydman, tr.), revised one-volume ed., 1982.

15. In his article "Double Vision: Duality and Nonduality in Human Experience," in *The Sacred Mirror: Nondual Wisdom & Psychotherapy,* ch. 6, John Welwood writes of this as "becoming fully human," beyond subhuman egoity or transhuman egolessness. With students/clients, I have termed this "the poignant

dignity of God playing the role of human being"—to be deeply honored in "oneself" and "others."

16. I recommend the delightful experiential exercises ("the science of the 1st Person") shared by British sage Douglas Harding for authentically realizing Awareness (beyond mere abstract concept) as one's imperceptible but quite *be*-able Self. See www.headless.org and bibliographic references.

SELECTED BIBLIOGRAPHY

Abhayananda, Swami (1989). *Jnaneshvar: The Life & Works of the Celebrated Thirteenth Century Indian Mystic-Poet*. Olympia, WA: Atma Books.

Abhinavagupta (1991). *Essence of the Exact Reality or Paramarthasara of Abhinavagupta* (B. N. Pandit, tr.). New Delhi: Munshiram Manoharlal.

Adams, W. (1995). "Revelatory openness wedded with the clarity of unknowing: Psychoanalytic evenly suspended attention, the phenomenological attitude, and meditative awareness." *Psychoanalysis and Contemporary Thought* 18(4): 463–94.

Adyashanti (2003). "Love returning for itself," in *The Sacred Mirror: Nondual Wisdom and Psychotherapy* (ed. J. Prendergast, P. Fenner, and S. Krystal). St. Paul: Paragon House.

Anandamayi Ma (1959). *Matri Vani* (Br. Atmananda, tr.). Varanasi: Shree Shree Anandamayee Sangha.

———— (1971). *Words of Anandamayi Ma* (Br. Atmananda, tr.). Varanasi: Shree Shree Anandamayee Sangha, 2d ed.

———— (1973). *Sad Vani* (Br. Atmananda, tr.). Varanasi: Shree Shree Anandamayee Sangha.

Anonymous (1979). *Sadguru Gnanananda*. Bombay: Bharatiya Vidya Bhavan.

Assagioli, Roberto (1965). *Psychosynthesis: A Manual of Principles and Techniques*. NY: Viking.

Atmananda (Sri Krishna Menon) (1963). *Notes on Spiritual Discourses of Sri Atmananda (of Trivandrum)*. Vol. 2, 1953–59 (Nitya Tripta, ed.). Trivandrum: Reddiar Press.

Atwood, G., and R. Stolorow (1984). *Structures of Subjectivity: Explorations in Psychoanalytic phenomenology*. Hillsdale, NJ: Analytic Press.

Avadhuta Gita (See various translations by Swamis Abhayananda, Chetanananda, Ashokananda.)

Ashtavakra Samhita or *Gita* (See various translations by Swami Nityaswarupananda, Hari Prasad Shastri, Radhakamal Mukerjee.)

Bahirat, B. P. (1984). *The Philosophy of Jnanadeva*. New Delhi: Motilal Banarsidass ed. (first published in 1956).

Batchelor, S. (2000). *Verses from the Center*. New York: Riverhead Books.

Bayda, E. (2003). *Being Zen*. Boston: Shambhala.

Becker, E. (1973). *The Denial of Death*. New York: Free Press.

Benoit, Hubert (1959). *The Supreme Doctrine: Psychological Studies in Zen Thought* (Terence Gray, tr.). NY: Viking (first published in France, 1951).

———— (1973). *Let Go! Theory and Practice of Detachment According to Zen* (Albert Low, tr.). NY: Samuel Weiser (first published in France, 1954).

Beres, D. (1980). "Certainty: A Failed Quest." *Psychoanalytic Quarterly* 49: 1–26.

Berger, P., and T. Luckmann (1967). *The Social Construction of Reality: A Treatise in the Sociology of Knowledge*. NY: Doubleday.

Bhagavad Gita (Many translations, by S. Radhakrishnan, Winthrop Sergeant, David White, F. Edgerton, Eliot Deutsch, R. Minor, W. J. Johnson, J.A.B. Van Buitenen, and Laurie Patton.)

Blackstone, J. (2002). *Living Intimately*. London: Watkins Publishing.

———— (2007). *The Empathic Ground: Intersubjectivity and Nonduality in the Psychotherapeutic Process*. Albany: State University of New York Press.

Blakney, R. (1941). *Meister Eckhart*. NY: Harper & Row.

Bollas, C. (1987). *The Shadow of the Object: Psychoanalysis of the Unthought Known*. New York: Columbia University Press.

Brahma-Sutras (*Vedanta-Sutras*) (See various translations, usually with Sankara's commentary, by Swami Vireswarananda, George Thibaut, S. Radhakrishnan.)

Bugental, J. (1978). *Psychotherapy and Process*. NY: Addison-Wesley.

Cabezon, J. (1992). *A Dose of Emptiness: An Annotated Translation of the* sTong thun chen mo *of mKhas grub dGe legs dpal bzang*. Albany: State University of New York Press.

Caplan, M. (2002a). *Do You Need a Guru?: Understanding the Student-Teacher Relationship in an Era of False Prophets*. London.

———— (1999). *Halfway Up the Mountain: The Error of Premature Claims to Enlightenment*. Prescott, AZ: Hohm Press.

———— (2002b). "Adventures of a New Age Traveler," [in] *Radical Spirit: Spiritual Writings from the Voices of Tomorrow*. Novato, CA: New World Library.

Casper, M. (1976). "The psychology of meditation," in *Garuda IV: The Foundations of Mindfulness*. Ed. C. Trungpa. Berkeley: Shambhala.

Cenkner, William (1983). *A Tradition of Teachers: Sankara & the Jagadgurus Today*. New Delhi: Motilal Banarsidass.

Chandrakirti (2004). *Introduction to the Middle Way: Chandrakirti's* Madhyamakavatara *with commentary by Jamgon Mipham*. Padmakara Translation

Group. Boston: Shambhala.

Chang, Garma C. C. (gen. ed.) (1983). *A Treasury of Mahayana Sutras: Selections from the Maharatnakuta Sutra.* Penn State University.

———— (tr.). (1977). *The Hundred Thousand Songs of Milarepa (Mila Grubum)* (2 vols.). Boulder, CO: Shambhala.

Chogyam, Ngakpa (1995). *Wearing the Body of Visions.* London: Aro Books.

Chogyam Trungpa Rinpoche (1973). *Cutting through Spiritual Materialism.* Boston: Shambhala Books.

Comans, Michael (2000). *The Method of Early Advaita Vedanta (A Study of Gaudapada, Samkara, Suresvara and Padmapada).* New Delhi: Motilal Banarsidass.

Conze, Edward (tr. & ed.) (1975). *The Perfection of Wisdom* [Prajna-Paramita] *in Eight Thousand Lines* [Ratnagunasamcayagatha] *& Its Verse Summary* [Astasahasrika]. Bolinas, CA: Four Seasons Foundation.

Conze, E., David Snellgrove et al. (eds.) (1964). *Buddhist Texts through the Ages.* Harper Torchbook ed. (first published in 1954).

Deikman, Arthur (1982). *The Observing Self: Mysticism and Psychotherapy.* Boston: Beacon.

Deutsch, Eliot (1973). *Advaita Vedanta: A Philosophical Reconstruction.* Honolulu: University Press of Hawaii ed.

Deutsch, E., and Rohit Dalvi (ed.) (2004). *The Essential Vedanta: A New Source Book of Advaita Vedanta.* Bloomington, IN: World Wisdom.

Dogen, E. (1985). *Moon in a Dewdrop: Writings of Zen Master Dogen* (ed. K. Tanahashi). San Francisco: North Point Press.

Doumoulin, Heinrich (1963). *A History of Zen Buddhism* (Paul Peachey, tr. from the German 1959 edition). Boston: Beacon.

Dyczkowski, Mark (1987). *The Doctrine of Vibration: An Analysis of the Doctrines & Practices of Kashmir Shaivism.* Albany: SUNY.

Eckhart, M. (1957). *The Essential Sermons, Commentaries, Treatises, and Defense.* (trans. E. Colledge and B. McGinn). London: Paulist Press.

Fenner, P. (1990). *The Ontology of the Middle Way.* Dordrecht: Kluwer Publications.

———— (1995). *Reasoning into Reality: A Systems-Cybernetics and Therapeutic Interpretation of Middle Path Analysis.* Boston: Wisdom Publications.

———— and P. Fenner (2001). *Essential Wisdom Teachings: The Way to Inner Peace.* York Beach, ME: Nicholas Hays.

Ferguson, Andy (2000). *Zen's Chinese Heritage: The Masters and Their Teachings.* Somerville, MA: Wisdom Publications.

Ferrer, J. (2006). "Embodied Spirituality: Then and Now." *Tikkun* (May/June).

Forman, R.K.C. (ed.) (1998). *The Innate Capacity.* New York and Oxford: Oxford University Press.

Freud, S. (1912). "Recommendations to Physicians Practicing Psycho-Analysis," in *The Standard Edition of the Works of Sigmund Freud.* London: Hogarth.

Fromm, Erich (1963). *The Art of Loving.* NY: Bantam (first published in 1956).

———— (1976). *To Have or To Be?* NY: Harper & Row.

————, Richard De Martino, and D. T. Suzuki (1963). *Zen Buddhism and Psychoanalysis.* NY: Harper & Row.

Giorgi, A. (1970). *Psychology as a Human Science: A Phenomenologically Based Approach.* NY: Harper & Row.

Godman, D. (ed.) (1992). *Be As You Are: The Teachings of Sri Ramana Maharshi.* New Delhi: Penguin Books India.

Gyamtso, T. (2001). *Progressive Stages of Meditation on Emptiness.* Auckland, New Zealand: Prajna Editions, Zhyisil Chokyi Ghatsal Publications.

Harding, Douglas (1986). *On Having No Head: Zen and the Rediscovery of the Obvious.* NY: Arkana, rev. ed. (first published in 1961).

———— (1974). *The Science of the First Person.* Nacton, Ipswich, UK: Shollond.

———— (1988). *The Little Book of Life & Death.* London: Arkana.

———— (1996). *Look for Yourself: The Science and Art of Self-Realisation.* London: Head Exchange Press.

Hart, T., P. Nelson, and K. Puhakka (eds.) (2000). *Transpersonal Knowing.* Albany: SUNY Press.

Heidegger, M. (1977). "On the Essence of Truth," in *Basic Writings* (ed. D. Krell). NY: Harper & Row.

Hirst, Jacqueline Suthren (2005). *Samkara's Advaita Vedanta: A Way of Teaching.* London/NY: Routledge.

Hixon, L. (1993). *Mother of the Buddhas: Meditation on the Prajnaparamita Sutra.* Wheaton, IL: Quest Books.

Hopkins, J. (1983). *Meditation on Emptiness.* Cumbria: Wisdom Publications.

Huang-po (1958). *The Zen Teaching of Huang Po* (trans. J. Blofeld). London: Buddhist Society,

Husserl, E. (1970). *The Crisis of European Sciences and Transcendental Phenomenology.* (Originally published in 1954). Evanston, IL: Northwestern University Press.

Isayeva, Natalia (1995). *From Early Vedanta to Kashmir Shaivism: Gaudapada, Bhartrhari, & Abhinavagupta.* Albany: SUNY Press.

James, William (1958). *The Varieties of Religious Experience.* NY: New American Library (first published in 1902).

Jones, Rufus (1909). *Studies in Mystical Religion.* London: Macmillan.

Kapleau, P. (1966). *The Three Pillars of Zen.* Tokyo: Weatherhill.

Kingsley, Peter (2004). *Reality.* Inverness, CA: Golden Sufi Center.

Kohut, H. (1984) *How Does Analysis Cure?* Chicago: University of Chicago Press.

Krishnamurti (1998). *Sayings of J. Krishnamurti* (ed. S. Weeraperuma). New Delhi: Motilal Banarsidass.

Laing, R. D. (1990). *The Divided Self.* NY: Penguin Books.

Lankavatara Sutra (D. T. Suzuki, tr.). (1932). Routledge & Kegan Paul.

Lewis, Franklin (2000). *Rumi: Past & Present, East & West.* Oxford, UK: Oneworld Publications.

Lin-Chi (1993). *The Zen Teachings of Master Lin-Chi.* (tr. B. Watson). Boston: Shambhala.

Longchenpa (1987). *You Are the Eyes of the World.* (tr. K. Lipman & M. Peterson). Novato, CA: Lotsawa.

Loy, D. (1998). *Nonduality: A Study in Comparative Philosophy.* Amherst, NY: Humanity Books.

——— (1990). "A Zen Cloud? Comparing Zen Koan Practice with the Cloud of Unknowing," in *Buddhist-Christian Studies* 9.

——— (1996). *Lack and Transcendence: The Problem of Death and Life in Psychotherapy, Existentialism, and Buddhism.* NJ: Humanities Press.

Madhyamakavatara, with commentary by Jamgon Mipham. Boston: Shambhala.

Maharaj, Sri N. (1982). *I Am That.* Durham, NC: Acorn Press.

Maharshi, R. (ed. M. Greenblatt) (2001). *Essential Teachings of Ramana Maharshi.* La Jolla, CA: Inner Directions Press.

Meher Baba (1995). *Discourses.* North Myrtle Beach, SC: Sheriar Foundation, 7th rev. ed. (1 vol.).

Merleau-Ponty, M. (1968). *The Visible and Invisible.* (Originally published in 1964). Evanston, IL: Northwestern University Press.

Mumon, Y. (trans. Sogen Hori, V.). *Lectures on the Ten Oxherding Pictures.* Honolulu: University of Hawai'i Press.

Murphy, Paul (1986). *Triadic Mysticism: The Mystical Theology of the Saivism of Kashmir.* New Delhi: Motilal Banarsidass.

Nagarjuna (1995) *Mulamadhamakakarika: The Fundamental Wisdom of the Middle Way* (trans. and commentary by Jay L. Garfield). New York: Oxford University Press.

——— (1997). *Master of Wisdom: Writings of the Buddhist Master Nagarjuna* (Christian Lindtner, ed. & tr.). Berkeley, CA: Dharma Publications, rev. ed.

Nalanda Translation Committee (tr.) (1980). *Kagyu Gyutso: The Rain of Wisdom.* Boston: Shambhala.

Nishitani, K. (1982). *Religion and Nothingness.* Berkeley and Los Angeles: University of California Press.

Nityananda, Swami (1985). *Nitya Sutras: The Revelations of Nityananda from the Chidakash Gita* (M.U. Hatgendi & Swami Chetanananda, ed. & tr.). Cambridge, MA: Rudra Press.

Norbu, N. (1984). *Dzog Chen and Zen* (ed. K. Lipman). Grass Valley, CA: Blue Dolphin Press.

Norbu, C. N. (1996). *Dzogchen: The Self-Perfected State.* Ithaca, NY: Snow Lion.

Orange, D. M. (2000). "Zeddies Relational Unconscious." *Psychoanalytic Psychology* 17: 488–92.

———, G. E. Atwood, and R. D. Stolorow (1997). *Working Intersubjectively: Contextualism in Psychoanalytic Practice.* Hillsdale, NJ: Analytic Press.

——— (1995). *Emotional Understanding.* New York: Guilford Press.

Pande, Govind Chandra (2004). *Life & Thought of Sankaracarya.* New Delhi: Motilal Banarsidass.

Pandey, K. C. (1963). *Abhinavagupta: An Historical & Philosophical Study.* Varanasi: Chowkhamba, 2d rev. ed.

Potter, Karl (ed.) (1981). *Advaita Vedanta Up to Samkara and His Pupils (The Encyclopedia of Indian Philosophies*, Vol. 3). Princeton University Press.

Powers, J. (tr.) (1995). *Wisdom of the Buddha: A Translation of the Samdhinirmocana Sutra.* London: Dharma Publications.

Prendergast, J. (2000). "The Chakras in Transpersonal Psychotherapy" in *International Journal of Yoga Therapy*, N. 10.

———, P. Fenner, and S. Krystal (eds.) (2003). *The Sacred Mirror.* St. Paul: Paragon House.

Puri, J. R. (2000). *Guru Nanak: His Mystic Teachings.* Punjab: Radha Soami Satsang Beas, 3d ed.

Rabjam, L. (2001a). *A Treasure Trove of Scriptural Transmission* (R. Barron, trans.). Junction City, CA: Padma Publishing.

——— (2001b). *The Precious Treasury of the Basic Space of Phenomena* (R. Barron, trans.). Junction City, CA: Padma Publishing.

Ramdas, Swami (Papa) (1968–73). *Ramdas Speaks* (5 vols.). Bombay: Bharatiya Vidya Bhavan, 2d ed.

——— (1969, 1975). *God Experience* (2 vols.). Bombay: Bharatiya Vidya Bhavan/ Kanhangad: Anandashram.

Ranade, R. D. (1983). *Mysticism in India: The Poet-Saints of Maharashtra.* Albany: SUNY ed. (first published in 1933).

Ribhu Gita (1995). (H. Ramamoorthy, tr., with Master Nome). Santa Cruz, CA: SAT/Society of Abidance in Truth.

Rogers, C. (1959). "A theory of therapy, personality, and interpersonal relationships, as developed in the client-centered framework." In S. Koch (ed.), *Psychology: A Study of Science,* New York: McGraw-Hill.

Rumi, J. (1999). *The Glance* (trans. C. Barks). NY: Penguin.

Sana'i (1976). *The Walled Garden of Truth, Hadiqat al-Haqiqa* (David Pendlebury, tr. and abridged). NY: E. P. Dutton.

Sangharakshita (1985). *The Eternal Legacy: An Introduction to the Canonical Literature of Buddhism.* London: Tharpa.

Sankara (1975). *Atma-Bodha (Self Knowledge)* (and devotional hymns) (Swami Nikhilananda, tr.). Madras: Sri Ramakrishna Math.

————— (1992). *A Thousand Teachings: The Upadesasahasri of Sankara* (Sengaku Mayeda, ed. & tr.). Albany: SUNY Press.

Sarvapelli Radhakrishnan, Swami Nikhilananda, Patrick Olivelle et al. Online translations of more than eighty major and minor *Upanishads* are posted (*sans* commentary or Devanagiri script) at www.celextel.org.

Schimmel, Annemarie (1975). *Mystical Dimensions of Islam.* Chapel Hill, NC: University of North Carolina.

Sogyal Rinpoche (1990). *Dzogchen and Padmasambhava.* Junction City, CA: Rigpa.

Stambaugh, J. (1999). *The Formless Self.* Albany: State University of New York Press.

Stolorow, R. D., G. E. Atwood, and B. Brandchaft (1987). *Psychoanalytic Treatment: An Intersubjective Approach.* Hillsdale, NJ: Analytic Press.

—————, and G. E. Atwood (1992). *Contexts of Being: The Intersubjective Foundations of Psychological Life.* Hillsdale, NJ: Analytic Press.

—————, G. E. Atwood, and D. M. Orange (2002). *Worlds of Experience.* New York: Basic Books.

Suzuki, D. T. (1956). *Zen Buddhism.* New York: Anchor.

Tansey, M., and W. Burke, *Understanding Countertransference.* Hillsdale, NJ: Analytic Press.

Thich Nhat Hanh (1999). *Collected Poems of Thich Nhat Hanh.* CA: Parallax Press.

Thompson, B. M. (2002). *The Odyssey of Enlightenment.* Mt. Shasta, CA: Wisdom Editions.

Thondup, T. (1996). *The Healing Power of Mind.* Boston: Shambhala.

Thurman, R. (1984). *Tsong Khapa's Speech of Gold in the* Essence of True Eloquence*: Reason and Enlightenment in the Central Philosophy of Tibet* Princeton: Princeton University Press.

Tolle, E. (1999). *The Power of Now.* Novato, CA: New World Library.

Tripura Rahasya. (Various translations by Sri Munagala Venkataramaiah, Pandit Rajmani Tigunait.)

Trungpa, C. (1973). *Cutting through Spiritual Materialism* (eds. J. Baker & M. Casper). Boston: Shambhala.

————— (2005). *The Sanity We are Born With: A Buddhist Approach to Psychology.* Boston: Shambhala.

Tsoknyi Rinpoche (1998). *Carefree Living,* Hong Kong & Kathmandu: Rangjung Yeshe.

Underhill, Evelyn (1961). *Mysticism.* NY: E. P. Dutton (first published in 1911).

Upanishads. (Various translations by Thompson, B. M. (2002). *The Odyssey of Enlightenment.* Mt. Shasta, CA: Wisdom Editions.

Utpaladeva (1987). *Shaiva Devotional Songs of Kashmir: A Translation & Study of Utpaladeva's Shivastotravali* (Constantina Rhodes Bailly, tr.). Albany: SUNY Press.

—— (2002). *Isvarapratyabhijnakarika of Utpaladeva with the Author's Vrtti* (Raffaele Torella, tr.). New Delhi: Motilal Banarsidass, rev. ed.

Vaudeville, Charlotte. (1998). *A Weaver Named Kabir: Selected Verses with a Detailed Biographical & Historical Introduction.* London: Oxford University Press.

Venkatesananda, Swami (tr.). (1993). *Vasishtha's Yoga.* Ithaca, NY: SUNY Press (first published in 2 vols. in 1976 as *The Supreme Yoga: A New Translation of the Yoga Vasishtha*).

Watson, Gay (2001). *The Resonance of Emptiness: A Buddhist Inspiration for a Contemporary Psychotherapy.* New Delhi: Motilal Banarsidass.

Welwood, J. (2003). "Double Vision: Duality and Nonduality in Human Experience," in *The Sacred Mirror.* St. Paul: Paragon House.

—— (2000). *Toward a Psychology of Awakening.* Boston: Shambhala.

White, John (ed.). (1972). *The Highest State of Consciousness.* Garden City, NY: Doubleday.

—— (1984). *What Is Enlightenment? Exploring the Goal of the Spiritual Path.* Los Angeles: J. P. Tarcher.

Wilber, Ken. (1979). *No Boundary: Eastern and Western Approaches to Personal Growth.* Boulder, CO: Shambhala.

—— (1996). *The Atman Project.* Wheaton, IL: Quest Books, rev. ed. (first published in 1980).

—— (1996). *A Brief History of Everything.* Boston: Shambhala.

—— (1997). *The Eye of Spirit: An Integral Vision for a World Gone Slightly Mad.* Boston: Shambhala.

ABOUT THE CONTRIBUTORS

COEDITORS

John J. Prendergast, Ph.D., is a psychotherapist in private practice in San Rafael, California. He is also an Adjunct Associate Professor of Psychology at the California Institute of Integral Studies in San Francisco, where he has taught since 1990. He is senior editor (with Peter Fenner and Sheila Krystal) of *The Sacred Mirror: Nondual Wisdom and Psychotherapy,* author of "The Chakras in Transpersonal Psychotherapy" in the *International Journal of Yoga Therapy* (2000), and coauthor (with S. Krystal, P. Krystal, P. Fenner, and I. and K. Shapiro) of "Transpersonal Psychology, Eastern Philosophy and EMDR", in F. Shapiro (ed.) *EMDR as an Integrative Psychotherapy Approach: Experts of Diverse Orientations Explore the Paradigm Prism,* American Psychological Association Books (2002). He is also one of the main organizers of the Conference on Nondual Wisdom and Psychotherapy, which has met annually since 1998 (please see www. wisdompsy.com for details). He began a regular meditation practice in 1970; traveled to India on three occasions to be with various teachers, including Ammachi; and spent fifteen years with Dr. Jean Klein, a European sage who synthesized elements of Advaita Vedanta and Kashmiri Saivism. He has studied with Adyashanti since 2001. He currently offers several self-inquiry groups and can be contacted at (415) 453-8832 or johnprendergast@comcast.net .

G. Kenneth Bradford, Ph.D., is a licensed psychologist in private practice in the San Francisco Bay area. He is an adjunct professor at John F. Kennedy University and the California Institute of Integral Studies, where he teaches courses on Existential-Contemplative Psychotherapy and psychological assessment integrating mindfulness and phenomenological perspectives. He offers advanced training, workshops, and lectures in the United States and Europe, integrating existential therapeutic sensibilities with the principles and practices of Buddhadharma. Ken studied Existential Psychotherapy as a protégé of James Bugental beginning in 1988, joining him as a teaching associate in 1994. His clinical background also includes training in European and relational Psychoanalysis, Focusing (with Eugene Gendlin), and Nondual Therapy (with Peter Fenner). Ken has been a *vipassana* student since 1975, being most indebted to the instruction of Joseph Goldstein and Ruth Denison. He met his root Dzogchen master, Chogyal Namkhai Norbu, in 1980, and has also studied with other masters of Vajrayana Buddhism, including, Tsoknyi Rinpoche, Tarthang Tulku, and Dudjom Rinpoche. His recent publications address "Natural Resilience," "Therapeutic Courage," "Unconditioned Presence," "Psychotherapeutic Eros," and "Romantic Love as Path: Tensions Between Erotic Desire and Security Needs." He can be contacted at 925-283-9377 or ken@bradfordphd.com.

OTHER CONTRIBUTORS

Judith Blackstone, Ph.D., is author of *The Subtle Self, The Enlightenment Process, Living Intimately,* and the upcoming *The Empathic Ground: Intersubjectivity and Nonduality in the Psychotherapeutic Process* (SUNY Press, 2007). She has also contributed to *Inner Directions* journal and to the anthology *Finding a Way.* Judith developed Realization Process, a method of nondual realization that includes psychological and relational healing. She has taught this work at Esalen Institute in California since 1987. She is also on the faculty of the Institute of Transpersonal Psychology and of Empire State College, SUNY. Judith has been a meditation practitioner and student of contemplative traditions for thirty years. She is a psychotherapist and Realization Process teacher in private practice in New York City and Woodstock, New York.

Mariana Caplan, Ph.D., is the author of six books, including *Halfway Up the Mountain: the Error of Premature Claims to Enlightenment* (Hohm Press, 1999), and *Do You Need a Guru? Understanding the Student-Teacher Relationship in an Era of False Prophets* (Thorsons, 2002). She is an adjunct professor at the California Institute of Integral Studies and the Naropa Institute, and has a private practice in spiritual guidance and counseling. She is a long-term practitioner in the Western Baul tradition under the guidance of her spiritual teacher Lee Lozowick. www.realspirituality.com

Timothy Conway, Ph.D., lives in Santa Barbara with his wife and three cats. His perspective is informed by a deep study of nonduality in all sacred traditions, a B.A. in Psychology & Religious Studies (UC Santa Cruz), M.A./Ph.D. degrees in East-West Psychology (CIIS in San Francisco), and trips to Asia and Europe starting in 1980. Encouraged in winter of 1980–81 to share the nondual/Advaita perspective by Ramana Maharshi's disciple Annamalai Swami, by Nisargadatta Maharaj, and other sages, he waited until the late 1980s before openly adopting this work. Based in Santa Barbara, he has for nearly twenty years facilitated nondual *satsangs,* taught classes at various institutions (ongoing free classes for seventeen years through the acclaimed SBCC Adult Education Department), and coached persons wanting a more authentic applied spiritual understanding. Author of *Women of Power & Grace: Nine Astonishing, Inspiring Luminaries of Our Time* (including rich nondual teachings of Anandamayi Ma, Anasuya Devi, and Amritanandamayi), Timothy is preparing a comprehensive two-volume work, *India's Sages* and *India's Sages Sourcebook,* together featuring over 150 esteemed adepts and texts of nondual wisdom/devotion in Hindu, Buddhist, Tantric, Jaina, Nirguni Sant Bhakti, Sikh, and Indian Sufi traditions. A book of *satsang* talks dating to the early 1990s and a trilogy of books applying nonduality to religion, science, and politics are also in preparation. Timothy may be reached at t.conway1@cox.net or 222 Meigs Road #8, Santa Barbara, CA 93109; 805-564-2125.

Penny Fenner, MAPsS, is a psychologist, teacher, writer, mother, and executive coach to CEOs and their teams. She has been steeped in Buddhism since the 1970s. In her work she distills the essence of nondual wisdom, integrating this with Western therapeutic and development processes. Her work directly helps dispel many myths arising in the spiritual and psychological journey. Based in Australia and traveling regularly to the United States, Penny provides therapy, executive coaching, spiritual guidance, and group work globally. Coauthor of *Essential Wisdom Teachings: The Way to Inner Peace,* Penny is currently writing a book based on the synthesis underscoring her life work, of which this chapter offers a slice.

Peter Fenner, Ph.D., is a leader in the adaptation of Mahayana nondual wisdom for Western needs. He was a celibate monk in the Tibetan Buddhist traditions for nine years. His main teachers include Lama Thubten Yeshe, Lama Zopa Rinpoche, Namkhai Norbu Rinpoche, and Sogyal Rimpoche. He has a Ph.D. in the philosophical psychology of Madhyamika Buddhism. His books include *Radiant Mind, The Edge of Certainty: Paradoxes on the Buddhist Path, Reasoning into Reality, Essential Wisdom Teaching* (with Penny Fenner), and *The Ontology of the Middle Way.* He was a Senior Lecturer in Asian philosophy at Deakin University for twenty years. Peter is founder and spiritual director of the Center for Timeless Wisdom (www.wisdom.org). Since 2003 he has been offering an innovative and comprehensive ninth-month course in nondual presence, called Radiant Mind, in the U.S. and Europe. Peter has taught at Naropa University, Omega Institute, Open Center-Tibet House, Spirit Rock, Trimurti (France), Les Cormettes (France), ZIST (Germany), and the Center for Mind-Body Medicine (Israel). He has presented his work at Stanford University, Columbia University, the University of California at Berkeley, CIIS, ITP, Saybrook College, the University of Hawaii, and JFK University. Peter's way of teaching is known for its dynamic and engaging deconstruction of all fixed frames of reference that block entry to the unconditioned mind, and for the purity and depth of natural, uncontrived silence that emerges in his work.

Dorothy S. Hunt, A.M., L.C.S.W., is the founder of the San Francisco Center for Meditation and Psychotherapy, and has practiced psychotherapy since 1967. Following a series of ever-deepening realizations, she was invited by her spiritual teacher, Adyashanti, to teach within his lineage. Dorothy now serves as President and Spiritual Director of Moon Mountain Sangha, Inc. offering *dokusan,* satsang, meditation intensives, and retreats in the San Francisco Bay area as well as elsewhere by invitation. She has taught extensively at her Center as well as workshops at Esalen, the Association for Transpersonal Psychology annual conferences, and at the Nondual Wisdom and Psychotherapy annual conferences.

Dorothy is the author of *Only This! (Poems and Reflections)*, a contributing author to *The Sacred Mirror: Nondual Wisdom and Psychotherapy*, and editor of *Love: A Fruit Always in Season*. Her poems have been published in the journals, *Advaita-Satya-Amritam, Nectar of Non-Dual Truth, Your Head in the Tiger's Mouth, Talks in Bombay with Ramesh S. Balsekar,* and the on-line journals, *Groundwater,* and *Mystic Poets*. She lives with her husband in San Francisco and Sonoma, California, and is both a mother and a grandmother. She may be contacted through her website at www.dorothyhunt.org.

Sheila Krystal, Ph.D., likes to garden and design altars, inside and outside. She admires Andy Goldsworthy and likes to dance and do yoga. She has been a licensed psychologist since 1974. She has a B.A. from Barnard College, an M.A. and Ph.D. from Columbia University (1970), was in Jungian analysis in New York City, spent four years as a postdoctoral fellow in the Human Development Program and the Psychiatry Department of the U.C. San Francisco Medical School, was in Reichian analysis, and finally is a continual student in the University of Life. She has sat with many teachers in her life, most notably Sai Baba, Ammachi, Papaji, Adyashanti, and Krishnamurti. She is a caretaker of a small collection of Sacred art, some of which has given *darshan* at various *satsangs* in the Bay Area. She has a business matching people with sacred objects and gems and textiles, feng sui and garden and interior redesign. She has edited several of her mother's eleven books, coauthored and published several articles in the *Journal of Substance Abuse Treatment* and *Maturitas,* coauthored a chapter in Francine Shapiro's *The Paradigm Prism* (2002), and coedited *The Sacred Mirror: Nondual Wisdom and Psychotherapy* (2003). Her e-mail address is shekrystal@aol.com and her telephone number is: 510-540-0855.

David R. Loy, Ph.D., a Zen student for many years, is qualified as a teacher in the Sambo Kyodan tradition. His present academic position is Besl Professor of religion and ethics at Xavier University in Cincinnati, Ohio. His work is primarily in comparative philosophy and religion, particularly comparing Buddhist with modern Western thought and social issues. His books include: *Nonduality: A Study in Comparative Philosophy* (1988), *Lack and Transcendence: The Problem of Death and Life in Psychotherapy, Existentialism, and Buddhism* (1996), *A Buddhist History of the West: Studies in Lack* (2002), and *The Great Awakening: A Buddhist Social Theory* (2003). E-mail: loyd@xavier.edu

Kaisa Puhakka, Ph.D., is Professor of Psychology at California Institute of Integral Studies and has previously taught at the Institute of Transpersonal Psychology and the State University of West Georgia. She also works as a psychotherapist in Palo Alto and in San Francisco and supervises students in psychotherapy training. A student of Hindu and Buddhist philosophical and spiritual systems, Dr. Puhakka is a longtime practitioner of Buddhist meditation and Zen and has written numerous articles and book chapters on Buddhist and Hindu thought and spiritual practice and on the interface between these and contemporary Western psychotherapy. She is former editor of the *Journal of Transpersonal Psychology* and coeditor of and contributor to *Transpersonal Knowing: Exploring the Horizon of Consciousness* (SUNY Press, 2000).

INDEX

A

Absolute awareness, 241

Absolute bodhicitta, 207–208

Absolute reality, 198–199

Absolute truth, 71–74, 240–241

Acceptance, practice, 193–194

Activity, observation, 154

Adhyatma-yoga, 235

Advaita Vedanta, 32, 79, 197
  nondual wisdom, 22
  secret doctrine, 233
  top-down approach, 186–187

Adyashanti, 50–51

Aha experience, 161–162

Aja (One Truth), 231

Ajata-vada (no-creation view), 238

Ajnana, 233

Aletheia, 14–15

Anatta (selflessness), 174
  absence, 175–176

Anxiety/calm, 227

Aranyakas, 232

Articulate contradictions, 143–144

As if condition, 42–43

Attunement, 43

Authors, involvement, 19–33

Avatamsaka, 238

Avidya, 233

Awakening, 6–11. See also Initial
    awakenings; Nondual awakening
  experience, 7
  expression, 173
  modes, 243–245

questions, 246–250
triple method, 236
Awareness
  awakening, 244
  coming from, 164
  discovery, 115
  field, 123
  mode, 243–244
  sense, expansion, 250

B

Badha, 239

Bauls (Bengal), embodied spirituality
    practice, 184

Being. See Home; Inter-being
  consciousness, 103
  illusion, stopping/dropping/
    releasing, 243
  immensity, 55
  Mystery, 101

Beliefs, filtration process, 44–45

Bhagavad Gita, 237

Bhakti heart, filling, 213

Blackstone, Judith, 19, 22

Bodhi Tree, 195

Bodhicitta, 207. See also Absolute
    bodhicitta

Bodian, Stephen, 167

Bodily grounding, absence, 204

Body, integration, 213

Body-based therapy, 217
  case study, 222–228
  conclusion, 228
  endnotes, 229

Body-mind
  conditioning, holding, 13
  transformation, 16
Body-sensing, 89
Bodywork
  focus, 225–226
  impact, 224–225
  process, 221–222
Bondage (bandha), 238
Bradford, G. Kenneth, 1, 21, 55, 124
Brahman, 233–236, 239
  existence, 240
  formlessness, 237
  state/mood, 232
Brahma-Sutras, 236–237
Breathing (pranayama), 31, 217, 220
  type, 223
Brhadaranyaka, 233
Buddhata, existence, 240
Buddhism
  nondual wisdom, 22
  question, 178
  spiritual texts, 129
Burke, Walter, 47

C

Capacious no-thingness, 246–247
Caplan, Mariana, 27–28, 181
Casper, Marvin, 63–64
Changeless Principle Right Here, 247
Chest-belly-out breathing, 223
Chogyam, Ngakpa, 189, 190
Classical psychoanalysis, neutral
  stance, 124
Clear-through space, experience, 89
Cocreator, process, 249
Complementary experience, 47

Complete Perfection teachings, 197
Concluding dialogue, 144–146
  example, 144–146
Concordant experience, 47
Conditioned consciousness, grounding
  (problem), 175
Conditioned states (sankhara), 174
Conditioning
  disappearance, 109
  identity, 110–111
  structures, dismantling, 128
Conscious expectations, relaxation, 58
Consciousness, 82. See also Nondual
  consciousness
  division, 157
Contact capacity, deepening, 90
Contentless conversations, 25, 141–143
Contentlessness (nihsvabhavata), 121
Continuous consciousness, 108
Conversations. See Contentless
  conversations; Deconstructive
  conversations; Unfindability
  conversations
  paradoxes. See Nondual
  conversations
Conway, Timothy, 31–32, 231
Core distinctions, location, 128–129
Cosmic Source/Witness, 237
Creative heat, 231

D

Deconstruction, ethical implication,
  173
Deconstructive conversations, 128–129
  types, 129
Deconstructive inquiry, usage, 132–
  133

Deep empathy, nondual dimensions, 20

Delusions, 179

Depth psychology, reach/range, 73

Depth psychotherapy, 2–3, 58
purposes, 4

Deutsch, Eliot, 81

Diamond Sutra, 172

Direct contact, making, 156

Direct introduction, 141

Disconnected emptiness, 20–21

Discriminating wisdom, cultivation, 211

Disintegration, fear, 161–164. See also Self

Divine Atman/Self, 232, 233

Divine immanence, expense, 239–240

Divine Mystery, manifestation, 112

Doing
evaporation, 171–172
kinds, 166–167

Dualistic thought, artifact, 71

Duality
direction, 102
nondual expression, 189

Dukkha. See Suffering
types, 174

Dzogchen, 12, 15, 141, 197

E

Eckhart, Meister, 103
poverty sermon, 4–5

Ego
desire, experience, 106–107
experience, 106–108
mystery, transition, 108–110

Egoic need, 107

Ekam satyam, 231

Eknath, 239

Embodied nonduality
approach, 1
endnotes, 33–34

Embodied spirituality, 184
principles/practices, 181

EMDR, 167, 220
usage, 222–223

Emotional connection, 36–37

Emotional construct, reality (inquiry), 130–131

Emotional responsiveness, 84

Empathic introspective inquiry, 60–63

Empathic resonance, 42–47
cultivation methods, 44
endnotes, 52–53
reflections, 35

Empathy
clinical applications, 38–42
emphasis, 61–62
session, 38–40
comments, 40–42
survey, 43

Emptiness, 4–6. See also Disconnected emptiness; Sunyata
feeling, 248–249
requirement, 100–101

Empty essence, 203

Energy, feeling, 249

Energy flow, facilitation, 221

Enlightened duality, 192
danger, 193

Enlightenment. See Gradual enlightenment; Sudden enlightenment
clarity, 195
underbelly, 182

Entrainment, 25–26, 125–127

Environment, information, 105

Erring, extreme, 200

Essential relationship, 37–38
   endnotes, 52–53
   reflections, 35

Evil, roots, 178

Exclusive disidentification, 51

Existence, question, 247

Existentially independent entity, 78

Experience
   manipulation, push-pull, 198
   mind control, 114
   transposition, 199
   unspiritual aspects, 193

Eye-gazing, 167

F

Fast-food-spiritual technologies,
   caution, 28

Fear, movement agenda, 111

Feeling, 166
   need, 210

Fenner, Penny, 29–30, 197

Fenner, Peter, 24–25, 121

Ferrer, Jorge, 184

Fixated self, 152–153
   expression, 164
   reactions, 160

Fixating, 152
   capacity, 69

Flowing out, 154–155

Forms, behavior, 105

Foundation, strength, 200–201

Free association, practice, 57

Free Awareness, 245

Freud, Sigmund, 57–58
   advice, 59–60

Friend-client, other (absence), 241

Fully human, 243

G

Gaudapada, 137, 238–239

Gautama Buddha, 195

Gestalt psychotherapy, 77

God, dwelling, 184

God-ing, 242

God-Self, presence, 250

Gradual enlightenment, 168

Greed
   capacity, 191
   institutionalization, 178–179

Groundlessness, 175–176

Group self, sense, 177–178

Guest, receiving, 37–38

Gurdjieff, G.I., 181

H

Hane, Staci, 186

Hart, Tobin, 43–44

Hearing, neutral attitude, 3

Heart, healing, 197
   case studies, 205–206, 208–212
   conversations, 208–212

Heart, matters, 40

Heidegger, Martin, 14

Helper-rescuer-savior-liberator, 242

Helplessness, facing, 196

Higher Knowledge, 240–241

Higher Self, ordinary self (expansion),
   26

Hinduism, spiritual texts, 129

Home, being, 37–38

Honesty, cultivation, 202

Human discourse, context shift
  (elimination), 86
Hunt, Dorothy S., 23–24, 99, 167

I

I, concept, 105–106
I, question, 108
Impersonal, term, 85–86
Inclusive disidentification, 49–52
Initial awakenings, 7–8, 208
Inner child, addressing, 9
Inner stability, helpfulness, 8
Instant enlightenment, 201–202
  neo-Advaitic paths, caution, 28
Institutionalized poisons, nature
  (realization), 179–180
Insubstantial, coemergence, 201
Integration. See Body
  process, 14
  question, 191–193
Intensity, distinction, 247–248
Inter-being (pratityasamupada), 21,
  63–64
Interpretation
  making, 114
  process, 125
  unreality, inquiry, 129–136
Intersubjectivity. See
  Psychotherapeutic relationship
  nonduality, relationship, 84–88
  theory, 77–79, 84
  anit-Cartesian project, 88
  perspective, 87
Intrinsic meaning, unlocking, 131
Introjective identification, 47–48
  conscious/unconscious empathic
  resonance, 48

J

Jnana, 233
Jnanesvar, 239
Judgments, exasperation, 117–118
Jung, Carl, 228

K

Kashmiri Saivism, 12, 32
  doctrines, 190
Kaya sadhana, 184
Kensho, 7
Klein, Melanie, 47
Koans questions, timing/process, 138
Kohut, Heinz, 42, 61
Kornfield, Jack, 183, 185–186
Krystal, Sheila, 30–31, 167, 217

L

Lack, sense. See Sense of lack
Lankavatara, 238
Letting-go, 173
Levine, Peter, 186
Life force, 231
Lila (Divine pasttime), 237
Limiting world horizons, 85
L'intelligence du coeur (Jung), 3
Listening, 2–4. See also Negative
  listening; Nothing; Positive
  listening; Pure listening
  heart of Silence, 3
Living, untruth (impact), 116
Longchenpa, 199, See also Rabjam,
  Longchen
  paradox, 12
Loving-kindness, 200
  elixir, 207–208

fostering, 212
invocation, 209
practice, 212
Loy, David, 27, 71, 171
Lozowick, Lee, 182, 192
Lumiere, Lynn Marie, 186

M

Madhyamika, Mahayana, 15–16, 71
Madhyamika Buddhism, 79
Mahabharata, 237
Mahamudra, 197
Maharaj, Nisargadatta, 51, 219, 241, 245
Maharshi, Bhagavan Ramana, 51, 103, 242
  teachings, 86
Mandukya Upanishad, 238
Margas (spiritual paths), 237
Materialism. See Spiritual materialism
Maya (illusion), 51, 190
Meaning, 99, 112–113. See also Psychotherapeutic meaning
  endnotes, 119–120
Meaning-making process, 125
Meditation, usage, 223
Meditative techniques, usage, 172
Mental dukkha (repression), 174
Mental reality, creation, 226
Mental-emotion fixations, 63
Merging, intimacy/space sense (impact), 36
Militarism, institutionalized ill (example), 179
Mind, 99, 105–106
  deconditioning, 172
  distraction, 225

endnotes, 119–120
judgment, 108
psychology, 194
spaciousness, 202
Mind-body entity, 78
Misguided openness, 203–205
Mystery, 99
  bright face, 103–104
  dark face, 102–103
  discovery, 104
  endnotes, 119–120
  self-reflecting quality, 105–106
  transition. See Ego
  understanding, 100

N

Namdev, 239
Naropa, 238
Nasadiya, paradox, 231
Natural koans, 136–137
Natural resilience, capacity, 74
Neediness, facing, 196
Negative listening, 122
Neng, Hui, 218
Neo-Advaita approaches, 187
Neurotic, anguish/despair, 175
Neutrality, 55
  analytic attitude, 55–56
  conception/usage, 56–60
  detachment, 61
  endnotes, 74–75
  function, 21
Nibbana/nirvana, bliss, 237–238
Nirguni (formless God), 239
Nirvana, 11, 12, 72, 257
No practice, 167–168
No-mind (mushin)
  endnotes, 147–149

listening/speaking, 121
speaking, 127–128
initiation, 143
Nondual awakening
endnotes, 251–254
source/applications, 231
Nondual awareness
aspects, 41
facilitation, 167
Nondual coming/going, 153
Nondual consciousness
background, 93–97
clinical illustration, 93–97
comments, 97
connection, ability, 93
realization, 88–90
spaciousness, 88
Nondual conversations, paradoxes, 143–144
Nondual embodiment, 11–17
Nondual experience, 172
description, 80–81
Indian Vedantic teachings, 80
Nondual inquiry, 137
Nondual insight, 185–189
Nondual psychospirituality, 232
Nondual psychotherapy, value, 166–167
Nondual reality, 159
Nondual realization, 83
embodiment, 29
historical Indian sources, 231
process, gradualness, 87–88
Nondual theology, 231–232
Nondual therapy, 24–25
practice, 138
Nondual therapy-satsang situation, 241
Nondual understanding, 72–73

Nondual wisdom, 217
embodying, 197
endnotes, 214–215, 229
introduction, 197–198
schools, 191
traditions, 165–166
Nonduality, 17–19. See also
Psychotherapeutic relationship;
Self/lack; Self/other; Self/society
appearing/disappearing, 151
coming from, 158–161
defining, 79–82
direction, 102
discussion, 164–168
duality, inseparability, 189–191
experience, 152
going into, 161–164
individuality, relationship, 88–90
introduction, 151–153
therapeutic applications, 240–242
therapeutic relationship, connection, 90–92
Nonfixating therapeutic exchanges, 26
Nothing. See Sunyata
communication, therapeutic value
(confidence development), 141–142
listening, 122–125
occurrence, 140
resistance, 110
speaking, 141
talking, 141–143
thinking, 138–141
No-thing definable, 110

O

Objective reality, historical influences, 91
Object-Relations psychotherapy, 77
Ogden, Thomas, 47
One Self/Awareness, 232

Oneself
    centering, 155
    discovery, 104
    forgetting, 172
Ontological difference, 71
Ontological existence, 153
Openness (shunyata), 121. See also
    Misguided openness; Revelatory
    openness
    sense, 42
Openness-Emptiness-Fullness,
    permanence, 243
Original speech, 158–161
    clarity/vividness, 161
Ourselves, dimension, 89
Overindulgence, 195

P

Pain, distinction, 247–248
Pain/difficulty, manifestations
    (overanalysis), 213
Paradox, 164–168. See also Nasadiya;
    Nondual conversations
    communication, 143
Paranoid schizophrenia, diagnosis,
    163–164
Past conditioning, impact, 213–214
Perception, 80
Personal history, illusion, 185
Personal life, abstract ideas (distance),
    161
Personal Lord (Isvara), 238
Personality, impact, 109–110
Perspectival realism, 78–79
Physical body, information, 105
Physical sensation, 84
Positive listening, 122

Prajna, 233
Prajna-Paramita Vajracchedika
    (Diamond-Cutter), 241
Prajna-Paramita-group, 238
Prasthana-traya, 236–237
Pratyabhijnahridayam, 190
Preference, attachment (absence),
    202–203
Prendergast, John J., 1, 35, 167
Pre-personal psychological work, 11
Projective identification, 47–48
    clinical applications, 38–42
    endnotes, 52–53
    reflections, 35
    session, 38–40
    comments, 40–42
Psychoanalysis, impossible profession,
    60
Psychological transformation, focus, 10
Psychology, illusion, 185
Psychotherapeutic encounter, self
    (presence), 153
Psychotherapeutic meaning, 113–166
Psychotherapeutic relationship
    intersubjectivity, 77
    introduction, 77
    nonduality, 77
Psychotherapy. See Depth
        psychotherapy
    clinical approach. See Somatic
        psychotherapy
    collaborative nature, 90–91
    division, absence, 110–111
    dual understanding/nondual
        understanding, relationship, 38
    enrichments, 19
    forms, 77–78
    nondual wisdom, role, 1
    practice, change, 113–114
    problems, reality, 118

types, danger, 192

Psychotic state, 163

Puhakka, Kaisa, 26, 69, 151

Pulling in, 154–155

Pulling-in activity, 154–155

Pure awareness (vidya), 121

Pure listening, 122–125
  exploration, 123–124

Pure Solid Being-Awareness-Bliss, 242

Pure speaking, 122, 127–128
  origin, 127

R

Rabjam, Longchen, 83, See also
    Longchenpa

Ratnakuta-group, 238

Real identity, recognition, 243

Reality. See Absolute reality; Relative
    reality
  cocreation, 116–119
  glimpses, 7–8
  illusory nature (maya), 124
  revelation, 102

Realization Process, development,
    93–97

Reflexive sense of self, alienation, 177

Reiki, 220

Reincarnational/samsara dream, 236

Relative reality, 198–199
  absolute reality, interplay, 201

Relative truth, 71–74

Religion, institutionalization, 177

Resilience, helpfulness, 8

Revelatory openness, 57

Rg Veda oral scripture, 231

Rigpa, 15, 56

Rinpoche, Tsoknyi, 199

Rinpoche, Tsultrim Gyamtso, 82

Rolf, Ida, 220

S

Sacred mirroring, 167

Sahaja (inborn/intrinsic), 245

Sahaja samadhi, 239

Sakyamuni Buddha, 174–175

Samadhi, 10
  group, 238

Samsara, 11

Sandhinirmocana, 238

Sanity, 63–64

Sankara, 238–239

Saraha, 238

Satapatha Brahmana, 233

Satsang, 225
  therapy, 242

Seeing, 166

Seeing through (vipashyana), 139–141

Self (jiva), 238–239. See also Fixated
    self
  arising, 158
  coming/going, 156–158
  disappearance, 151
  disintegration, fear, 163
  dissolution, 162
  fixation, 153–156
  moments, 162
  natural coming/going, examples, 157
  nonexistence, 206
  perception, problem, 246
  sense. See Sense of self
  silence, 245

Self Psychology, 77

Self-abandonment, facing, 196

Self-acceptance, helpfulness, 8

Self-annihilation, path, 4

Self-centeredness, permeability, 59

Self-consciousness, involvement, 155

Self-defeat, weight, 72

Self-denial, facing, 196

Self-deprecation, weight, 72

Self-destruction, capacity, 191

Self-disintegration, fear, 26

Self-hatred, facing, 196

Self-honesty, promotion, 198

Selfhood, paradox, 69–70

Self-image, inflation/deficiency, 37

Self-improvement agenda, 74

Self-inquiry (atma-vichara), 249
    Hindu form, 137

Self-judgment, trance, 99

Self-knowing awareness, 81

Self/lack, nonduality, 174–177

Selfless awareness, interference, 57–58

Selflessness, 70

Self-liberation agenda, 74

Self-love, helpfulness, 8

Self-obsessing thoughts, entanglement,
    248

Self/other, nonduality, 171–173

Self-preoccupation, freedom, 173

Self-reflecting mind, survival, 107

Self-reflection, emphasis, 61–62

Self/society
    endnotes, 180
    nonduality, 171, 177–180

Self-soothing techniques, usage,
    222–223

Self/world image, appearance, 6

Sense of lack, elimination, 176–177

Sense of self, 106. See also Group self
    alienation. See Reflexive sense of self

analysis, 175
birth, 107–108
construct, 171
internalization, 176

Sensory perception, 84

Sensory phenomena, experience, 81

Separation/alienation, inner sense, 2

Serenity (shamatha)
    cultivation, 139–140
    experience, 125–126
    seeing through, relationship, 140

Sesshin (meditation retreat), 159–160

Shakyamuni Buddha, 11

Shame, facing, 196

Shankara, 137

Shobogenzo, 171, 172

Silence, impact, 103

Sokushinzebutsu, 171

Somatic and Trauma work, 186

Somatic Experiencing, 186

Somatic impulses, ignoring, 213

Somatic psychotherapy, clinical
    approach (overview), 219–222

Soto Zen, 168

Spacious intimacy, 35
    experience, 123
    introduction, 35–37

Spacious meeting, 41

Spiritual alchemy, 13–14

Spiritual awakening, focus, 10

Spiritual bypassing, 9–10
    danger, 185–189

Spiritual data, 182

Spiritual language, mind-made
    concepts, 205

Spiritual life, purposes, 195

Spiritual materialism, 201–202

Spiritual teachers/practitioners, shortcomings (misinterpretation), 183–184

Spiritual traditions, recognition (importance), 186

Spirituality. See Embodied spirituality
fast-food seekers, 187
pursuit, 182–183

Status symbols, 176

Story, listening, 130

Subjectivity. See Intersubjectivity
components, 79
dimensions, 60–61

Subject-object, integration, 82–84

Subject-object structure, unraveling, 165

Substantial, coemergence, 201

Subtle energy (prana/nadis/chakras), 15, 23

Suchness (tathata), 121, 159

Sudden enlightenment, 168

Suffering (dukkha), 27, 173
collective selves, connection, 178
existence, question, 247–248
inflicting, 179
institutionalized forms, 178
liberation, clearing, 126–127
preoccupation, 177
translation, 174

Suicide, contemplation, 115

Sunyata, 5
existence, 240
nothing/emptiness, 158–159

Supreme Reality, 234

Swami Prajnanpad, 194

Systems theory, 78

T

Talk, walking, 181, 195–196

Tansey, Michael, 47

Tantric initiation, 183

Taoism, 79

Tat Tvam Asi, 234

Teaching relationship, 132

Therapeutic exchange, lightly conditioned presence (impact, case example), 65–68

Therapeutic relationship, 132

Therapeutic resonance, 31, 221

Therapist
nondual dimension, living, 91
primary role, 129

Therapy, nondual approaches, 139

Theravada, 168

Thoughts, thinning out, 138–139

Thought-stream, 127

Tibetan Buddhism, 168
Mahamudra/Dzogchen schools, 81

Tilopa, 238

To/fro
endnotes, 169
introduction, 151–153
spontaneous movement, 151

Tolle, Eckhart, 45–46, 49

Totality, expression, 112

Transference
definition, 87
phenomena, 86

Transformational approach, 192

Transmission, 47

Transubjective field, 92–93

Trauma. See Unhealed trauma
application, 186
psychological/physical patterns,

nonverbal inquiry, 220–221

True embodiment, 213–214

Trungpa, Chogyam, 56, 194

Truth, devotion, 109

Tukaram, 239

U

Uddhava Gita, 238

Unborn nature, 101

Unconditional exchanges, impulses, 73

Unconditional openness, maintenance
(difficulty), 74

Unconditional presence
endnotes, 74–75
play, 55, 68–71
skillful means, 64–65

Unconditioned mind (asamskrta-
citta), 121
experience
betrayal, 143–144
impact, 130
presence, 127

Unconditioned presence, 121

Unconscious fixations, 74

Unconscious organizing principles,
illumination, 62

Understanding, capacity, 84

Unenlightened thought, 242

Unfindability conversations, 129–136

Unfolding process, example, 133–136

Ungroundedness, 27

Unhealed trauma, 204

Unintentional attitude, practicing,
73–74

Universe, experiencing (yourself), 171

Unworthiness, facing, 196

Upanishad, 232–233

aphorisms, 234–236
secret doctrine, 233

V

Vakyapadiya, 238

Vedanta-Sutras, 236–237

Victim, identity, 113

Vidya, 15, 233

Viewspace, 152

Vimalakrti-nirdesi, 238

Violence, capacity, 191

Vipassana, 5

Visualizations (guruyoga), 15

W

Waking down
approach, 191–192
phase, 15

We-ego (wego), 71, 177
types, 178

Welwood, John, 183, 185, 190
"Double Vision," 194

What Am I, question, 108

What Is, 201
acceptance, 207

What Is This, question, 137–138

Whitman, Walt, 6, 51

Who Am I, question, 108, 137

Whole body, inhabiting, 95

Wilber, Ken, 13–14
causal state, comments, 18
nondual copresence, discussion,
21–22

Wisdom (spontaneous movement),
mystery (impact), 99–101

Witness, emptiness, 18–19

Witness consciousness (sakshin), 121

Witnessing, 49–52
    endnotes, 52–53
    power, 49–50
    reflections, 35
Word salad, 164
World (jagat), 238

Y

Yajnavalkya, 233
Yang-shan, 171
Yoga Vasishtha, 248

Z

Zen boyfriends, example, 187–189
Zen Buddhism, 79
    koan, 137–138
Zen koan practice, example, 172–173
Zen Saivism, 12